COACHING THE

4-2-3-1

BY WAYNE HARRISON

Library of Congress
Cataloging - in - Publication Data

COACHING THE 4-2-3-1
by Wayne Harrison

ISBN-13: 978-1-59164-158-2
ISBN-10: 1-59164-158-6
Library of Congress Control Number: 2011939049

Art Direction and Layout
Bryan R. Beaver

All the diagrams in the book were created using Session Planner 2.0 software from SoccerSpecific.com. This software is available for purchase and download at www.soccerspecific.com

CONTENTS

Thank you to my parents Harry and Betty, my wife Mary and my children Sophie and Johanna for all the love and support they have given to me in my career; this book is dedicated to them.

INTRODUCTION

The 4-2-3-1 is now a very popular system of play in world football incorporating four units of players instead of the usual three.

This means all the units are closer together and there is less chance for them to lose contact with each other and be spread too far part.

Spain has won both the European Championships and the World Cup in 2008 and 2010 respectively so everyone has to take notice of this development in team play. Barcelona, the best club team in the world currently, plays a similar style to this; perhaps a little more offensive with three very mobile interchanging strikers but with a particular development of play from the back that we will explore in this book.

Real Madrid under Jose Mourinho employs a similar system of play. Arsene Wenger at Arsenal is another famous head coach who is working more in this style.
The interchange of players between units of play is what stands out for me to discuss and explore the methodology.

Of course you need the players to make this system of play work but if done properly opponents will find it difficult to recognize who to pick up and where on the field to do it as there is so much interchange and movement of players within the team framework.

This book will present ideas on coordination and combination play between players in the same units but also between players in different units, which is the true secret of the system.

Coupled with this method of play, ideas on the shadow striker will be incorporated in the playing scheme. This player will play in the middle of the three attacking midfield players and is a pivotal position in the team that needs to be discussed in full. Other players will interchange WITH HIM AND PLAY IN THE ZONE 14 SHADOW STRIKER PART OF THE FIELD ALSO.

The system will be explored through Functional and Phase Plays, as well as Small Sided Games Situations and ultimately many 11 v 11 situations, often against different systems of play.

When discussing certain positions on the field of play I will use the traditional numbers from 1 to 11 for clarity.

Enjoy the book.
Regards,
Wayne Harrison

HOW TO SET UP A SMALL - SIDED GAME

This is a game of less than 11v11 that can be any number from 3v3 to 9v9. Generally, games to establish team coaching themes are 6v6 or 8v8.

Session Plan

1. Try to work with all the players on the team you are coaching, affecting each performance in a positive way.
2. Divide the field into thirds (defending, middle, attacking third) for easier points of reference (for 6v6 and upwards). Use cones to show the boundaries.
3. Use specific start positions to get the session going.
4. Develop your theme using the key coaching points and use them as a reference to check you have covered them in the session.
5. List the key points in the order you perceive them in the process of building the session. For example, in defending, pressure on the ball comes before support.
6. Move from simple to complex as you develop the session. For example, in the theme "Defending from the Front", coach individual play within the team concept first (working with one striker), move to coaching a unit of players (it could be the two strikers working together), then extend the numbers (it could be working with the strikers and midfield players), then finish with coaching the whole team (strikers, midfielders, defenders, keeper).
7. Individual, then unit, then team, in this order, building up the session from simple to complex.
8. This is just an example of how it can be done in a logical order; it is up to the individual coach to develop his own method to suit his own style.

HOW TO BUILD A FUNCTIONAL SESSION

1. Work with all the players, but primarily with those players in the specific areas you are trying to affect. On a percentage scale consider 75% of the time with the specific players and 25% of the time with the supporting players on the same team.
2. Try to isolate the area of the field and the players who function within that area you are trying to affect. For example, the area to work in with central defenders would be centrally around the edge of the penalty area up to the half way line. For wide midfielders it would be on the wings of the field.
3. Use start positions to determine how the session begins. Servers can be used to start the session and also double up as targets to play to.
1. Develop your theme using the key coaching points and use them as a reference to check you have covered them in the session.
2. List the key points in the order you perceive them in the process of building the session.
3. Work with the individual then the pair or unit, building up the number of players you work with at any one time.
4. Use the functional practice to work with a small number of players in key areas of the field. A functional practice is more specific than a small – sided game, phase play or an 11v11 and it isolates the players being coached.

HOW TO PRESENT A PHASE OF PLAY

1. Try to work with all the players on the team you are coaching, affecting each performance in a positive way.
2. Include key coaching points you want to get into the session and list them with the session plan. Try to cover each point within the session itself.
3. Use specific start positions to begin the session.
4. The phase play is attacking one set of goals only with target goals for the opponents to play to should they win the ball.
5. In defending phase plays where you are working with the defending team who protect the only goal, the attacking team needs to have the ball most of the time as it is the defending team's job to win it back. Once they win it they should get the ball to a target goal quickly and in as few passes as possible as we are coaching them when they haven't got the ball, not when they are in possession. As soon as they have won it and have got it to a target the ball goes back to the attacking team and they begin a new attack. You can condition this by allowing the defending team only so many passes (maybe 5 passes) to get the ball to a target, then they lose the ball and a new phase play is set up.
6. It can be numerous combinations of numbers of players ranging from 4v4 to 9v9; this can depend on the number of players you have to work with on any given day. Often the best number is a 7v7 or with an overload with the team you are working with to help gain initial success in the session (it could be a 7v5). For example, in an attacking phase play have 7 attacking players against 4 defending players and a keeper to help the session have the chance be a positive experience for the players you are coaching and the theme to be successful.

Coaching styles – Command, question and answer and guided discovery are the three methods of coaching to be used. Guided discovery is the most used as it gets the players to think for themselves though there are always situations where each style is required. Command is telling and / or showing players what to do (doesn't leave a lot of room for the players to think for themselves and understand). Question and answer is just that; asking them to tell you what they think should happen. Guided discovery is asking them to show you they understand a coaching point by moving themselves to the position you require them using their own decisions.

11v11 GAME SITUATIONS: As it sounds; and much of the focus in the book will be clinics in this format. Training can be using single themes or double themes.

4-2-3-1 TEAM SHAPE

ATTACKING PLAY: FUNCTION / PHASE PLAY / AN 11v11 SHADOW PLAY

A) WARM UP

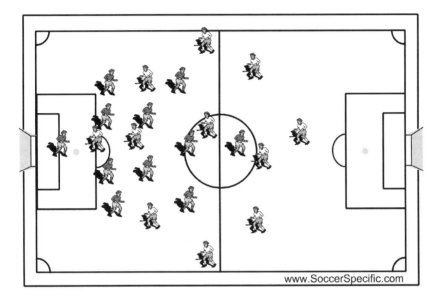

1. Start with two sets of cones for defensive shape and then attacking shape. This gives a good point of reference for each player, especially when you are coaching younger players You can also EXAGGERATE the difference by making the defensive shape very short and tight so the recovery is much longer in order to emphasize the importance of recovery runs to defend quickly.

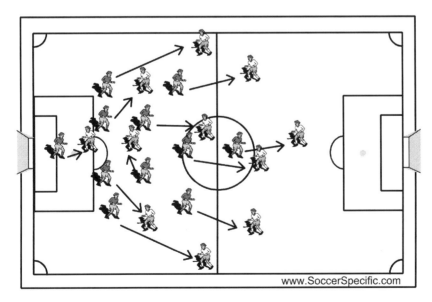

1. This shows the movements of each player. Progression: use cones of the same color for both defensive and attacking positions to further challenge the players.

B) GETTING USED TO THE TEAM SHAPE

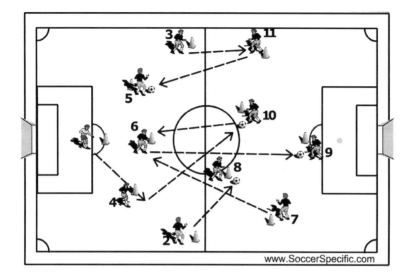

1. Development: Have the players pass the ball through the team staying in THEIR ATTACKING position while doing so. Introduce 2, 3 then 4 balls all going at the same time between players, playing one and two touch. The distances between players are big as we need them to use the whole width of the field. This gets them accustomed to this by passing several balls to each other and passing each time to a different player who is free.

2. Four balls ensure their attention is focused. As one ball goes the next one comes and they have to be focused on their next pass in advance. Play two touches then one touch when it is on to do so; keeping all the balls moving quickly. Long passes; short passes, diagonal passes, forward passes; back passes, switching play passes and so on, just as in a real game.

C) PASS AND FOLLOW

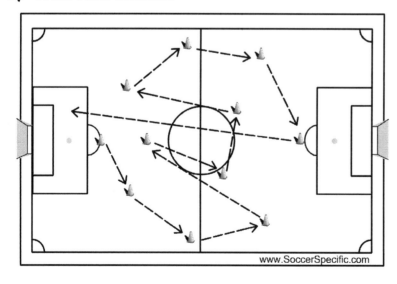

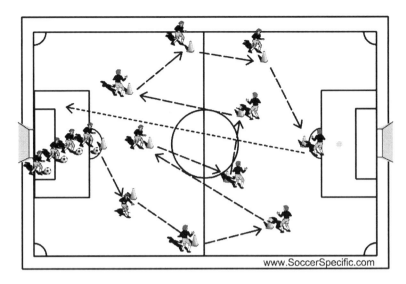

D) REHEARSAL OF MOVEMENTS

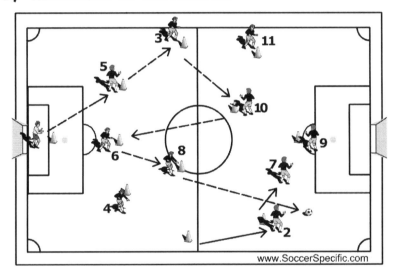

1. Using a numbering system to determine who passes to whom in a shadow play. This is continued REHEARSAL of movements.
2. Looking to make angled passes all over the field but in a set routine.
3. Alternatively tell the players before each one receives the ball where the next pass is to go. This will make it easier for them to remember the routine.
4. Routine here is the keeper to (5) to (3) to (10) and then back to (6). Next, a forward pass to (8), interchange by (7) and (2) creating space wide for a pass to overlapping (2). The coach can determine this as the ball is moving at each pass in advance so the players know where to go next. You can do many different routines with the players, eventually having them create their own.
5. So; have them move up and down the field as a team in a shadow play passing one ball. The coach determines where the ball has to go initially. Play the ball into the keeper and from there we pass through the team with the coach calling a name or number out before each player receives the ball for them to know where the next pass has to go. This way the coach can dictate the plays exactly as he wishes and create the buildup he wants.

No interchange of players and units initially to keep the movements simple but as above you can begin to develop interchanges with players.

E)   THE FINISH

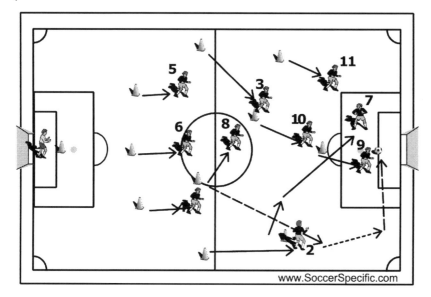

www.SoccerSpecific.com

1.   The finish. All the movements as (2) is running with the ball are shown and then (2) crosses. It can be a different set up with (9) going far and (7) near but this gives the gist of it. (8) slides across centrally to add balance defensively should the opponents win possession and counter attack. (3) and (10) position around the box for a pullback from (2) or clearances from defenders. (11) attacks beyond the far post should the cross be played long. Now we have a good attacking shape and a good defensive shape should the opponents start a quick counter attack. Have the keeper push up also so for any ball played in behind the back three he can act as a sweeper.

F)   TWO TEAMS AT ONCE

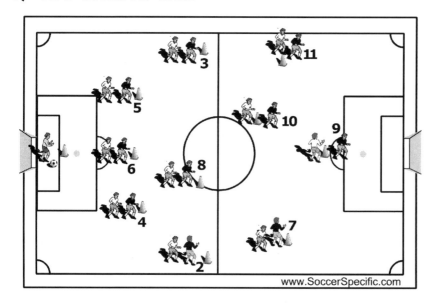

www.SoccerSpecific.com

1. If you have a surplus of players for the session assign two players for each position. As one team has gone and finished the next team go as the first team recovers.

2. Routines can be varied to include all players, to change direction, to go from one side of the field to the other and so on. (7) and (11) need to be involved a lot in the build up as you develop the idea as they will act as both midfield players and strikers supporting (9) and are involved with overlapping play.

3. The recovering team gets in the way of the other team and so they can act as a passive opposition.

4. Use a second ball to check their shape. As they attack they have to forget the first ball and get back into their defensive shape quickly. Then start again.

5. Introduce a VISUAL CUE for movements off the ball. For example, pick a central midfield player who on receiving the ball is the VISUAL CUE for (7) and (11) to cut inside and (2) and (3) to overlap. Again the coach can dictate when it goes to one of these players by calling the next pass. It could be player (6), (8) or (10) depending on how far up the field you want the movement to begin. Have both sides make these movements at the same time so the player on the ball has options going both ways. Several passes may be made throughout the team until the coach decides it is time to pass to the CUE player.

6. Let the players work it out for themselves now, and when the ball gets to the player you have identified the wide movements and interchanges begin and the player on the ball has 4 passing options.

7. Play to a finish against a keeper and show team shape from back to front, ensuring we have cover if we get a counter in an actual game. You can show how the team is set up and if it needs adjustment or not based on the opponent's ability to break away. Lay down a team of cones as a back four and middle four for the attacking wide players to have a guide. Use the back four cones as an offside line too.

8. Isolate a cone and create and show a 2v1 situation. For example, (7) cuts inside, (2) overlaps and they both attack the wide cone representing the position of the opposing fullback. Likewise, if (7) receives the pass INSIDE he can attack the central cone representing the nearest opposing center back and can work with (9) to create a 2v1 more centrally. Or play into (9)'s feet and (7) can receive back from him but facing forward and attacking the center back with perhaps (9) moving off the center back's shoulder to create the 2v1 situation.

9. You can rotate the (2) and (7) and (3) and (11) combinations also, where (7) can go wide and (2) comes inside and the same for (3) and (11). Good communication between these two sets of players is vital for this to work.

10. Introduce Defenders: Build it up from the back against two defending players. You can break it down to just the keeper and 6 players; a back four and two central midfielders against two defending strikers who, if they win the ball, have to run it over the half way line to score.

11. Build this idea up until you have all eleven players on the field and you play against 2 then 4 then 6 then 8 and ultimately an 11v11.

12. Where you put the defenders depends on your area of attacking focus. Initially we want to develop play from the back and affect the wide players on our team so you could have a back four, midfield central two and two strikers against you so the wide areas are freer to play in to ensure we get success with these movements. Do NOT try to do too many movements at once or the players will be confused.

The pass selection will be determined by the positioning of the defenders. You can ask the defending fullbacks to track the wide players inside; and sometimes not, so the player on the ball is tested with his decision making.

13. If the defending team wins the ball they must pass the ball to the coach. This is the visual cue for the attacking team to sprint back into their defensive shape and we start again with a pass into the keeper.

14. Once you have had success with these movements you can begin to try other combination movements as shown later, but initially have the coach determine where the ball goes each time. It may be from (4) at the back straight to (9) at the front and then midfield support from behind and so on.

15. Use the second ball often to ensure their concentration is good and the transition from an attacking mentality to a defensive mentality is developed and taught.

START POSITION IS A 4-2-3-1

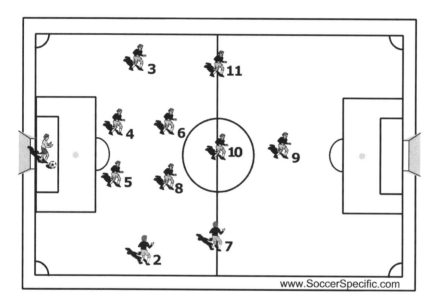

www.SoccerSpecific.com

1. Leave the cones down for reference and assume for the following diagrams they are down. The basic starting position of the 4-2-3-1 with the team in readiness to attack having just won the ball.

TEAM GAME PLAN AND INDIVIDUAL ATTRIBUTES NEEDED BY PLAYERS PLAYING THIS SYSTEM OF PLAY

The 4-2-3-1 is a flexible way to play employing four units rather than the usual three. It can transform quickly into a more offensive pattern of play of 4-2-1-3 by moving the wide outside midfielders forward and with this push on the two fullbacks to fill the spaces they have left.

THE BEAUTY AND FLEXIBILITY OF THIS SYSTEM

1. Our wide players can attack the space between the fullback and the center back on both sides. Left on right, right on left; coming onto their stronger foot is an advantage because they come in against the full back's weaker foot.

2. Our fullbacks attack wide to get crosses in and can cut inside also to do the job of the wide player

3. Our center backs are spread wide to open up the attack from the back
4. Our defensive midfielder (6) drops back in to cover and to start the movement also; he can fill in centrally or to the side.
5. Our attacking midfielder (10) plays between the opponent's defense and midfield and works in the shadow striker zone. He can interchange with the wide players or the striker (9).
6. Our 2nd defensive midfielder (8) is more offensive and creates support between the back and the front.
7. Our two defensive midfielders can interchange.
8. (8) positions off center to (10) and off center to (6) to maintain angles of support when attacking.
9. The most important thing we need when we play with such great flexibility and movement is GREAT COMMUNICATION BETWEEN THE PLAYERS so each knows in advance what the other will do. By training the players using particular movements, these movements in real game situations will become automatic and when a certain set up of players occurs they will recognize the movements beyond this. Almost like a set play in open play, which is to our advantage.
10. Attacking Midfielder (10) and striker (9) position off center to each other and often interchange positions.
11. An alternative way to get out from the back through a fullback is for one center back to break wide right (for example) into the right fullback position and the right fullback on that side of the field to attack forward into a wide right midfield / right winger position. The other center back moves into the middle and you have a standard back three. In this case the number (6) plays more distinctly in front of the back three and not between the center backs; when both fullbacks would attack at the same time.

INTERCHANGING OF POSITIONS BETWEEN UNITS SHOULD BE EXPLORED
CHOICES OF PERSONEL
- (7) and (11); wingers or wide midfielders?
- Winger on one side and a midfielder on the other?
- Particular match ups with fullbacks on either side?
- Attacking fullback and attacking winger, or attacking fullback and defensive midfielder?
- Defensive fullback and defensive midfielder?
- Defensive fullback and an attacking winger?
- Changes depending on the opposition?
- Fullbacks or wingbacks?
- More attacking or more defensive type players?
- Wingers at wing back and not traditional fullbacks?
- Defensive midfield players: strong or technical or one of each?
- Converted center back for the number (6) position so he is comfortable dropping back into the defense?
- Determining who plays where depending on the personnel we have?

I am using approximate percentages to define the amount of attacking and defending certain positions require. Plus it will vary depending on how coaches perceive each position or the type of player they have in each position. This is just a rough guide to how I see it.

THE ATTACKING AND DEFENDING ROLES AND RESPONSIBILITIES OF EACH PLAYER IN THE 4-2-3-1

THE ROLE OF THE KEEPER

In Possession / Without Possession
1. Technical
2. Tactical
3. Psychological
4. Physical

Technical Qualities: In Possession
1. Speed and quality of distribution.
2. Pass, kick, without hands and excellent on the floor technique.
3. Technique of releasing the ball with the feet and hands - distance (short, middle and long) with speed and direction.

Tactical: In Possession:
1. Speed - with ball TO START ATTACKS
2. Positioning - in a position to receive the back pass.
3. Choice - playing in depth - retaining possession of the ball.

Out of Possession:
1. Positioning: depending on where the ball is and who has it.
2. Communication - with their peers and with respect to the opponents.
3. Control of ways to defend - the goal - area (at the sides, in front of the back four and behind the back four)

Psychological:
1. The "Will" to avoid goals against.
2. Disciplined and responsible.
3. Stable / consistent performances - avoiding risk
4. A Leader and organizer.
5. Good Vocal Communication Skills - with defenders (especially) - with the midfielders - with the forwards (can see the WHOLE FIELD)

Physical Attributes:
1. Speed over short and middle distances.
2. QUICK Reactions (not anticipation).
3. Vertical Force - strong jumping ability - to attack the ball AT ITS HIGHEST POINT.
4. Duel - in the air - power in the 1v1

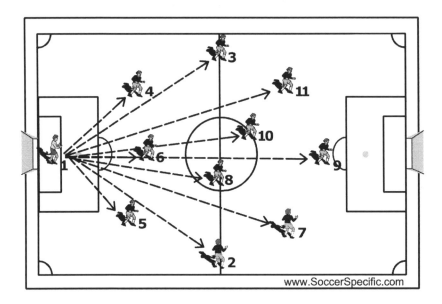

www.SoccerSpecific.com

THE ROLE OF DEFENSIVE MIDFIELDER NUMBER (6)
POSSIBLY THE MOST IMPORTANT PLAYER IN THIS SYSTEM OF PLAY

THE ROLE OF NUMBER (6)

In Possession / Without Possession
1. Technical
2. Tactical
3. Psychological
4. Physical

The number (6) is a vital player (perhaps THE main player) in the modern game; and the team often takes its shape around him.

Technical Attributes:
1. Excellent first touch control: A Great passer - short medium and long passing, ability to play ONE TOUCH.
2. Speed of play with the ball in all disciplines.
3. Heading ability
4. Shooting ability

Tactical Attributes: In Possession
1. Control at speed in tight situations; a great first touch, always moving the ball quickly when able.
2. Always in a position to receive the ball and always WANTING the ball.
3. Choice – preservation of the ball - change the direction of the game.
4. Direct quick passing. Create and save the space and distance.

5. Acting as a first, second or third man if needed in the build up.
6. Scoring goals

Out of Possession:
1. Orientation (Positioning according to the positioning of opponents; the ball and teammates).
2. Communication - with their peers and with respect to the opponents, particularly those immediately close to him, center backs, central midfielders and fullbacks (a position on the field of great responsibility for communication).
3. Insight in when and where to apply pressure on the ball.
4. Control of the different types of defending- between the lines, zoning, man marking, covering the passing lanes.

Psychological
1. Vocal leader and organizer.
2. Control over the pressure of the ball.
3. Disciplined and responsible - always in a position to receive the ball
4. Self-confidence
5. Authority
6. Charisma
7. Security for all the actions
8. Composure

Physical
1. Speed - in short and medium distances.
2. Change of pace - ability to play at three different speeds.
3. Strength of shooting and passing
4. Coordination with and without the ball
5. Agility
6. Power in the defensive 1v1 duel
7. Strength in the air

He must first have an excellent understanding with his centre backs.
Percentages for attacking and defending for each player are only approximate depending on how each team employs their players.

ATTACKING (40%)
He needs to read the game well, must keep possession and pass calmly.
He needs to be comfortable dropping back into a central defender's role (maybe a converted center back that is technically good can play here?).
Awareness: He must be able to anticipate his next pass or movement ahead and in advance of the ball; as often the space to play in where he operates is restricted.
Passing: He must have a high percentage success rate for maintaining possession; as losing the ball in his area of work is very dangerous. So, a very skilled passer and a strong physical player to protect the ball also.
Often this player is the player with the most time on the ball so he MUST be an excellent passer (especially over long distances).
Discipline and Personality: Finally the number (6) has to have an incredibly DISCIPLINED MIND as he must resist the urge to venture too far from his area of work; unless he is

sharing the position with his number (8) and he has more freedom (most number (6)'s will have the one role as it is so specialized these days). He is the player who must always want the ball, never hiding from the action; so he has to be super confident and a player with a strong dominating character

Game Intelligence: Ultimately, the most interesting thing about this role, is when (6) drops between the centre-backs, allowing them to spread into a back three from an initial back four with the fullbacks' starting positions, and giving the full-backs license to get forward and provide width. It is great to see the defensive midfielder (6) switching seamlessly between these two systems from a back four to a back three.

He is a major decision maker in the team, defensively breaking up the opponent's final attacks into our attacking third and offensively starting off the team's build up play, often with just a simple pass to maintain initial possession.

DEFENDING (60%)

Screening: He positions in front of the center backs to screen passes into the opponent's strikers. He must get into their passing lanes to prevent the pass to them, thus be a good reader of the other team's intentions.

Heading: Must be VERY GOOD IN THE AIR. Many balls into the strikers will be in the air and his job is to cut them off, so he's expected to be dominant in the air (which is vital for a holding midfield player so he is not targeted when up against a tall striker).

Double teaming: He can act as a double teaming player with his center back if the ball gets past him to their striker

Man Marking: Part of his job "may" be to stop the opponent's play maker too, who, because he is an attacking player may not do the same job defensively on our number (6), in which case (6) has freedom when we have possession.

If the number (6) gets drawn away from his position, by tracking the playmaker going short for example, then (8) can drop in and fill the same role.

Tackling: He must be a good tackler also, who is able to win the ball and set up the attacks simply.

Pressure: Able to press quickly and effectively in a 1v1 situation

Physical: He needs to be a tremendous physical presence in front of the back four, a strong and determined player.

AN EXAMPLE OF THE RELATIONSHIP BETWEEN THE DEFENSIVE MIDFIELD PLAYER AND THE TWO CENTER BACKS:

BARCELONA OF SEASON 2010 / 2011

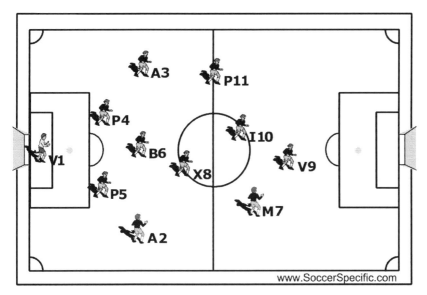

www.SoccerSpecific.com

Sergio Busquets (6), Gerard Pique (4) and Carles Puyol (5) do this so well at Barcelona as well as for Spain.

Busquets: The real point of interest in tactical terms of the defensive midfield player is the role of Sergio Busquets. He plays extremely deep, dropping between Pique and Carles Puyol to form a back three, allowing the Barcelona full-backs to push on extremely high up the pitch.

A three-man defense with the ball...

There's nothing particularly new about this, of course. Barcelona has seen a defensive midfielder drop in at centre-back when in possession for much of the past few years under Head Coach Pep Guardiola. Yaya Toure did it frequently on the way to Barcelona's Champions League win in 2008/09, and Busquets himself showcased it many times in season 2009/10 and beyond, with the Pique-Puyol-Busquets trio also featuring together for Spain in the World Cup win of 2010.

Sometimes a more permanent three: Busquets' position as a centre-back is also far more permanent in some games. It is frequently used when Barcelona are in possession, to get out of the natural press of opposing formations using two strikers, or a 4-2-3-1 when the central player in the '3' closes down a centre-back. Dropping a central midfielder in to make a three-man defense results in Barcelona being able to build up play from the back more easily, widening the active playing area, and allowing the full-backs to become wing-backs.

FORWARD TEAM DEVELOPMENT FROM THIS BASIC BEGINNING OF THE INTERCHANGES OF THE DEFENSIVE MIDFIELDER AND THE CENTER BACKS

A three in midfield of Busquets (6), Xavi (8) and Iniesta (10)

Xavi plays a more traditional passing role of number (8) and Iniesta the more advanced number (10) role. Again we see this lopsided triangle in midfield.

Dani Alves (2) is probably the most attacking full-back in the world, and Barcelona's centre-backs are used to coming over to the flanks when in possession. So they can attack two ways; down one side only with a fullback or down both sides with both fullbacks where the positioning of number (6) is more specialized.

Although the central midfielder (6) moving backwards happens a long way from the opponents' goal, it's actually a very good attacking tactic.

Switching to a back three means that the full-backs can become wing-backs and motor on forward.

The Advantages of the Number (6) role?

It widens the active playing area at both ends of the pitch, making it easier to keep possession, and tougher for the opposition to cover the space. It also creates a difficult situation for the opposition in terms of picking up players.

So it is likely that the equivalent of a sweeper in future years will be a defensive midfielder (6) dropping into the backline – with the centre-backs moving wide – rather than a centre-back who pushes forward into the midfield.

Barcelona's three-man attack narrows..

In turn, this means that the forward trio no longer has to provide width high up the pitch, and the wingers can instead come inside and play very close together. Naturally, this narrows the opposition defense and opens up space on the flanks for the wing-backs. It also means the opposing wide midfield players (generally attackers) are forced into extremely defensive positions.

Messi (7) and Villa (9) are often so close together that they can resemble a front two, with Pedro (11) offering a little more width whilst arguably the biggest threats in open play are attacking fullbacks becoming wingbacks, namely Abidal (3) and Dani Alves (2), who frequently get into good crossing positions.

Pedro's role (11), rather than playing on the shoulder of the opposing full-back, sometimes instead finds him playing deeper in an advanced midfield role, which helps compensate for Barcelona's loss of a spare man in the centre of midfield through Busquets (6) dropping into the back three.

Alternatively, based on the playing personnel on any given day, Barcelona may attack with three strikers; one being central (9) and two wide cutting inside to support him (7) and (11).

Barcelona will tweak their formation depending on what game it is and who they play; with very subtle position changes within the 4-3-3 / 4-2-3-1 / 4-2-1-3 framework. Once the game is in motion the formation only really represents a starting position anyway.

ANOTHER EXAMPLE:
REAL MADRID OF SEASON 2010 / 2011 UNDER JOSE MOURINHO

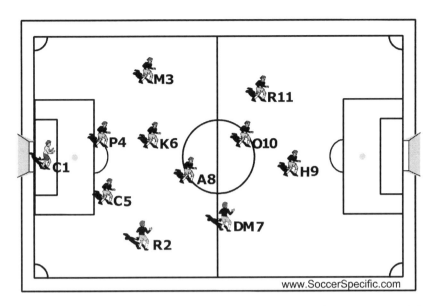

www.SoccerSpecific.com

Real Madrid in this modern era play a 4-2-3-1 with two very solid and powerful defensive center backs, Carvalho (4) and Pepe (5), and two very offensively minded overlapping fullbacks in Ramos and Marcelo.

Khedira (6) and Alonso (8) are a two in central midfield. Khedira is the ball winning number (6) and the "fill in" player to offer the fullbacks the opportunity to attack, and Alonso is the great passing number (8). Ozil plays in front of them in the number (10) role.

Add to this mix that center back Carvalho (4) likes to attack also. When he does so, Khedira (6) will sit in for him and the fullback (2) will stay home, which makes their build up from the back even less predictable.

The two wide players have very different styles. Da Maria (7) is a more traditional wide midfield player on the right and Ronaldo (11) a more traditional winger/wide striker on the left (hence the differences in percentages for attacking and defending with different types of players in these same roles)

Ronaldo is particularly dangerous coming inside onto his better right foot to shoot (he has scored many goals with this outside to inside movement) though he shoots well with both feet.

Higuain (9) is the lone striker but is ably supported by 3 players in Ronaldo (11), Ozil (10) and Da Maria (7).

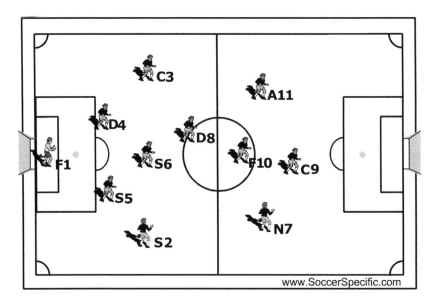

Arsene Wenger changes his team around but this is a regular set up of his personnel. Fabianski in goal (when Almunia is injured) and a back four of fullbacks Sagna (2) and Clichy (3) and center backs Squillaci (4) and Djourou (5).

A more lopsided midfield three in attack also with the traditional numbers of (6), (8) and (10) in that order from back to front in the lopsided triangle.

In this midfield trio it is often a combination of Song (6), Denilson or Wilshere (8) and Fabregas (10).

Wide players are Nasri (7) and Arshavan (11) with striker Chamakh (9) if Van Persie is injured.

Freddie Ljungberg was a player who played this wide role (7) or (11) very well in the past for Arsenal and was very difficult to pick up. Of course Dennis Bergkamp was the master of the number (10).

Slightly lopsided middle three again. You could even break this down to a five unit set up instead of four. Perhaps a 4-2-1-2-1 (depending how you look at it), but this would be a little too much to take in.

Other Top Players in this Number (6) Role

Arsenal have Alex Song, Manchester United have Michael Carrick, Chelsea have Jon Obi Mikel, Manchester City have Gareth Barry or Vincent Kompany, Tottenham have Tom Huddlestone – all of whom would be comfortable dropping back to allow the fullbacks to venture forward.

THE ROLES OF FULLBACKS (2) AND (3)

Technical Qualities:
1. Ability to play at speed with the ball
2. Control of the ball – excellent first touch control
3. Technique of the pass - short, medium and long distance
4. Crossing Technique

Tactical Qualities: In Possession
1. Speed control - With the ball
2. Decision making – when to pass, run with the ball, cross the ball, dribble, shoot and so on
3. Positioning - Always in position to receive the ball, with a desire to receive the ball

Out of Possession
1. Orientation: (positioning determined by the ball, the opponent, his teammates)
2. Communication – with teammates with respect of the opponents, particularly with those players always around him: closest center back, wide midfield player in front of him and central midfield beside him (so, 2, 4, 6 and 7)
3. Understanding of the different forms of defending; zoning and man marking; 1v1

Psychological
1. Disciplined and responsible - always with an attitude to receive the ball - first pass without risks – maintaining possession
2. Willingness to work for the team - in attack - defense
3. Understanding - when and where to attack; as a fullback with defensive duties he must have good decision making on this.

Physical
1. Speed - In short, medium and long distance
2. Great endurance / stamina – covering the whole of the flank
3. Strength of passing / crossing
4. Strong in the tackle / in the air
5. Agility

ATTACKING (50%)
Offensively, in this system of play the fullbacks have incredible freedom to attack, and unlike many systems of play which only allow for one fullback to attack at any one time this system allows for both of them to attack at the same time with the security of the defensive midfielder (6) becoming the third center back behind them and central midfielder (8) staying in front of them.

For normal full backs, the percentage between defending and attacking would be far higher on the defending side; but this system allows them to attack much more.

Crossing: An ability to cross the ball well is a must for these modern day wingbacks as they will find themselves in many crossing positions during a game. They will be crossing with a moving ball so they need to learn several techniques for crossing the ball. This will include driven crosses, lofted crosses, cut back crosses, bending whipped crosses and so on, depending on the situation.

DEFENDING (50%)
1v1: First priority is to be a good defender; so he needs to be good in 1v1 confrontations.

Physical: Physically strong to be able to compete against powerful players and quick of foot as he usually comes up against wide players with pace.

Heading: Good in the air is a bonus

Game Intelligence: He has to build a good relationship and understanding with his immediate center back and wide midfield player in front of him; and with his inside central midfield player.

THE ROLES OF CENTER BACKS (4) AND (5)

Technical Qualities:
1. Heading skills.
2. Passing Technique - distance (short, medium and long) - direction (left and right)

Tactical Qualities: In Possession
1. Speed - with the ball
2. Always in a position to receive the ball.
3. Simple Choices- first pass - retain possession of the ball – ability to change the direction of the game

Out of Possession:
1. Orientation: (positioning determined by the ball, the opponent, his teammates)
2. Communication - with their peers (especially as a center back pairing) and with respect to the opponents.
3. Understanding of the different forms of defending; zoning and man marking; 1 against 1
4. Knowing when to press / when to cover

Psychological:
1. Killer mentality (Take no prisoners).
2. Vocal leader and organizer
3. Disciplined and responsible, ensuring the first pass is a safe one; always in a position to receive (confident) - orientation - preserving the position – great positional sense.
4. Ability to focus on man marking and stick to the task (1 to 1 and 1 more)

Physical Attributes:
1. Speed in short and medium distances
2. Strength on and off the ball
3. Jumping ability
4. Strength in the challenge: On the ground: In the air.
5. Agility

ATTACKING (10%)

Depending on the adventure of the head coach and the technical ability of the center backs they may start the build up at the back by bringing the ball out of defense themselves and running with it. This is not a big part of their game; but again, depending on the type of center back; their game may be more than just 10% offensive.

They must be VERY comfortable on the ball and be very good passers to have the confidence to always look to build play from the back.

DEFENDING (90%)

Heading: Of course they must be good in the air first of all.

1v1: They must have the usual defending skills of having the ability to delay and be patient, plus anticipate situations ahead of the ball and pick the right moment to tackle with the right timing and pace to close down.

Pace: It always helps if they are quick but if they read the game well this is not vital
Game Understanding: They must also have a great understanding as a pair able to cover each other effectively and be good communicators. They must be very good readers of the game, especially if they are not the quickest of players.

THE ROLE OF CENTRAL MIDFIELDER NUMBER (8)
Physically strong, this is probably the most physically strong position on the field.

ATTACKING (50%)
He can be the link player between defensive midfielder (6) and offensive midfielder (10), the passer working between them and sharing his duties between defense and offense equally, whereas (6)'s duties are primarily defensive and (10)'s duties are primarily offensive. Perhaps we can have an approximate calculation of 70% - 30% for (6) in favor of defending, 70% - 30% for (10) in favor of attacking; and 60% - 40% for (8) in favor of attacking.

DEFENDING (50%)
He plays a balanced role with the defensive midfielder number (6). He is usually the more offensive of the sitting central midfielders. Sometimes he may switch and does the defensive number (6) job depending on the coach's method of playing. Most coaches will choose one or the other to do the specific job; but some may allow them to alternate roles.
Pressure: Ability to press quickly and effectively in a 1v1 situation
Understanding: Ability to work defensively within a unit and position correctly in support.

THE TWO CENTRAL MIDFIELDERS AS A UNIT (6) AND (8)

ATTACKING (Number (6); 40% attacking; Number (8); 50% attacking)
They must play off each other, always offering up angles of support to help each other. They must constantly find space to receive the ball.
They will tend to not spread out too far offensively, though (8) pushes on more in the attack.
They can switch positions to enable each to move forward, but always with one holding the team shape.

DEFENDING (Number (6), 60% defending, Number (8) 50% defending)
The two central defensive midfielders in front of the defense give tactical balance to this pattern of play to allow for offensive movement and also to keep a sense of stability defensively. They also work to delay opponents to allow for the three attacking midfielders to recover.
With the security of the central midfield two, the fullbacks have a more offensive game plan than normal and must have good fitness to apply this fully and effectively.
The two central midfield players can fill in for defenders attacking from the back, be it center backs bringing the ball out or, more likely, fullbacks attacking with width.
With this role in mind they cover more of the width of the field than normal center midfielders in a midfield four. One is usually a more advanced player (8) and one a definite number (6) defensive role becoming the pivot which the team takes its shape from, a very important player.

THE ROLES OF (8) AND (10)

Player (8) can play slightly different to (10), (8) being more the link player between (6) and (10), more the passer; and (10) being the more offensive creative player. They may interchange depending on the team methodology.

Technical:
1. Speed with the ball
2. Control of the ball – excellent first touch
3. Passing Ability - short, medium and long distance
4. Dribbling Ability - to create a situation of 2 to 1 to score goals
5. Long distance shooting on goal
6. Heading Ability

Tactical: In Possession
1. Change of pace - be able to play at 3 different speeds.
2. When and where to pass (very important as they will have the ball a lot)
3. Coordination with the ball
4. Game head – when and where to move – making third man runs

Out of Possession
1. Orientation (Ability to read movement off the ball)
2. Communication - with their peers and with respect to the opponent
3. Attitude to pressure as team
4. Control of the different types of marking - between the lines, 1v1 pressing

Psychological
1. Quick thinker
2. Disciplined and responsible - always in the position of receiving the ball. Assessing options before receiving the ball. First check - First pass –
3. Orientation: Movement off the ball recognition
4. Will work for the team - on offense - on defense
5. With confidence - to go deeper - to score goals - to return to his position - To defend

Physical
1. Speed - In short (especially), medium and long distance
2. Change of pace - be able to play at 3 different speeds.
3. Good coordination and balance with and without the ball
4. Strength of passing
5. Shooting power
6. Endurance / stamina

THE ROLES OF WIDE ATTACKERS (7) AND (11)

Technical:
1. Speed with the ball
2. Control of the ball - first control – great first touch

3. Crossing Ability – cross with pace: on the ground or by air, with a curve out of the reach of the goalkeeper and between the goalkeeper and defenders. Where to Cross can depend on the position of goalkeeper, defenders and attackers (to the near post, to the far post, the pull back, beyond the far post)
4. Also dribbling inside and outside to shoot at goal or to cross
5. Passing ability
6. Scoring - balls on the floor - balls in the air

Tactical: In Possession
1. With ball - speed control with the ball
2. Positioning- always in a position to receive, open stance, and facing towards the goal, and as open as possible
3. Know how to choose (when and where) - Cross, 1 to 1 dribble; when to pass, when to shoot.
4. Understanding of when and where to break outside to inside.

Tactical: Out of Possession
1. Orientation: Movement off the ball - to attack - to defend
2. Communication - with their peers and with respect to the opponent
3. Attitude to close spaces as a team player
4. Ability to press and hold the position.
5. Retrieve balls

Psychological
1. Disciplined and responsible - make the field as large (and deep) as possible.
2. Orientation. Will work for the team - on offense - on defense: close spaces and prevent deep passes.
3. Confidence - Create actions for goals - Passing and crossing

Physical
1. Speed - in short, medium and long distance - technical in speed (with great coordination)
2. Endurance
3. Change of pace - be able to play at three different speeds.
4. Ability in Passing and Crossing; Dribbling; Shooting ability; Heading ability
5. Agility

ATTACKING (55%)

Depending on the way the coach plays the 4-2-3-1, the types of players in these roles may be quite different team to team. A more defensive minded coach may use defensive midfield players here while an attacking coach may choose wingers, producing totally different effects within the same system.

Or, the coach may pick certain players in these positions based on how the opponents will play.

A big part of the switch is the role of the wide players. Rather than stay wide (which would hamper the ability of the full-backs to get forward), they narrow and become almost a conventional front three with the lone striker (9). This has the effect of narrowing the opposition defense, as their natural markers (full-backs) follow them into the centre.

Tactical Understanding / Game Intelligence: So, wide players must be comfortable drifting into the centre of the field and coming inside, not just being skilled going outside and crossing as is the traditional role of the wide player. Therefore they must be better all round players than the traditional wide player (whether it be a defensive minded or attacking minded player, now it is best if they can be good at both). Of course, this opens up a huge amount of space on the flanks, which the full-backs can exploit. This presents a further problem for the defending team, as their wide midfield players are suddenly charged with almost a solely defensive job. If the attacking full-backs get to the byline and the defending wide midfielders track them all the way, the defending team will end up with something approaching a flat back six. *Opposites:* An added advantage is a right footed player who can play on the left and cut inside and have a good shot, and vice versa. They attack the fullback inside, and they have an advantage from this as they cut inside onto their strongest foot and inside against the fullback's weakest foot. *Shooting and Crossing:* having the ability to shoot on goal. Traditional wide players usually are good at crosses and tended to stay wide, the modern wide player has to be better at so many more skills than previous generation's of players. So; they need the ability to stay wide and cross the ball and the ability to cut inside and shoot at goal.

DEFENDING (45%)
Understanding: Must defend in front of their respective fullback and develop a defensive relationship with them. This player can defensively cover for the fullback attacking. Must have a good tactical understanding to be able to combine with his fullback and know when and where to cover for him; when the fullback breaks forward.
Recovery: Recovery runs are vitally important for this player in this system of play. When recovering they can become a part of a defensive four in midfield.
1v1: Must be good at 1v1 defending

ATTACKING MIDFIELDER NUMBER (10) IN ISOLATION
ATTACKING (70%)
The number (10) is another very important position in the team, often playing in the Shadow Zone 14 between the opponents' back four and midfield. Advanced receiving and turning skills are very important here and great awareness of surroundings and an ability to find space in congested areas.
Technique: Good technical skills are at a premium for this player as often the team will play through him further up the field (where the number (6) starts the movements the number (10) is often the finisher of them or the creator for the striker or strikers).
Tactical Understanding / Game Intelligence: Must be able to read SPACE well, knowing where to move to between the lines of the opponent's defense and midfield. Past Players who come to mind are Dennis Bergkamp, possibly the best ever number (10), Zinedine Zidane, Eric Cantona, Totti, and Allesandro Del Piero. All different types of players but fulfilling the same role in their own style.
Passing: His passing skills must be of a high quality as he is usually the provider. He must be able to make penetrating passes in tight spaces, with great timing.
Dribbling: Likewise creative dribbling skills in tight places are a prerequisite.
Awareness: Finally he is usually the attacking pivot of the team so his vision and awareness must extend to assessing his options in advance of the ball, due to having little time and space to work in, and having the ability to see and change the point of attack in a moment.

The question for the number (10) position can be this:

Do you field a striker or an attacking midfielder?

It may depend on the game situation on any given day but most teams will employ one or the other to keep continuity that best suits the team system of play.

Do you play Rooney or Gerrard in the number (10) position for England for example? These are two totally different players; one being a striker and the other an attacking midfielder. It will likely depend on the players around them and their strengths and weaknesses as to which player the coach picks for this role, or it may be based upon the opposition and how they play.

So, Rooney who is really an extra striker or Gerrard an attacking midfielder making late runs into the box? Rooney dropping back into the hole or Zone 14, or Gerrard pushing up into the hole or Zone 14 behind the main striker?

It can be termed the Shadow striker dropping in, or the attacking midfielder pushing up.

But it shows there is more to picking the right player for this position than one might realize.

DEFENDING (30%)

Defensively this player is used in different ways based on the beliefs of the coach.

Some number (10)'s have few if any defensive responsibilities and they are allowed to be the free man. Totti of Roma would fit into this category. I believe this is becoming less the case in the modern game and coaches want the number (10) to at least make a contribution to the defensive team shape.

For example, if opponents have a playmaker patrolling in front of their back four, our number (10) can be the player to close him down. Or, if we are a team who presses high defensively we can have the number (10) push forward and help number (9), especially if our opponents like to try to build up play from the back. That said, some number (10)'s hardly contribute to defending at all.

THE RELATIONSHIP BETWEEN NUMBERS (6), (8) AND (10)

We are looking for three different players to play these roles. It is difficult to exactly define, but (6) is more defensive and solid, (8) is a link player and good passer so more attacking and (10) is the more creative attacking player.

In the middle of midfield these three will set up a certain way based on the coach's philosophy, so it will not always be a straightforward set up of a 2 and 1 in front.

ATTACKING SET UP OF THE MIDFIELD THREE

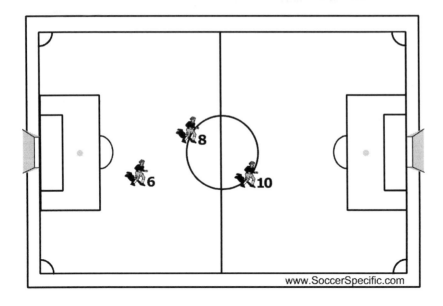

A lopsided triangle; with three distinct positions. This is more the Barcelona way, not a "PURE" 4-2-3-1, though the principle movements remain the same. Most teams have one of the two slightly deeper than the other, (6) deeper and (8) in front of him. Some teams may rotate the two so each has a chance to be more offensive but most will have specialists in each position.

DEFENSIVE SET UP OF THE MIDFIELD THREE

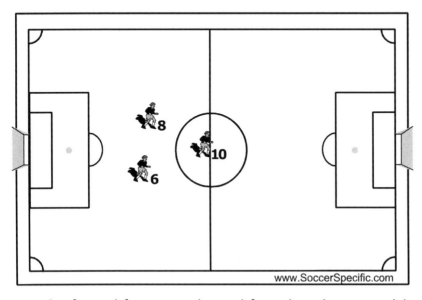

A regular forward facing triangle set defensively to be more solid and routine. Most teams fall back into this when they lose possession of the ball with two players in distinct positions to protect the back four and get in the passing lanes in front of the striker or strikers.

Depending again on the way a particular team will play, (10) will drop in to cover in front of them also though some teams will play their number (10) higher, even when defending. It also can depend on how solid these two are without this help.

A Functional Midfield: (6), (8) and (10)

We can take the ideal midfield trio as possessing (a) a ball-winner (b) a passer and (c) an attacking creator. Think of the old Liverpool with Mascherano-Alonso-Gerrard, Barcelona with Busquets-Xavi-Iniesta, Chelsea with Makelele-Essien-Lampard, Inter with Cambiasso-Motta-Sneijder, Arsenal with Song-Wiltshire-Fabregas. There are exceptions, of course, but in 4-3-3 and 4-2-3-1 formations this seems to be the general model.

ATTACKING

Try to set them up offensively at angles to each other, like a lopsided attacking triangle. This way they have good vision for each other's position.

DEFENDING

While defending (6) is likely already in a good defensive position, (8) may need to recover back and work with or alongside him. (10), who is the most offensively minded, should still provide some defensive help higher up the field in front of these two.

THE ROLE OF CENTRAL STRIKER (9)

Technical
1. Speed with the ball
2. Control of the ball - first control – great first touch in all directions
3. Ability to keep the ball; dribbling ability
4. Ability to play Give and go's- pass to the side (left and right) - cut pass (chip)
5. Passing ability
6. Shooting and heading ability

Tactical: In Possession
1. Speed - with ball - control without the ball
2. Positioning- without ball to receive it: always in position to receive 1 v 1, in depth and always in a position to receive
3. With the ball: choose direct / indirect play, create chances for others or retain possession of the ball

Tactical: Out of Possession
1. Orientation (Creative movement without the ball)
2. Communication - with their peers and with respect to the opponents
3. Attitude to pressure as a team player
4. Control of the different types of pressure - between the lines

Psychological
1. Killer mentality.
2. Self-confidence - (to create AND SCORE goals)
3. Disciplined and responsible
4. Willingness to work for the team - in attack AND defense
5. Self belief to KEEP going back after missing chances

Physical

1. Speed - in short (especially), medium and long distance - technical in speed (Great coordination and first touch control at pace)
2. Change of pace - be able to play at THREE different speeds.
3. Ability in passing and dribbling
4. Ability in the air
5. Strength in 1 v 1; in the air, on the ground to keep the ball under pressure
6. Agility

ATTACKING (80%)

The lone striker has to have good mobility and an ability to hold up the ball until support arrives, so physically very strong and difficult to knock off the ball.

Obviously the usual characteristics of being a good goal scorer, a great shooter and header of the ball, able to link up well with supporting players in front and behind him. Great pace is a bonus.

Good technical ability is required as he will often be trying to control the ball in tight spaces, especially when he is the only striker.

Also key is the ability to play with his back to goal and also to play facing the goal and get in good side on positions to receive and attack. He must know where and when to come off his marker and get free (not dissimilar to the number (10) in this regard).

Must be able to create space for himself or for others through intelligent movement off the ball.

Often the coach will choose between a tall, physically strong player, one who is able to hold the ball up and is good in the air, a "great wall" to play off for supporting players, or opt for a quicker, smaller and shorter limbed player with the ability to dribble and run at center backs and expose them 1v1.

Again it depends on the personnel and also the type of player the coach prefers in this position.

DEFENDING (20%)

He is the "first line of defense" on the team and so it is useful if he is good at pressing. He needs to pick when and where to press to conserve energy, but if supported by teammates and not isolated alone he can be very effective. So, a willingness to close down players when the opportunity arises to help the team defensively is a good asset.

THE RELATIONSHIP BETWEEN (9) AND (10)

ATTACKING:

They must develop a good understanding of movement off the ball to complement each other. Interchanging of positions can cause much confusion in the opponent's defense, so they have to develop good mutual timing of this movement.

Angled positions off each other will help them in a supporting capacity.

At the same time they will link up together and form a formidable unit of two.

Generally (10) is positioned behind (9) but it can be the reverse at different moments in the game to confuse defenders.

DEFENDING:

They can help each other by pressing as a unit high up the field. Better to work as a pair if possible with early pressing. The reward will often be winning the ball in an area where they can shoot immediately on goal.

THE RELATIONSHIP BETWEEN (7), (9) AND (11)

ATTACKING:

These three form a three pronged attack. The 4-1-3-1 becomes a 4-2-1-3 and often the two wide attackers tuck in to support the central striker (9). They may do it at the same time to form a three or, depending on which side of the field the ball is on, one will tuck in to form a two pronged attack. These three may interchange to confuse the defenders.

They need a good understanding of how to work as a three and also a two, and when to tuck in and when to stay wide. Barcelona again show this perfectly with the interchanges of Messi, Pedro and Villa with no real set positions for any of them. They have the freedom to interchange and move aroiund which makes it very diffcult for each defender to know who to pick up.

DEFENDING:

The central striker (or whoever is filling that role at the time between the three strikers) must be the first line of defense. Usually the two wide attacking players drop back to form a midfield four with the two central players and tuck back into a 4-4-1-1 defensive team shape. There again, when the time is right they will press as quickly as possible wherever the ball is, but from the basis of a unit of four.

START POSITIONS, PHASES OF PLAY AND VARIATIONS

THE START POSITIONS OF A 4-2-3-1 AGAINST A 4-4-2

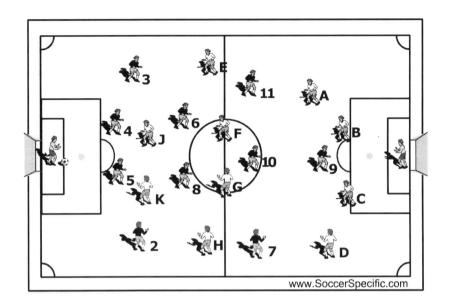

www.SoccerSpecific.com

1. This is the initial set up of the team, 4-2-3-1. The wide front two squeeze inside and closer to the striker, leaving space for the fullbacks to move into, though Barcelona on attack often have a lopsided midfield three with (6) deep, (8) in between (6) and (10) pushed on but not in a straight line.
2. At the same time the defensive midfielder drops back into the position between the center backs.
3. It only really makes sense against a team who play with two strikers, which is the problem with three-man defenses in general.

HERE IS HOW THE BUILDUP CAN LOOK OVER 4 PHASES OF DEVELOPMENT TO EMPHASIZE THE POINT:

PHASE ONE

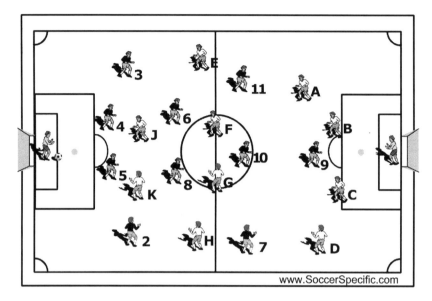

1. The start position of 4-2-3-1. Assuming the ball is being played forward through the team.

PHASE TWO

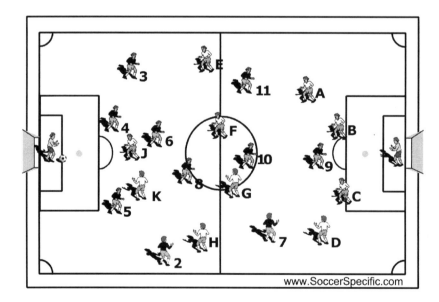

1. First phase of development and movement.
2. Team shape is changing and all our movements are affecting the opponent's positions.

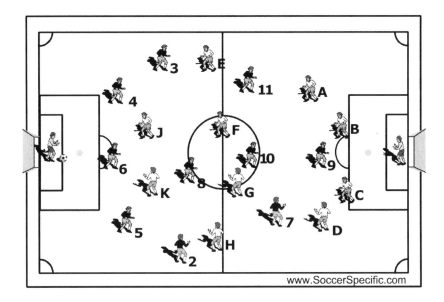

1. The next phase showing the fullbacks (2) and (3) moving forward and wider, the center backs (4) and (5) moving wider, the defensive midfielder (6) positioning between them as a sweeper; center midfielder (8) moving forward but keeping the shape in the middle, (number (10) pushing on to support (9) and wide midfielders (7) and (11) starting their cutting inside movements to create space outside.

2. Wide midfielders cut inside and the opponent's fullbacks (A) and (D) move inside also to leave the flanks open for (2) and (3) to run into. If they are tracked back by the opponent's wide midfielders (E) and (H) then our two center backs (4) and (5) are free to bring the ball forward.

PHASE FOUR

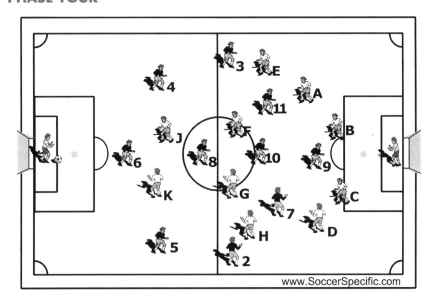

1. The final set up. A tight front three, central support from (10), two overlapping fullbacks, (8) keeping the defensive authority and (4), (5) and (6) giving defensive cover should the opponents win the ball and try to counter attack. These three can push up to the half way line and take their positions from there.
2. A VERY ATTACKING SITUATION, but balanced by a 3v2 at the back and a center midfielder in front of them to screen the opponent's strikers should we lose possession. Opponent's center midfielders will likely get goal side of (10) also.
3. So the fourth phase of play is the end product of a shot or header on goal.
4. The diagram above shows how a switch from a four to a three-man defense when in possession can outwit the opposition. The problem with attacking full-backs at the moment is that they are never completely free to attack; they are always concerned about their defensive responsibilities, especially with the tendency for sides to deploy their most creative players as wingers. With a more reliable three-man defense, they can get to the opposition byline without leaving a huge hole at the back.

AGAINST A LONE STRIKER

Against a lone striker, one of the center-backs in theory has a license to attack. But the reality is that it is suicidal to leave your defense equipped with just one center-back. Considering how popular one-striker formations are today, it is still extremely rare to see a center-back constantly looking to power forward to bolster the midfield – it is simply too risky.

Furthermore, the evolved shape makes it relatively easy for the attacking team to keep possession – the three defenders and holding midfielder should be able to play their way around the two defending team's strikers at the back.

So the advantages can be summarized as:

- It allows the full-backs freedom to join the attack knowing the defense is covered
- It makes keeping possession in defense easier
- It stretches the play high up the pitch
- If the opposition is playing creative players in wide areas, the center-backs will be in a position to pick them up immediately.
- It results in a system with three central forwards, an obvious goal threat
- The opposition will be confused about who to pick up in wide areas

In theory, this system should work extremely well against a two-man attack, although it might face similar problems as the traditional three-man defense against one-man/three-man attacks. But the difference comes because the traditional three-man defense is a completely different system to the traditional four-man defense, which necessitates a different way of defending, and most likely a different selection of players. These shifts, as shown by Barcelona, are more flexible, and happen within games, rather than the players lining up specifically like this in their start positions which are 4-2-3-1.

The system doesn't have to shift against one- or three-man attacks, and therefore is free to adapt into a three-man defense when required, and stay as a four-man defense when that is more appropriate.

Our OWN more regular way is to start with the wide players in wide positions on both sides to affect the opposing fullbacks' positions more clearly.

PHASES OF ATTACKING PLAY

- When gaining possession
- The buildup play
- The End Product

1. When gaining possession we go from a defensive shape to an offensive shape. By having a CLEAR TEAM OFFENSIVE SHAPE, the player winning the ball already knows approximately where his teammates will be. BUT, he has regained possession in the TEAM'S DEFENSIVE SHAPE, so we need the time through keeping the ball to allow the OFFENSIVE SHAPE to form.

2. To do this the players need time to adjust their positions, therefore with the initial gaining of possession the team must keep it long enough for our team to get positioned in an offensive shape. So the initial possession has to be kept, which means keeping play as simple as possible without any risk taking. This may include no risk back passes or sideways passes, giving everyone enough time to spread out and be offensively strong and find open spaces.

3. Build Up Play: Therefore initially on gaining possession, unless there is an obvious fast, safe and long pass forward and a quick counter attack on, we want players to keep the ball and not take the chance of a risky pass and immediately giving possession back to the opponents.

4. An example of this would be a clear immediate pass to the furthest forward player who is free in space (likely the lone striker) where he has to hold the ball up for support to come quickly.

5. A diagonally forward pass is better because it is to a receiving player likely side on and at an angle where his peripheral vision is superior to the long straight pass. The speed of building up play can also be determined by WHERE the ball is regained. If close to the opponent's goal then it is a short pass, run, cross or shot.

6. By examining the opponent's system of play you can see where the best areas for attacking are once we regain possession.

7. There again, if the player regaining the ball is put under immediate pressure, especially in a dangerous area, his best option is just to play the ball long and behind the opponent's defense to at least give us time to get reorganized and hopefully one of our front players will be near where he plays it. If not, at least we then have lost the next phase ball in a safe area.

8. The end product is of course a shot or header on goal from the buildup play.

REGAINING IN OUR DEFENSIVE AREA

1. So, as pointed out, in building up play from our defensive area, the player who gains possession should play a SAFE PASS first and not take risks in this area of the field. If no safe pass is on then he could play a long ball to the furthest player forward or wide into space (or if we have a player there also) to clear the lines and not get caught in possession in a dangerous area of the field. If this central player is strong and good in the air then a pass in the air may work. If he is very quick then a long pass into space either wide or in behind the last defender is another option to consider.

2. If the opponents win the ball back immediately at least we are well away from our goal and have time to get reorganized defensively.

VARIATIONS OF THE 4-2-3-1 DETERMINED BY WHO HAS THE BALL AND WHERE IT IS

I feel the 4-2-3-1 system of play is such a flexible system that it is worth considering as at any one time it can be a 4-2-1-3 in attacking action, or if you develop play from the back using the defensive midfielder number (6) as your pivotal player and we attack with both fullbacks it becomes a 3-3-1-3 (methodology of this is shown later). When we drop back in to defend we can instantly become a 4-4-1-1. So whilst we consider many systems; in actuality many are the same, they are just different depending on whether we are in an attacking phase or a defensive phase or even in between when the ball changes hands.

So if the Starting phase formation is 4-2-3-1:
The Attacking phase goes to 4-2-1-3 then 3-1-3-3, or 3-3-1-3; and the Defending phase is a 4-4-1-1 or 4-5-1, therefore:
We have five or six potential formations coming from one; depending on where the ball is and who has it.
I believe a team needs a regular way to play, an ultra attacking way to play, and an ultra defensive way to play to suit all these situations of winning and losing.
Try to make the changes as simple as possible.

Examples:
1. We are winning but are under great pressure, to ease that pressure for a short while we may need to switch to a very defensive set up to weather the storm and slow the opponents down. So we go from a 4-2-3-1 to a 4-5-1. This is an easy way to do it as all we change are the two wide players to play deeper and have more defensive start positions; the rest of the team positions stay the same.
2. We are losing and need to be more attacking and get more players forward, which may leave us exposed at the back, but we need positive action. So, again; as just an example, go from your regular 4-2-3-1 to a 3-3-1-3 system. If this is too complicated then just have the two wide players push on to become a front three so the rest of the team stays the same and we are a 4-2-1-3.

Most of the time our regular system of play will be all that we need; these reconfigurations are only to be considered at extreme times in a game.
Do NOT change a system of play for the sake of changing it if the regular way is working well, always do it with a reason in mind.
This is a good education for the players also for their future development.

PARTNERSHIPS ON THE FIELD

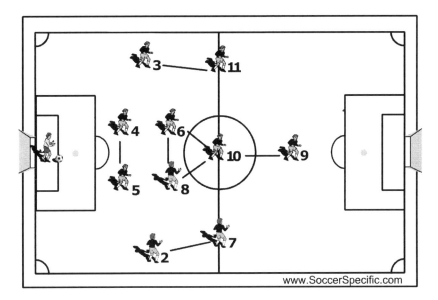

www.SoccerSpecific.com

The partnerships / relationships of players on the field.

1. (3) and (11): You can have a right footed number (11) cutting inside onto his strong foot to receive the pass going outside to inside..They can interchange offensively and provide defensive cover for each other.

2. (2) and (7): You can have a left footed number (7) cutting inside onto his strong foot to receive the pass going outside to inside. They can interchange offensively and provide defensive cover for each other.

3. (4) and (5): The center-back combination with great communication is a vital link for the team.

4. (6) and (8): Defensive Midfielder (6) drops in and the more attacking (8) pushes forward to support (10), but you can have them share this if they are both suitable for the role. Most teams have one defensive midfielder and one attacking midfielder.

5. (6), (8) and (10): A triangular relationship between these three players can create many options in attacking buildup play.

6. (10) and (9): (9) as the target striker and (10) as the shadow striker playing just behind him

7. (7) and (11) can cut inside to create space outside for the overlapping fullbacks (2) and (3) to receive and cross with their strongest foot.

OTHER POTENTIAL PLAYER COMBINATIONS

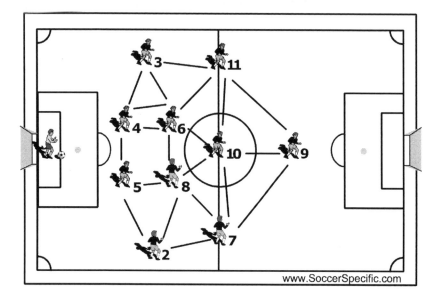

1. Looks complicated, but these show the possible combinations players can have on the field of play. Most are in triangular formations.
2. It is important to have these players playing together in training as much as possible to get familiar with each other, either in twos as previously shown (and simpler to create), or threes and fours as shown here.
3. You can design small sided exercises for each group to practice movements together.

1. Different combinations emerge as the team shape changes. Here we have diamond combinations. The 4 centrally positioned players (7), (9), (10) and (11) are fairly close together and this gives the team a big potential overload in this part of the field and many teams look to exploit this by playing through them.

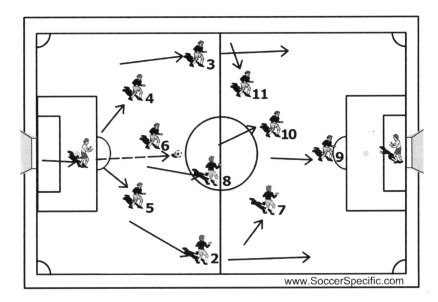

1. Where (6) passes will depend on how the opposing defenders react to these combination movements. But with the left footer on the right and right footer on the left plus the fullbacks we have two great options, one coming inside to attack the space inside and possibly shoot with his strongest foot; and one overlapping with width to get a good cross in, again with his strongest foot.
2. Wide players can come inside and position centrally to receive the pass; it does not have to be in sync with the fullback overlapping necessarily. These players are particularly difficult to pick up when they make these runs. Does the fullback track inside? Or the wide midfield player? Does the central midfielder pick them up? If the movement is quick then does the opposition have time to communicate this to each other? Do they track him or pass him on?

Let's say (6) is the passing player here.
- Full backs BOTH go forward up to around the half way line
- Center backs go AT LEAST as wide as the penalty area.
- Number (10) pushes forward into an attacking position
- Number (6) works initially as a sweeper in front of the center backs and if losing possession drops in behind them acting as a sweeper behind.
- Opponents likely will have one or two strikers pushed on so someone should get free to receive the ball, likely number (6).
- If they push three strikers on to go with a 3v3 then we have to play longer. So the back 3 just push up and condense the play.
- Starts off as a 4-2-3-1, goes to a 4-2-1-3 and finishes as an attacking 3-3-1-3 or 3-1-3-3.
- Visual Cues: When the ball is in the center of the field with (6) or (8) this is the visual cue for (11) AND (7) TO CUT INSIDE AND FOR (2) AND (3) TO OVERLAP.
- The player on the ball has to decide which pass to make depending on how the defenders react to the movements.
- So we have a staged pre planned movement in free play, but decision making based on the opponent's reaction to these movements. So the end product can be different in each situation.

- You can determine alternate moves you have practiced by one word signals or a number of whistles: 1 whistle: (7) and (11) cut inside, 2 whistles. (2) and (3) cut Inside, 3 whistles: Play the ball into the striker; 4 whistles: Interchange of (9) and (10) with (10) making a channel run to receive the pass down the side from wide.

CHOICES HERE "COULD BE":
1. Pass to (11)
2. Pass to (7)
3. Pass to (2)
4. Pass to (3)
5. Pass to (9)
6. Pass to (10)
7. Pass to (8)
8. Or (6) can run or dribble forward with the ball
9. Pass back if (6) can't pass forward to keep possession
10. So it is STILL DIFFICULT for the opponents to predict where the ball will go next despite it being the "same pre planned set up"
11. More phase plays develop from this initial buildup as shown later in the presentation

Coaching Points:
Observe:
- Initial team shape (4-2-3-1) moving to an attacking shape
- Timing of the runs (late and fast is best)
- Timing of the pass (if the choice is to pass)
- Where the pass goes (based on the opponent's set up and individual and team reactions)
- The next phase of play as each event (a pass, run; dribble etc) starts a new phase of play
- Buildup Phase of play, team shape (4-2-1-3) or (3-1-3-3 / 3-3-1-3)
- End Product Phase of play, team shape (3-1-4-2)

END POSITIONS IN ATTACKING PLAY

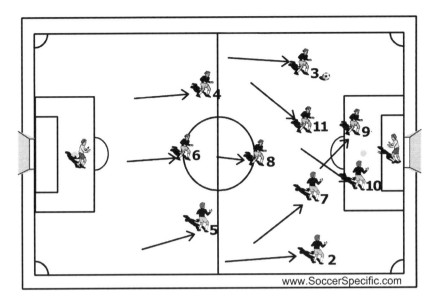

1. The team has attacked and this is the shape we can finish with.
2. Like a 3-1-4-2, with (8) keeping the defensive shape in front of the back three, screening passes into the opponent's strikers if they win the ball and try a quick counter attack.

1. The end product here with (9) and (10) being the two attacking strikers in the box.
2. Alternatively it can be the wide player who supports the striker (9).
3. If the ball comes in from the right then (11) is the second striker (and may even switch with (9) if time allows and attack the near post). If the ball comes from the left then it is (7) who supports (9). It will depend on who gets there earlier to support (9); perhaps (10)'s start position is closer so (7) or (11) will offer secondary support inside or on the edge of the box.

ATTACKING TEAM SHAPE

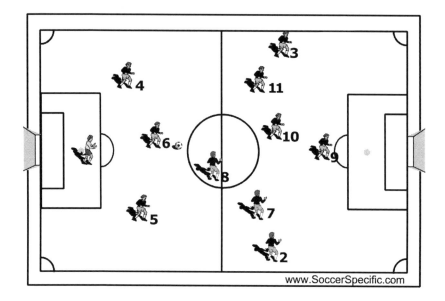

www.SoccerSpecific.com

1. Slightly over-exaggerated set up with both fullbacks attacking at the same time. It is presented like this to show some of the possibilities of this system. Possibly on one side of the field the wide player stays wide and on the other the wide player cuts inside. It all depends on the moment and how the opponents are set defensively.
2. Center midfielder (8) has to fill in as an attacking player with the view that if we lose possession he is close enough to get back to a good defensive position.
3. That said, players look to fill in for each other so the team is not open to a quick counter attack by the opponents. If the opponents are known to be good counter attackers you may only go with one fullback at a time to ensure we are secure defensively.
4. The strength of attacking in numbers like this will depend on the confidence of the team at that moment; and also the score. Likely we are in a good winning position when we are attacking with such flare.
5. (6), (8) and (10) may position at angles off each other so their set up is not in a straight line, and this offers better support positions for each of them. So we have (6) the play maker, (8) the supporting player and (10) the shadow striker all working together on and off the ball.

USING DIFFERENT PINNIES TO IDENTIFY THE LEVEL OF MOVEMENT BETWEEN THE FOUR UNITS OF PLAYERS

1. Having just gained possession of the ball this is the initial starting attacking situation of the team. Some players have different colored pinnies on to compare and identify the extent of their movements within the attacking phase of play.

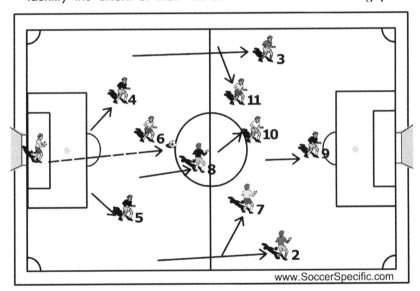

1. Here fullbacks (2) and (3) in red show big advances in movement. Defensive midfielder (6) in green stays in position or even drops back to receive the ball and dictate the play, (7) and (11) in yellow both cut inside at various times freeing the space up wide for the fullbacks. Shadow striker (10) in white pushes on the support (9).

2. I feel this is a good way to see more clearly the amount of variation in positioning you can get from the players.

3. ALTERNATIVELY (6) CAN DROP INTO A RIGHT CENTER BACK POSITION AND

THAT CENTER BACK (5) STAYS IN THE MIDDLE, AS THE BRAZILIAN NATIONAL TEAM DOES IT. So in the above diagram or the diagram below, (5) would stay central and (6) would drop into the right center back position to become a third center back.

Coaching Points:
Movements off the ball to create the INITIAL attacking shape
- Changing personnel between units with new combinations created by the forward motion of the team
- Balanced shape throughout the team with midfield players playing in angles off each other
- Good communication between (2) and (7) and (3) and (11) to determine who goes inside and who stays outside in the ADVANCED attacking shape
- Decision making by the passer; which player does he pass to of the several options he has?
- Timing and angle of the pass and the runs to receive
- Interchanges of the number (9) and (10) to create space for each other and for other teammates
- Team shape defensively; should the move break down we maintain cover behind the attack
- End Product of a goal scored

THE MOVEMENT OFF THE BALL OF THE PLAYERS IS THE KEY TO MAKING THIS SYSTEM OF PLAY WORK AS THERE IS SO MUCH INTERCHANGE BETWEEN THE FOUR UNITS OF PLAYERS

SECOND BALL INTRODUCTION

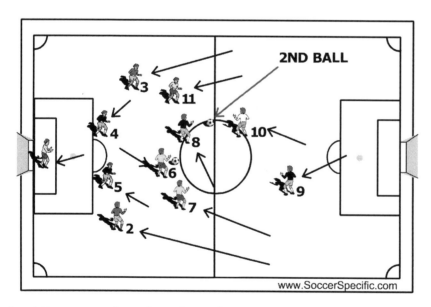

1. We are attacking through number (6) in the previous diagram but to test the defensive concentration of the team the coach can throw another ball into the field and the team then have to forget about the first ball and tackle their defensive shape against this second ball as if an opponent has it attacking forward.

2. Here we see the team drop back into a 4-4-1-1 defensive shape. (8) moves across to close the ball down (and delays in an actual game situation). The back four recover back to take up their usual shape. (7) and (11) drop back into a midfield four. (10) double teams with (8). (9) drops back into a space where the ball may be played in an actual game situation and the keeper recovers back to his goal line.

DEVELOPING PLAY THRU THE NUMBER 6

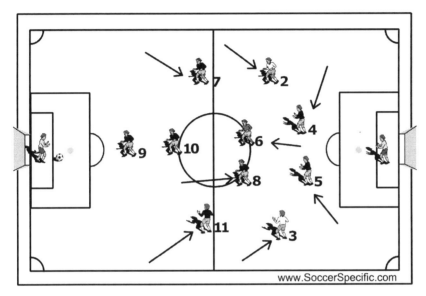

1. Here we show how the team gets organized defensively. It is more of a 4-4-1-1 now though (10) may be asked to drop deeper and therefore makes it a 4-5-1 depending on how the coach sees his tactics.

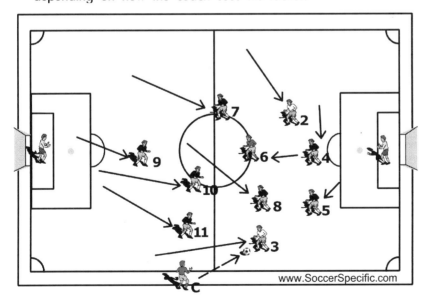

1. Here as the team is attacking and in the wide and long set up, the coach throws or passes another ball into another part of the field and the players have to leave the first ball and take their now defensive team shape off this second ball.

2. Now they have to arrange themselves into a defensive shape and defend like the opponents have the second ball. Here fullback (3) presses the ball as he is closest to it and the rest of the team takes their shape from him.

3. This is good to teach players to make recovery runs back towards their own goal and by the shortest route. Now they go from attacking wide and long to defending short and tight; and as quickly as possible.

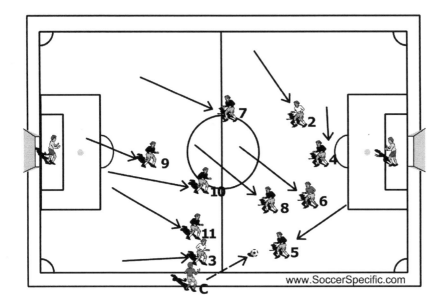

www.SoccerSpecific.com

1. If (3) and (11) cannot recover back quickly enough then center back (5) may need to close the ball down and be the first pressing defender delaying the forward attack. Defensive midfielder (6) drops in to cover at center back.

2. By delaying, (5) helps recovering players (10), (11) and (3) get back behind the ball or attack the ball from the other side. In a game situation (5) does not have to attempt to win the ball (and thus perhaps be beaten 1v1 and leave us exposed). Rather, take a safety first option and delay.

3. Alternatively if (8) is closest to the ball he can be the first pressing player and (10) can drop into his original more central position.

4-2-3-1 BECOMING A 4-2-1-3 IN ATTACK OR A 3-3-1-3 OR EVEN A 3-1-3-3 DEPENDING ON HOW YOU LOOK AT IT

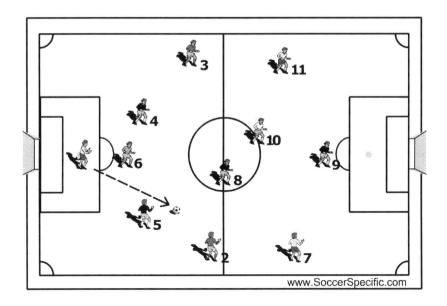

A) PLAYING THROUGH ZONE 14 - THE SHADOW STRIKER ZONE

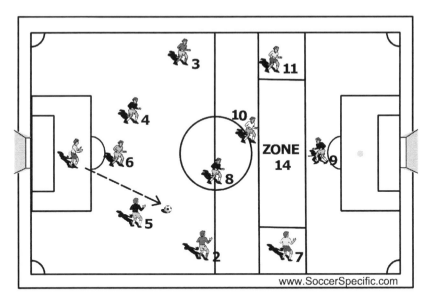

1. You can set out the field where we have a zone to play into. This is an important zone known as Zone 14; which is between the opponent's back four and midfield and a good area to exploit.

2. You can use this area as a guide for the movements of players, be it the striker (9) dropping into it to receive, or shadow striker (10) moving forward into it to receive, or (7) and (11) cutting outside to inside to receive; or even fullbacks (2) and (3) to cut inside to receive or (7) and (11) cutting inside to clear the space outside for (2) or (3) to receive still in or close to the shadow striker zone 14 if you extend it the full width of the field.

3. This at least gives players a space to observe and it can help as a guide to their runs.

B) USING CONES TO REPRESENT A BACK FOUR AND MIDFIELD FOUR

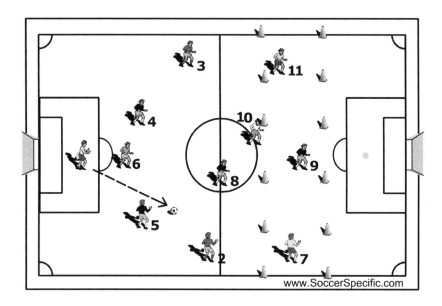

www.SoccerSpecific.com

1. Back line of four cones doubles as an offside line for the front players to time their runs against.

www.SoccerSpecific.com

1. (11) attacks the space between cones (A) and (B) and can create a 2v1 with (3) against cone (A), or a 2v1 against cone (B) with player (9). The same on the other side of the field creating two options of 2v1s. The development will apply when you put players in these positions. Defenders (A) and (D) may be taken inside by (7) and (11) to free up the flanks for (2) and (3) in the actual game situation.

C) PASSING OPTIONS

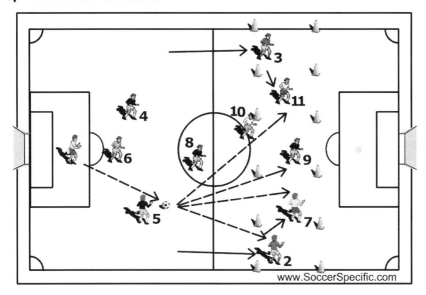

1. These movements create many good passing options. These are just a few to consider.
2. You can have a goalkeeper and cones for 10 outfield players to simulate the opponents if you like to show the gaps that you can play through.

D) FULLBACKS "UNDER"LAPPING

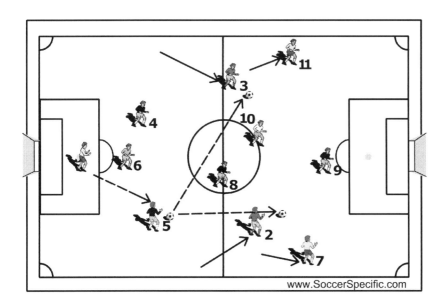

1. Imagine (11) breaking wide taking the opponent's fullback with him, creating space inside for our fullback (3) to underlap and receive the pass.

E) ADDING A BACK FOUR AGAINST US

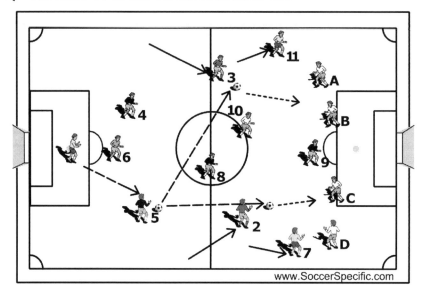

1. Here (11) does exactly that with (A) shadowing him outside, leaving a gap inside for our fullback (3) to advance into and attack between (A) and (B) with the possibility of creating a 2v1 with Striker (9) against (B). Encourage your fullbacks to be proactive.

F) MORE POTENTIAL PASSING OPTIONS

1. The player on the ball plays as positively as possible and as forward thinking as possible with the notion that he can go to the side or back if necessary in order to maintain possession.

Coaching Points:

- Composure on the ball
- Positioning of the players to offer a passing option for the player on the ball
- Movements off the ball to create space for oneself or a teammate
- Combination movements to create space for each other (example: (2) and (7) combining to create space for themselves and/or each other)
- Timing and Angles of runs to receive; or to create space for others (players must not go too early to close down their own spaces)
- Timing, accuracy and weight of the pass (trying to play into the path of the receiver so he does not need to interrupt his running pattern)
- All movement and passing will be determined by how the defending team reacts and where the spaces open up.

G) BOTH WIDE PLAYERS CUT IN AT THE SAME TIME

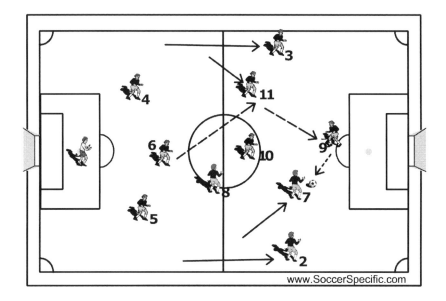

www.SoccerSpecific.com

1. Potential passing movements: (11) cuts inside and receives the pass from (6), and plays it to the feet of striker (9) who lays a first time pass off to (7) cutting inside to attack the goal or get a shot on goal.
2. The faster this movement is done with fewer touches on the ball (all one touch if possible if the timing of the passing and movements are in sync) the more likely it will be successful.
3. The coach dictates the movements initially, so have a few set phases of play with certain movements and certain passes to be performed in the shadow play. Once they have grasped the few ideas that you have created for them, let it go free and let the players determine the phases of play for themselves.

H) ONE WIDE PLAYER CUTS IN ONLY

www.SoccerSpecific.com

1. An example could be the phase of play above. The coach dictates the movements beforehand. The Keeper passes / throws to (5) who lays it back to (6). (6) passes to (4) who plays it into the feet of striker (9). In this phase of play (9) cannot turn so he has to lay the ball off to (8) who already has an angled approach off his position. (7) cuts inside, creating space wide for (2) to overlap and run into the space and (8) plays a ball in front of (2) to run onto and cross. The coach determines all these passes in advance.

2. Then we will work on the movements of (9), (7), (10) and (11) into or around the box for the finish.

3. As the ball comes back to (8) this can be a VISUAL CUE for (10) and (11) to move forward along with (7) and (2). You can make a rule that when the ball is passed back to one player, another player has to attack and run forward like a third man run. This will put them into good supporting positions. Here if (10) made the forward run as (9) is just passing the ball back, he is a good option for (8) to pass to also; as would be (11). There are so many combinations you can work on here but pick three or four and practice them as they may happen in a real game situation and the players will recognize it from training and make the correct runs and passes.

4. Having just one wide player cutting in is a safer way to play for some coaches if they are more comfortable with some defensive security in general or if the game situation calls for a more cautious approach, such as when your team has a lead.

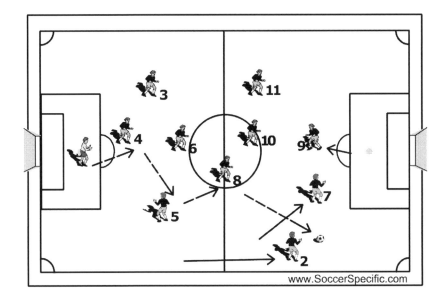

1. Here we show such a situation where only one fullback and wide player attack together down the side the ball is on. The other fullback (3) tucks in and stays in a defensive position. (11) can still provide attacking support on the other side of the field.

I) BECOMES A 3-1-3-3 (DEPENDING ON HOW FAR ADVANCED THE WING BACKS ARE)

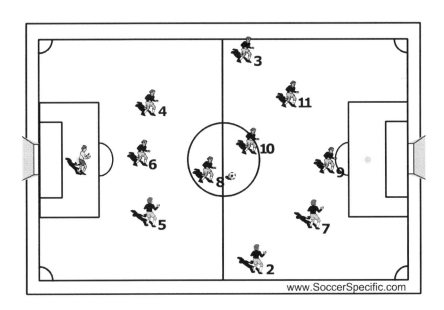

1. Front three tucked close together, creating space wide for the fullbacks (now playing as wing backs).

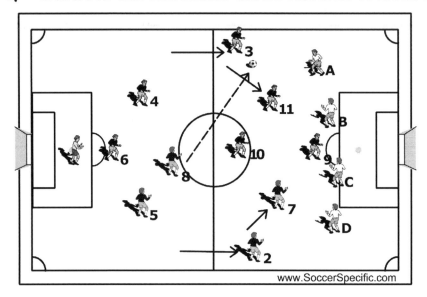

1. If the opponent's full backs are positioned too wide in dealing with the overlapping wing backs the opponents may even have a 3v2 against their two center backs, which is an ideal situation for our team. While this is unlikely to be allowed to happen, at any one moment if the attacking play by our team is fast enough the opponents may not have the foresight to adjust quickly enough to deal with it and for a moment or two we may create an overload centrally. Remember, we have the advantage of knowing what we will do in advance; the opponents do not and this may create the moment we are looking for.

2. Here (7), (9) and (11) outnumber (B) and (C). Likely (D) will tuck in to even it up and the opponent's midfield may track back to deal with this attack. However, if it is done quickly on the counter attack this situation may develop for us.

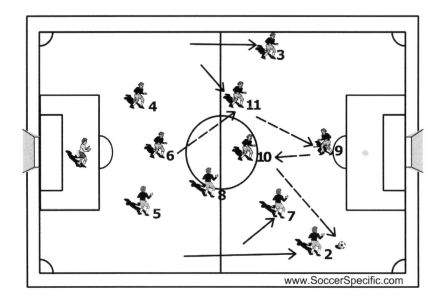

1. Another idea. (9) comes short to receive to feet and cannot turn. (10) supports behind (9) to advance the phase of play. (7) cuts inside and creates space outside for overlapping fullback (2) to receive the pass outside off (10). Whether he passes to (7) or (2) (or someone else) will depend on the defensive positioning and marking of the opponents in that split second.

2. This happens so quickly in the game that having the awareness we teach from a young age is paramount to identifying the playing options before receiving the ball, and can be the difference between a good player and a great player.

3. It may even be that there is no obvious pass on for (10) and his best option is to run forward with the ball and attack the goal, but it is crucial that he identifies this as being the best option as early as possible, preferrably before receiving the ball.

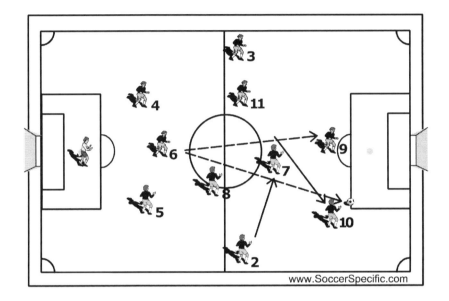

www.SoccerSpecific.com

1. Another example of movement, but this time with a different combination. Now we have (7) and (10) interchanging to help each other. The more the team practices and perfects these movements in training the better success they will have in the actual game situation.

2. Start in training with the more obvious ones such as the combinations of (2) and (7) and (3) and (11) and build the idea up as the players gain more knowledge and confidence in themselves and in each other.

K) SWITCHING THE POINT OF ATTACK QUICKLY

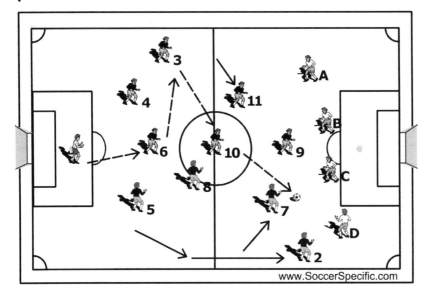

1. After a shadow play bring in a back four to play against. Often having defenders in to react to movements of the attacking players makes it "easier" to indentify the best passes rather than playing 11 v 0. Players defending can only intercept passes to begin and cannot tackle, but rather must jockey and try to delay.

2. Looking to switch the point of attack can be a great move to confuse the opponents if done quickly with few touches on the ball. Here we go from central to wide left, then across the field to wide right, exploiting the combination movements of (2) and (7).

3. Here (10) chooses to pass to (7) coming inside onto his strongest foot, running directly at the opposition. Fullback (2) makes an overlap run for two reasons; a) to receive the pass, or b) to occupy and draw defender (D) wide to allow space inside (7) to attack center back (C) 1v1; who in turn may be pulled out of a position of cover; which in turn may free up (9) or any other advancing player in the attack, possibly (10) or (11).

4. Good dribblers are perfect for this role.

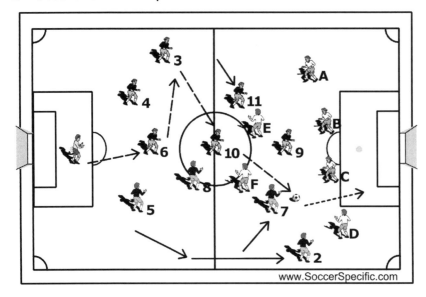

1. Same movement shown but building the opponent's numbers up. Now a keeper, a back four, a central midfield pairing and leading to eventually playing 11v11.

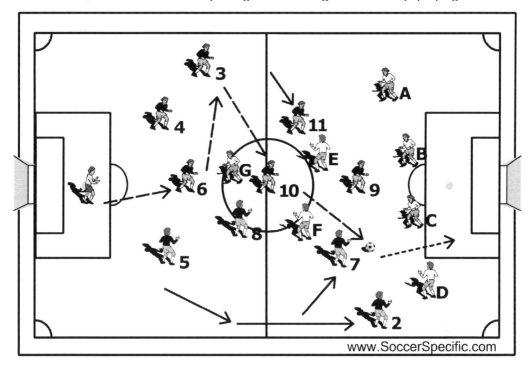

1. Now we go to an 11v8; a keeper, a back four, a central midfield pairing and and a lone striker to pressure the back players leading to eventually playing 11v11.

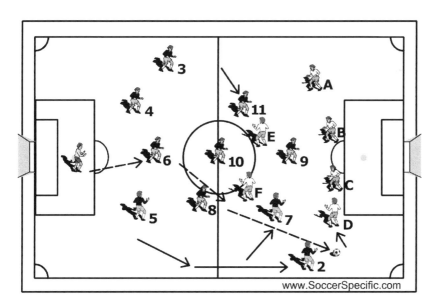

1. (7) attacks inside and takes defender (D) inside with him so he is marked and cannot receive the pass easily.
2. This frees up space wide for overlapping fullback (2) to receive and cross. (7) can continue his run into the penalty area to get on the end of the cross. As (D) is recovering he has his back to the ball tracking (7)'s run; so is in a poor and disadvantaged defensive position.

1. If both wide players come inside there are now two good pass options for (6) and / or (8). Here defender (A) comes inside to track the run of wide player (11) and this releases fullback (3) to receive the pass on the overlap.
2. Both (7) and (11) can continue their runs into and/or around the penalty area to get on the end of the cross.

L) A FULL 11 v 11 TRAINING PRACTICE

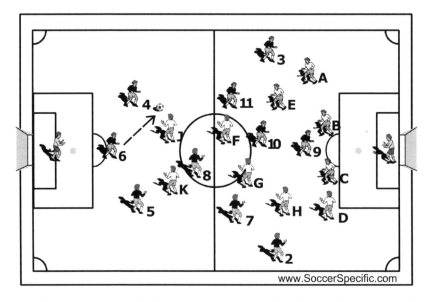

1. Finally have an 11v11 game, passive defending to begin; building up into a full scale practice.

2. Playing against a 4-4-2 here but if you know the next opponent's playing system you would prepare your team in training to cope with this.

3. It is imperative you prepare your team in training for the game situation. If players know some movements in advance and practice them, they will recognize certain situations that arise in the match and be able to deal with them accordingly.

4. Example: when a central midfield player, perhaps (6), is facing forward and has time on the ball to pass, this is a CUE for (2) and (7) and (3) and (11) respectively to work their combination movements and they can identify the moment in advance, which is to our advantage. Or it could be when (8) or (10) get the ball, depending on how far up the field you want this movement of the outside players to begin. The more movements like this you have the better. But be careful, doing too many can confuse the players.

5. This is now almost like a set play (where you have pre planned movements the opponents most likely will not know about; which gives us an advantage) within open dynamic play.

6. Obviously we do not want to stifle the creativity of attacking play and players need to be allowed to play "Off the Cuff" and be imaginative and creative, but having a set move or two in dynamic open play offers other options also.

M) WIDE PLAYER (11) CONTINUING HIS RUN ACROSS THE FRONT OF THE DEFENSE

www.SoccerSpecific.com

1. Showing the development in an 11v11 game situation. Here the build up is slower with more passes. (4) receives the pass but his forward pass is blocked by (J), so he lays the ball off to (8) who also has his forward pass blocked, by (G) this time. His pass back to (5) at last finds an opening to pass the ball forward. Defenders (H) and (D) are taken up giving attention to (2) and (7).

2. The time this phase of play has taken gives the wide player (11) time to not only cut inside but also to continue his run across the front of the back four and receive the ball centrally (Messi of Barcelona does this run all the time, going from the right and inside onto his better left foot. Ronaldo of real Madrid often does the same run left to right). Opponents are not quite sure who to mark here so this can

be a very productive run, especially if (11) is a right footed player coming in from the left onto his stronger foot to get a shot on goal and vice versa.

3. Striker (9) has moved out of the space to leave it free for (11) and hopefully in doing so has taken a defender out of that space as well. (7) continues his outside to in forward run also and can link up with (11) and perhaps create a 2v1 against (C).

N) TIMING OF THE PASS BY (4) AND TIMING OF THE RUN BY (11)

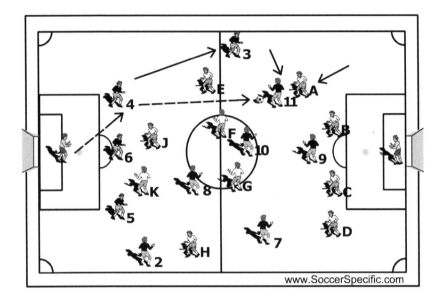

www.SoccerSpecific.com

1. Here the timing of the run by (11) is too early. So when (11) receives the ball he is already in his own space and has closed it down for himself and is receiving facing backwards. He is still in a position where we maintain possession but facing forward running at the defense would be better. He can still link up with (10) inside or perhaps receive and turn but timing his run better means he is facing forward when he receives it.

2. The run is best made as late as possible and as fast as possible to ensure the fullback (A) does not get there early either. If he goes early and has to wait for the pass then the fullback can read this move and follow him so he is marked when he receives the ball. He might even check wider and take the fullback with him, then check back quickly to catch him off balance.

3. Add to this the possibility that the run has been timed correctly but the pass is too late and you will see that success for this movement depends on both the passer and receiver being in synch with their timing in each phase of the process. Continual practice with the likely players to be in these positions will be needed to fine tune the timing of the run and pass.

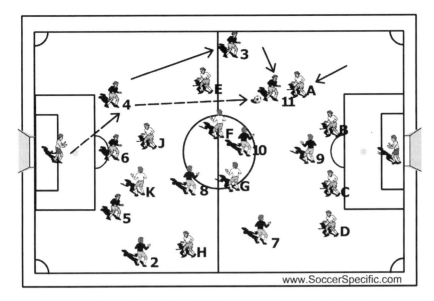

1. Here we show the timing of the pass and the timing of the run being in synch and successful. Now, (11) can receive the ball facing forward and attacking at pace. As previously suggested a right footer coming inside onto his strong foot can present a perfect opportunity for a shot at goal or a run inside against the fullback (A)'s weaker left foot.

O) DEFENSIVE PLAY

1. The 4-2-3-1 is a flexible way to play employing four units rather than the usual three. It can transform quickly into a defensive 4-4-1-1 or 4-5-1 by moving back the two wide outside midfielders. We have solid a defensive block of a back four and two central midfielders.

2. If you are playing a defensive type of 4-2-3-1 then the two players you must choose carefully will be the two wide players in the three. In an attacking set up you may play two wingers, in a defensive set up you may go for two more defensively minded midfield players, or, if you want a bit of both you may play a winger on one side and a defensive midfielder on the other side. Or, it may just depend on the players you have available as to how you set up the team.

3. At the same time you may balance each of these with the type of fullback they play with. It is all about getting the right balance between the two players on each side.

P) ATTACKING PHASE

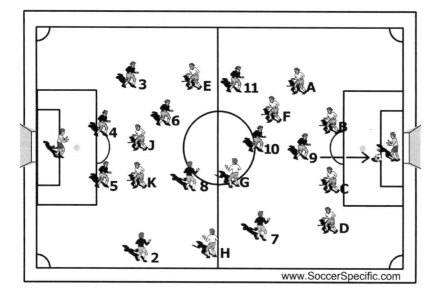

1.   We are attacking and (9) shoots at goal

Q) IMMEDIATE DEFENSIVE PHASE

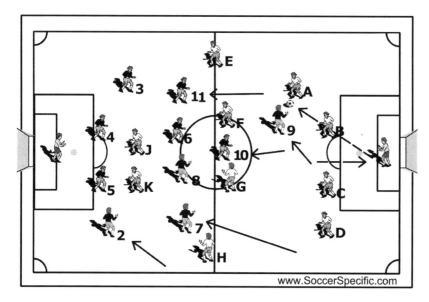

1.   Here (9) shoots at goal and the keeper saves the ball and immediately starts an attack through (A). If we are defending deep behind the ball we drop back into a 4-4-1-1 with the closest player (9) pressing the ball to try to delay the opponent's forward motion and give his team time to get defensively organized behind him.
2.   With this system also you can apply a defensive strategy based on offensive pressure in advanced areas of the field, especially from the wide midfield players (looking to regain possession in the attacking third of the field).
3.   So, alternatively if we are defending high then the previous forward position of (11) means he is closest to (A) and should push in to pressure and both (9) and (10) could slide over to support.

DEFENDING IN A 4-2-3-1 AGAINST DIFFERENT SYSTEMS OF PLAY

4-2-3-1 DEFENDING AGAINST A 4-4-2

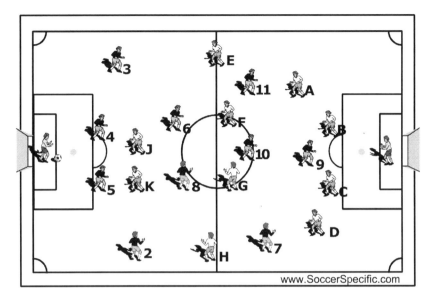

www.SoccerSpecific.com

1. The basic set up of each team. When attacking we may have number (10) free and should try to play through him. Do they drop a midfielder in to mark him or push a center back out?

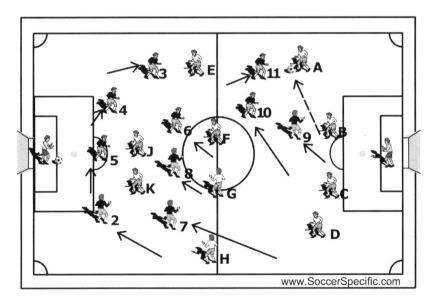

www.SoccerSpecific.com

1. Here we apply the previously discussed method of pressing high up the field with three players. When defending we can press close to the ball. (11) is the first pressing player and (3) presses the wide player (E).
2. (11) presses and shows inside to the strength of the team. (10) closes the next space off, (9) covers across to stop the back pass, (6) drops back in to stop the

pass through to strikers (J) and (K). Everyone slides across to fill the spaces closer to the side of the field the ball is on.

DEFENDING WITH OUR ATTACKING SHAPE WHEN GIVING THE BALL AWAY AGAINST A 4-4-2

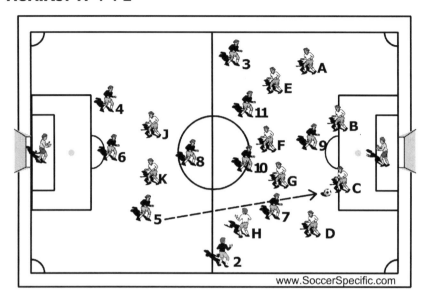

1. Here we have our full on attacking shape but we give the ball away with a bad pass. Even in our attacking shape we are well organized to be able to defend with a 3v2 at the back and (8) in front as a screen. Attacking fullbacks are close enough to get back as the opponents will have tracked them back anyway when we had the ball.

4-2-3-1 DEFENDING AGAINST A 4-3-3

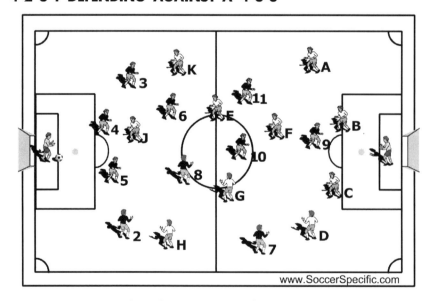

1. We are outnumbered in central midfield when they have the ball, so (10) must drop back in and make it a 3v3 in the middle. We still have a 4v3 advantage at the back.

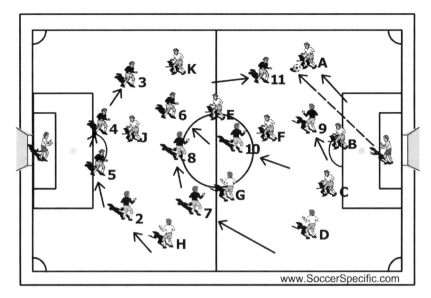

1. Our fullbacks can deal with their wide attackers (H) and (K); unless they are struggling 1v1, in which case you will need to ask the two wide midfield players to drop back and help. If the ball is at their fullback (as in the diagram) the first task of our wide midfielder is to press the ball (unless you are playing low pressure) so (3) must get tight and 1v1 with (K).

4-2-3-1 DEFENDING AGAINST A 3-4-1-2

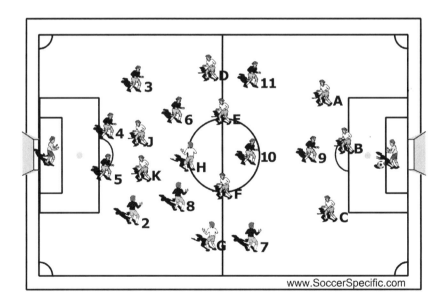

1. Their keeper has the ball so initially we can position positively.

1. The fullback (A) receives the ball and adjustments need to be made now. (11) presses showing inside again, (8) drops back to pick up their attacking midfielder (H), and (6) slides across to mark (E); and (10) drops back in to pick up (F). (7) makes it a midfield five with (11) as the pressing midfield player.

4-2-3-1 DEFENDING AGAINST A 3-5-2 (3-1-4-2)

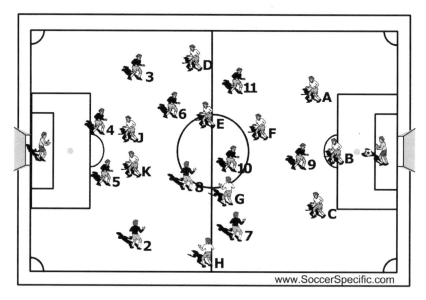

1. There is a danger of getting overloaded in midfield here. All three of our attacking unit need to defend and help out our two defensive midfield players, and all three also need to break quickly when we get the ball.
2. Here (7) and (11) mark slightly in advance of their immediate opponent, waiting to see if the opponents play from the back. With a 3v1 there, it is a possibility (unless we defend with low pressure and don't pressure them until the midfield line).

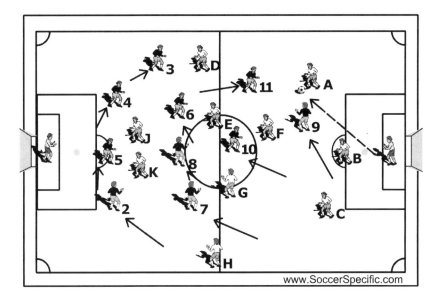

1. The ball is played to (A) and (11) has to close him down showing INSIDE and cutting the pass off to (D). (7) then slides across on the other side of the field and (10) must join in to help the defensive midfield unit.
2. We leave their wide player (H) free on the opposite side and our fullback (3) deals with (D).

4-2-3-1 DEFENDING AGAINST A 3-4-3

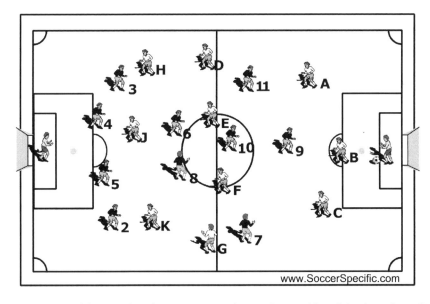

1. A possible overload against us down the width of both sides of the field, with three players potentially playing down each side (if their defensive players are comfortable creating space wide) so our adjustments may be slightly different to the 3-5-2 where they have more strength in the center of the field. Similar to the previous set up. (11) and (7) are ready to push in if necessary if (A) or (C) receive the pass. At the same time they are aware they may need to drop in and mark their immediate opponent should the ball be played to the other side of the field.

2.   This is anticipation defensive positioning and here (6) and (8) are ready to back them up, whichever side of the field the ball is played.

www.SoccerSpecific.com

3.   With three players down each side of the field (A), (D) and (H), and (C), (G) and (K), defensive midfielder (6) must slide across to mark their wide midfielder (D). Previously, with two opposing strikers only, it was (3) who pushed in, but he is now occupied by their wide striker (H).

ATTACKING IN A 4-2-3-1 AGAINST DIFFERENT SYSTEMS

It is important to note that changing the team shape does not happen in one instant as shown here but will just be one phase of several.

Below; as (5) receives the ball, (7) and (11) will not necessarily cut inside at the same moment but the ultimate phase idea is for them to do this as the ball travels forward.

4-2-3-1 ATTACKING AGAINST A 4-4-2

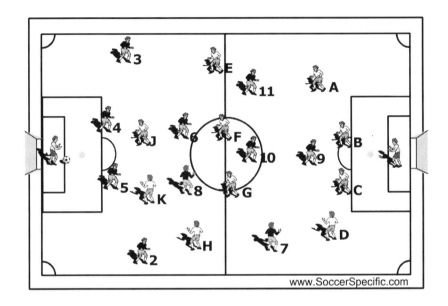

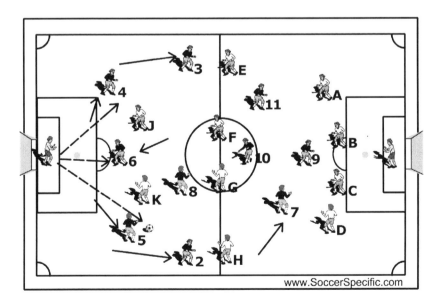

1.   This is just one idea of several that may happen based on what opponents do. The wide midfielders let (7) and (11) push into their fullbacks (A) and (D), still having a 4v3 in their favor.

2. We have a 3v2 in our favor at the back so can develop play from there. Who we get out though depends on how the two opposing strikers position. But they cannot mark three players, so someone will get free if they are confident to get wide enough. Here we show it as center back (5) starting the buildup play.

4-2-3-1 ATTACKING AGAINST A 4-3-3

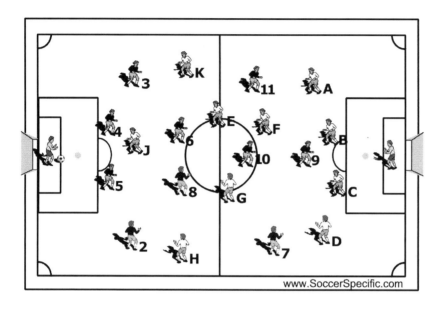

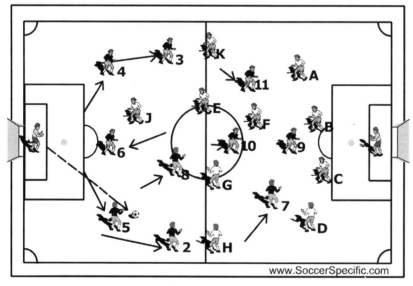

1. If the opposing front wide players (H) and (K) track back with our fullbacks, it leaves two players free at the back. If they stay forward and mark (4), (5) and (6) then our fullbacks get free. Alternatively their center midfield players (E) and (G) might go wide to deal with our fullbacks but this will leave the middle open for us to play through.

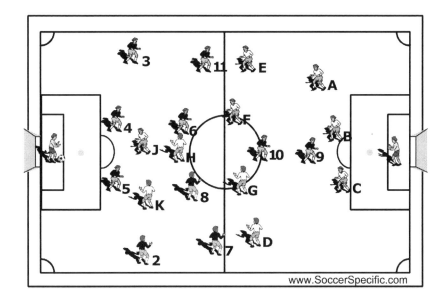

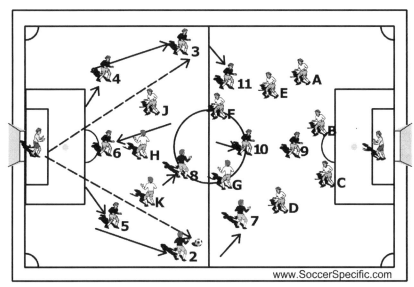

1. Their attacking midfielder (H) pushes in to make a 3v3 against us at the back. This means we cannot play from the back in this set up.
2. Their wide midfielders (E) and (D) cannot afford to let our two wide players (7) and (11) push onto their defenders and create a 3v3 so they track back with them. This means our fullbacks can get free to attack as wingbacks as shown through our fullback (2). They may or may not drop a player back to pick up our number (10).

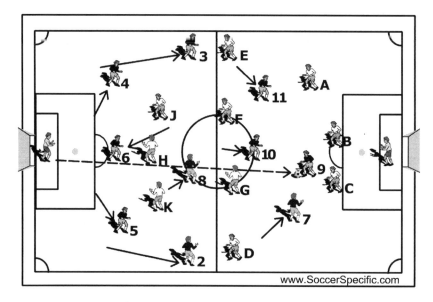

1. Their wide midfielders gamble and pass on our attacking flank players (7) and (11) to let us have a 3v3 against them up front. In this case, our keeper's best choice is to kick the ball long to our striker (9) for the 3v3.

2. Our number (10) can also help the attack and they may have to drop one of their center midfielders back to cope with this.

4-2-3-1 ATTACKING AGAINST A 3-5-2 (3-1-4-2)

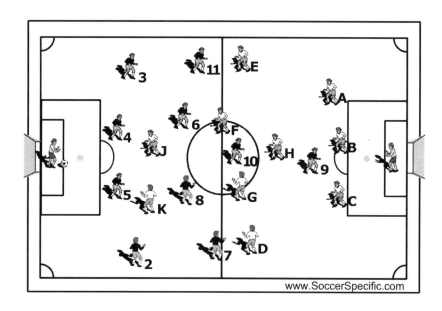

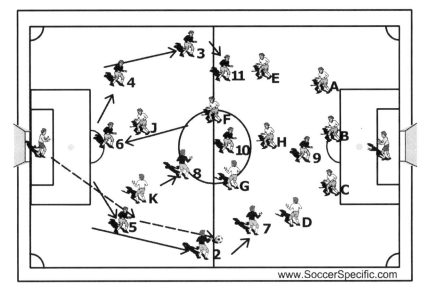

1. Here they have a defensive midfielder who can pick up (10). They are strong in the center so we can attack through the wide areas.
2. We have a 3v2 advantage to play from the back. We also have the advantage in wide areas with both fullbacks getting free is their wide midfielders track our wide midfielders (7) and (11) who clear the space for them. If they stay to pick up the fullbacks we can go to a 3v3 up front.

4-2-3-1 ATTACKING AGAINST A 3-4-3

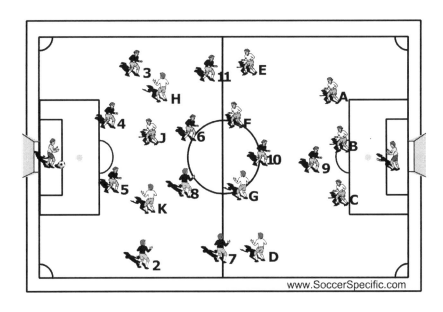

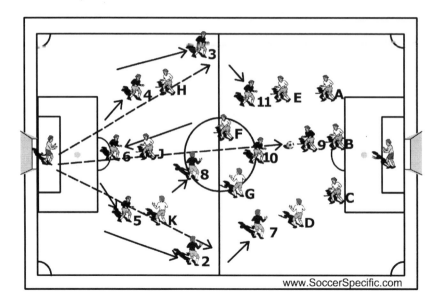

1. They go 3v3 against our back three. We get free in wide areas through our attacking fullbacks. They have a 2v1 in their favor in midfield so the best point of attack for us is through the wide channels.

2. We can also play with the long ball to the striker (9) and support quickly but we cannot safely play through the back three in this situation.

COACHING CLINICS TO USE FOR SPECIFIC TRAINING OF THE 4-2-3-1 SYSTEM OF PLAY

A) PASSING AND MOVING WARM UP

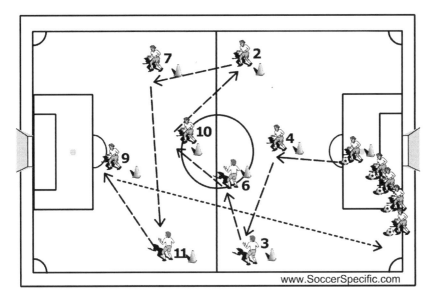

www.SoccerSpecific.com

1. Pass and follow in the team shape. You can do this for any team size, 6v6, 8v8, 9v9 or 11v11
2. Change the routines.
3. Several balls going at once and everyone moving.
4. Develop: Have players check to the ball to receive.
5. Develop: Have players check away to check back to the ball.
6. Play one and two touch.
7. This is getting the players to check and receive the pass. Check away to come back into the space created.
8. Follow the pass, lots of repetition. Two touch plays, receive and move the ball into space with a turn with one touch and pass with the second touch.
9. Pass to the back foot of the player or behind them to move them. Player receiving can point to where he wants the pass to go.
10. Develop: Give and go, 1-2 with the player passing to you.
11. Pass with the outside of the front foot.
12. Now playing give and go's to develop the play and get lots of touches for all the players.
13. Players pass and run to the next position.
14. Several balls should be going at once and everyone is moving.
15. Try different shapes with the players.

Make sure players check off at angles to receive the pass so they are side on and can go forward, to the side, and back with a run or a pass. You can start play from the keeper.

B) DEFENSIVE TEAM SHAPE

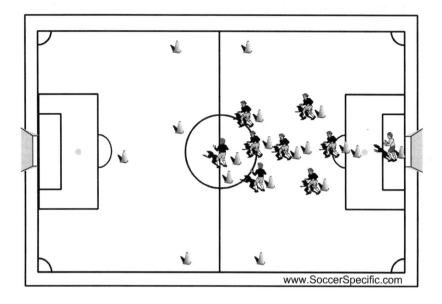

C) ATTACKING TEAM SHAPE FOR 9 v 9

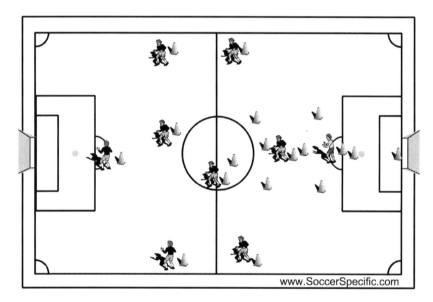

1. Players transition from a defensive shape to an attacking shape on the coach's command.

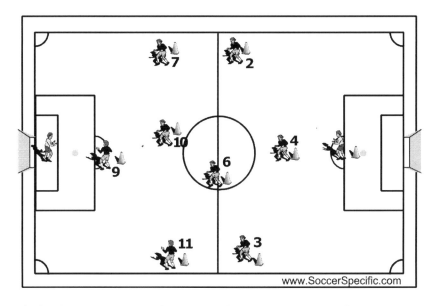

D) COORDINATED MOVEMENTS IN WIDE AREAS

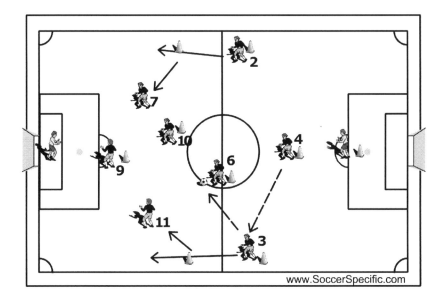

1. Wide players cut inside to create space outside for fullbacks to overlap or to receive to their feet running at the defense.
2. Have the players pass the ball around and then when it arrives at (6) that is the VISUAL CUE for the coordinated movements wide to make it easier for the players to understand when and where to make the runs.

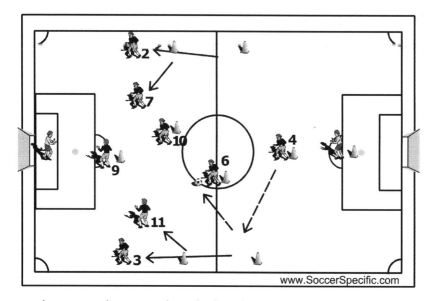

1. These two diagrams show both sides going at the same time but realistically it is better that one goes only to ensure we have stability at the back should the move break down.
2. When we go to an 11v11 with this system of play both fullbacks can go; as will be shown. We are preparing the players for these types of movements at a younger age so when they progress to the 11v11 they are already educated and trained in this.

E) SHADOW PLAY REHEARSAL

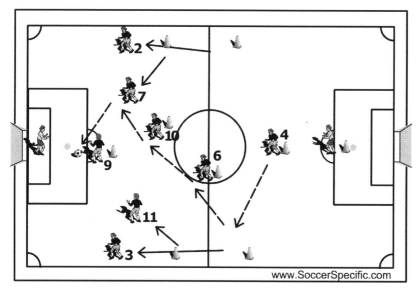

1. Here the coach dictates the movements to help the players more easily understand what to do. He instructs the players to pass from (4) to (3) to (6) to (10) to (7) to (9) to shoot on goal. At the same time he will have shown the players the interchanging movements to make to ensure this phase of play is developed correctly.

2. Once the players are comfortable with this they can then make their own movements and decisions on where and when to pass.

F) HIGH PRESSURE ON THE BALL

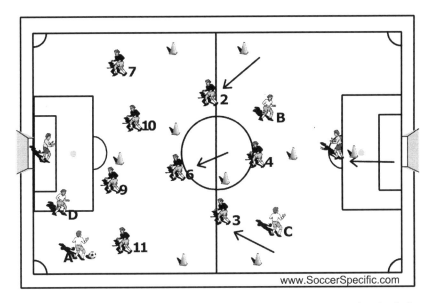

1. Here (11) has pressure on the ball. (A) cannot pass the ball forward, and this allows (2), (3) and (4) to push up to the half way line and condense the play from the back. Leave the opponents in an offside position (even though we do not play offside at 9 v 9).
2. If (2), (3) and (4) take their defensive shape off (C) and (B) and drop back, our team shape is wrong in this situation.

G) HIGH PRESSURE

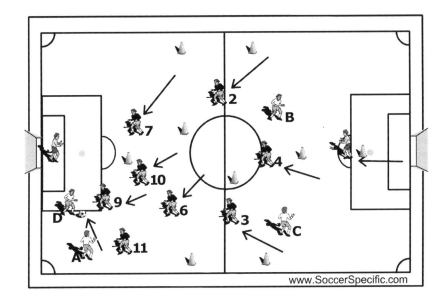

1. Let's say (9) is close enough to close down (D) as the ball travels to him. This is the BEST SOLUTION if it is possible to implement it quickly. High pressure close to the opponent's goal may result in a quick shot on goal when regaining possession.
2. High pressure like this also saves a lot of recovery runs for the rest of the team. They can push up and close down the spaces in front of them and don't need to worry about the ball in behind them because the delivery has been stopped by (11) and (9) at the source.

I) LOW PRESSURE

www.SoccerSpecific.com

1. Here, just as an example (because (9) would or should have closed down (D) already) we have (D) free and as the ball is played to him there will be no pressure on the ball, allowing the opponents to play it forward. As the ball is travelling (2), (3) and (4) have to anticipate long balls to unmarked (B) or (C). Practice: "When and where to Drop"
2. By the time the ball arrives forward they should have enough time to recover back into position. The rest of the team can use this situation to recover back for the next phase of play.

J) TEAM SHAPE DEFENSIVE POSITIONS

1. Players drop back into position to avoid the ball being played in behind them.

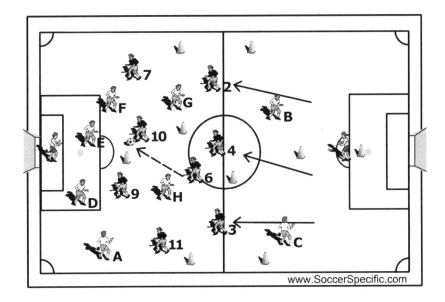

1. Here we have possession and are moving forward. (6) has passed to (10) who is now in a shooting position.
2. Use a CONDITION that the team cannot score unless all the players (except the keeper) are over the HALF WAY LINE. This teaches the team to push up from the back. This also trains any defenders who mentally switch off and do not push up, or are just too lazy to do the right thing and get up as a unit.
3. As they move to the 11 v 11 game and offside is applied, this will be a good lesson for them on pushing up and leaving players offside and forcing them to work back (something strikers do not like to do).

A COMFORT ZONE GAME DEVELOPING WIDTH IN THE PLAY IN A SMALL-SIDED GAME

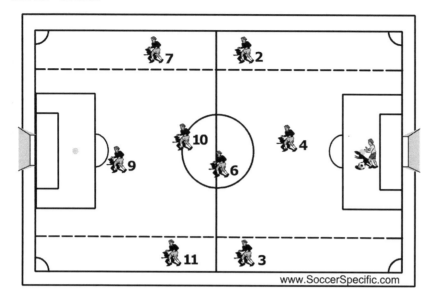

A) TO ENCOURAGE PLAYERS TO USE WIDTH AND OFFER AN AREA TO PLAY WITHOUT PRESSURE

1. If a player breaks wide into the outside channel on either side of the field and is in possession of the ball, he cannot be tackled. Defenders are not allowed into the channel.
2. The players on the team in possession of the ball can run the ball into the channel or have it passed to them into the channel.
3. This condition plants the seed in the minds of the players to immediately play with width when in possession. Numbers for this game can be 3v3 and upwards.
4. Our offensive team shape to begin. Four players give us width in attack.
5. Develop: The wide areas can be used to practice certain moves the players have been taught, especially at the younger ages where they need to be able to practice them without pressure. This allows them to play in a game while doing the move without pressure.

Coaching Points:
* Create space wide when in possession of the ball
* Building play from the back
* Using width to attack
* Developing overlap runs

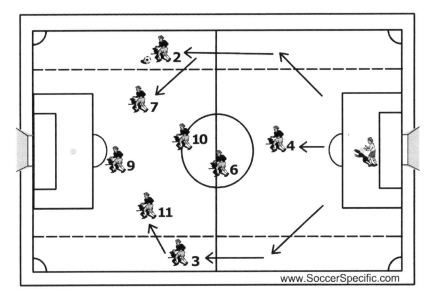

1. Both fullbacks (2) and (3) push forward. They interchange with the wide attacking players (7) and (11). (7) and (11) cut inside, forming an offensive three in attack with (9).
2. This is a big overload from both sides of the field so (6) needs to sit in and cover for this should the opponents win possession and counter attack.
3. Players make movements off each other. Overlapping fullback (2) gets the ball and has options in front of him. He can play a teammate in or run the ball to get into a crossing position.
4. Alternatively it could be the fullbacks (2) and (3) cutting inside and the midfield players (7) and (11) staying wide.

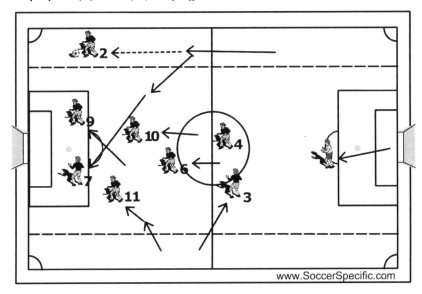

1. An alternative is to have both fullbacks break wide initially to offer to receive the pass in the buildup.
2. Once the side to attack down has been established we can then have our opposite side players adjust as shown, (11) still attacking but (3) dropping back in to cover in case of a counter attack. This gives more freedom to (6) to support the attack.

3. Here we see the continued movements of the players in the attacking phase of play. We are compact from the back as the players move up the field to get up to the half way line as their guiding position.

B) INTRODUCE OPPONENTS

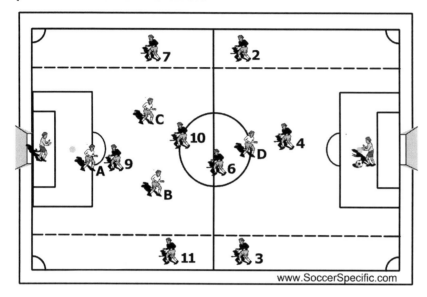

www.SoccerSpecific.com

1. Introduce 5 players to give an overload for the team you are coaching to give them the opportunity to have initial success.
2. Opponents can only "shadow" the outside players and cannot enter the outside comfort zone.
3. Players can only stay outside in the channel with the ball for a few seconds then must make their move inside, either passing it in or dribbling it in.
4. Build the session up using an overload situation to gain success.
5. Gradually increase the number of opponents until you finish with a 9v9. This should ensure a progressive situation where each stage of development is successful.

C) USING FOUR ZONES TO TEACH TEAM DEPTH IN A 9 v 9

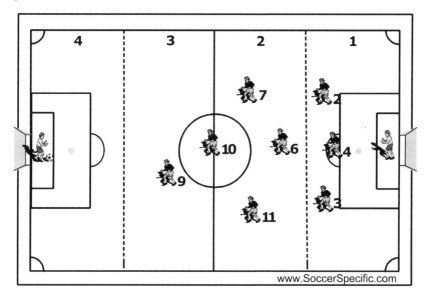

D) DEFENSIVE TEAM SHAPE:
1. The team maintains its shape by only occupying three of the four zones.
2. Short and tight. If we are ultra defensive and playing low pressure it may be only two zones we occupy.

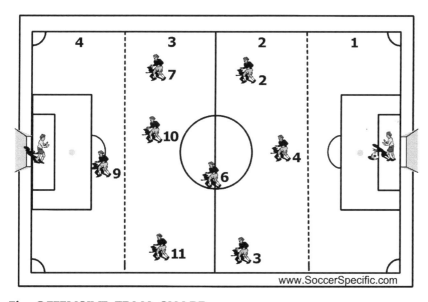

E) OFFENSIVE TEAM SHAPE:
1. Now we have our offensive shape and the team pushes up with all players still in three out of four zones (except the keeper).
2. Wide and Long.

ONE WORD COMMANDS FOR TEAM SHAPE AND MOVEMENT IN A SMALL SIDED GAME

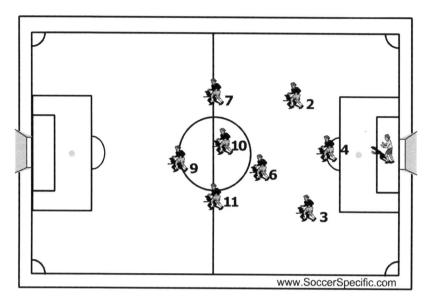

1. This is a 9v9 but the same principle applies for 11v11.
2. Just a one word signal can organize a back four defense so everyone knows what to do and reacts together as a unit. Also midfield players close by can react off the call too.
3. One word calls ensure everyone will know quickly and effectively what they should do as a unit and as a team.
4. Hence the back players (and the keeper) can organize their movement as a unit (and therefore influence those in front of them) from five one word commands. The momentum is triggered from the back and runs forward through the team to the strikers.

A) UP

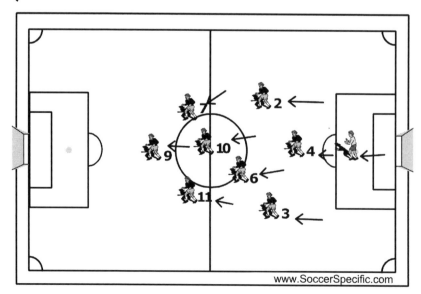

1. **Game situation:** The opponents have the ball and pass it back towards their own goal, or we pass the ball forward maintaining possession. The coach can move around the field with a ball and the team can take their shape from that also. All the movements are without a ball to begin.

2. Here the players move up the field only about five yards in distance (it may be only one or two yards), waiting to see if we win the ball, at which point they can apply the OUT call.

3. UP can also be used when we pass the ball forward and move up as a team. Units move up together maintaining the same distance between each other. They move up a short distance then reassess the situation and reorganize depending on where the ball is.

4. If it goes back again (we force them to play it back as a team) we can move a short distance up again.

5. If they pass it a long distance back then as the ball travels back we travel forward too and it can be the OUT call instead (see next slide).

B) OUT

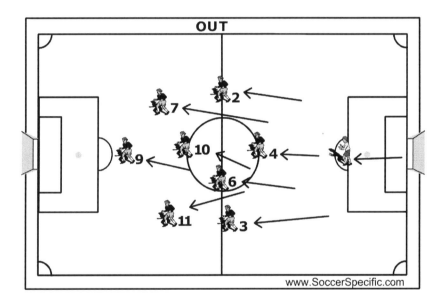

www.SoccerSpecific.com

1. **Game situation:** We have the ball and have played it forward into the attacking third and kept possession (or not, maybe just played it behind the opponent's defense and it takes time for them to get the ball and turn and pass it forward again). At Practice: the coach can move around the field with a ball and the team can take their shape from that also.

2. The team sprint out together on the OUT call until the coach says "sit" or "stop". All the players then stop moving and sit down and you assess their spacing (between players and between the three units).

3. As they get good at this, speed up the commands until they are moving around the field quickly and efficiently with correct spacing. Eventually have them stop and stand still (not sit) "stop" command (in practice) so you can move them around the field at a faster pace, working the transitions.

C) HOLD

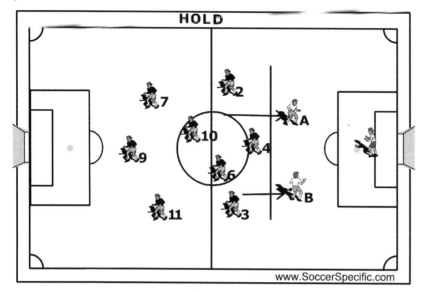

1. **Game situation:** Holding the line at the back of the defense and staying in the same place. The back defenders neither drop nor push up. This could be when the opponents have the ball but there is pressure on the ball so they can't play it forward. The two opponents are included to show how this situation works. You wouldn't necessarily use them in this practice, though it may help the players to understand it better. This is a difficult situation to identify for the players and relies on good officiating plus positive direction from the player in charge.
2. This can occur even if the opponents have the ball and are facing forward with it but the defending pressing player or players prevent the forward pass effectively. Decisions have to be instant here. Our team lets the opponent's strikers run offside.
3. Players can also use the UP call here, just pressing a little to work the opponents' strikers if there is pressure on the ball to prevent the forward pass. This makes it even more obvious when the opponents have run offside as the distance between them and the back four is greater.

D) DROP

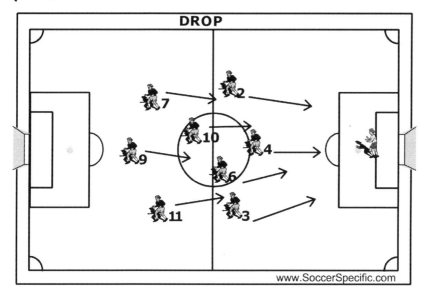

1. **Game situation:** Opponents have the ball and are moving forward with it playing left to right; we are playing right to left.

2. Here the team drop back together, recovering back to the goal. Again varying factors will determine when this happens but one situation could be when the opponents have the ball and are moving forward with no pressure on the ball, leaving us vulnerable to a pass in behind our back players for their strikers to run onto.

3. In the game, the closest player would go to the opponent on the ball, delaying the forward pass and allowing teammates more time to drop and get back behind the ball. For ease of practice to highlight the movement here we work all the players together to get the point across.

4. More attention to detail shows that you can break the situation down further to the player on the ball facing forward;

   a. Is his head up so he can see the forward run and play the ball in quickly? In this case the back four **must** DROP, or:

   b. Does he not see the potential run because his head is down? If so, we likely have time to weigh the options. We can DROP, HOLD the line or even press up with the UP call.

5. Another variable, if their highest striker is alongside our deepest defender, that defender can push up and play offside (and call UP) even with the opponent facing forward and ready to pass. We rely on good officials to catch this!

E) SLIDE

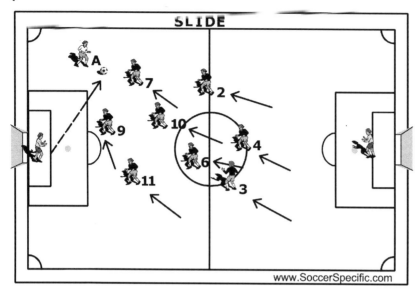

1. **Game Situation:** Here the opposition has played the ball into a very wide area and we all move across the field.
2. The SLIDE call can be used when the opponents are taking a goal kick so there are players around the area where the ball is to be kicked.
3. In the game the ball may have been passed wide in the opponent's possession and we move across the field as a team to close down all the spaces around the ball to try to win it back.

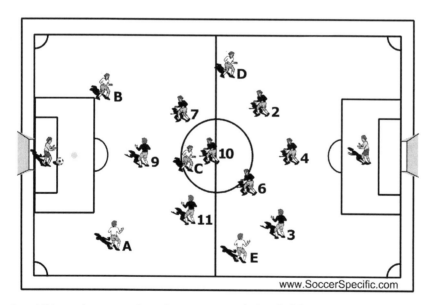

1. Ultimately move the players around the field with the various commands keeping them in motion. You can introduce other players to pass or run the ball around the field and they must adjust to where the ball is. The team can only intercept passes, not make tackles, as we want them to move around the field off the ball.
2. Once they intercept it they can attack the goal and try to score as a reward. Introduce this method into an 11v11 game situation as the final progression.

USING ALL COMMANDS

1. The players need to learn that these one word commands can be used in quick succession in a matter of seconds. For example, "SLIDE" as the ball goes out wide to their wing midfielder, then "UP" as he passes back, then "DROP" as they maintain possession and prepare to pass forward, then "OUT" as we win the ball and pass forward quickly, giving us valuable time to get out.
2. Train the players to make these decisions quickly and effectively. Offer lots of situations and have them practice it.
3. Mistakes are expected, so we have to correct them, and the time to make them and correct them is in training.

DEVELOPING PLAY FROM THE BACK USING THE 4-2 OF THE 4-2-3-1 TO BEGIN

Players must develop the play from the keeper and run the ball through the flag goals.

COACHING POINTS:
1. Spread out: Create space across the width of the field.
2. Technique – quality of pass (weight, accuracy, timing).
3. Skill: Decision – when, where and how to pass.
4. Support Positions – Movements off the ball and angles and distances.
5. Communication – TALK.
6. Running with the ball: Through the flagged goals

A)   WITH BOTH FULLBACKS ATTACKING AT THE SAME TIME:
With both fullbacks attacking from the back from both sides and a defensive midfielder staying back to drop in as a sweeper if need be. This is the usual method Barcelona and Real Madrid use as does the Spanish National team in this 4-2-3-1 system of play to build up the play from the back.

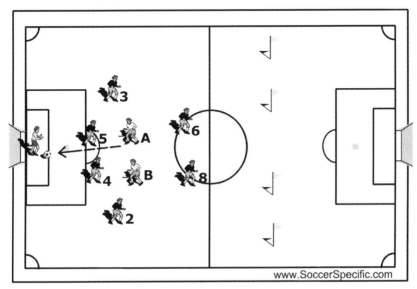

1. The back four spread out as much as they can and use the full width of the field.

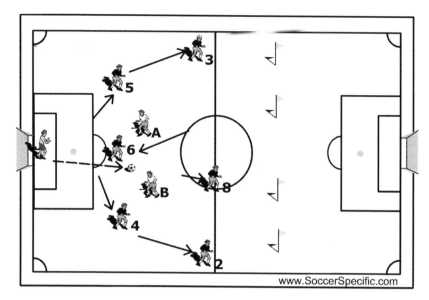

1. Change in shape as the players move forward. Defensive midfielder (6) drops in between the center backs as security, particularly if the opposition leaves 2 forwards up. Most often teams play directly through the number (6) in this situation.
2. Here 2 fullbacks break forward, the center midfielder (6) stays in front as we have possession, and as soon as possession changes and opponents win it and look forward, the center midfielder (6) drops back into the sweeper role. It is likely that our opponents will have two players up so it now becomes a 2v2 at the back, which is risky. Therefore we make sure a defensive midfield player, in this case (6), stays back to help them CREATE A 3v2 going forward but also should the opponents win the ball and counter attack quickly we have a 3 defenders against 2 attackers as security.

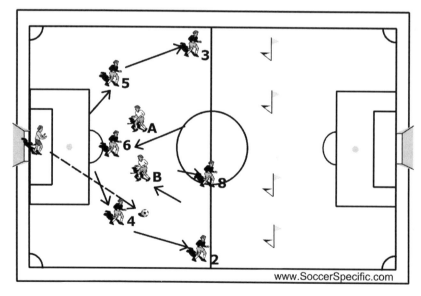

1. If (B) stays central and marks (6), (4) may be free to receive the pass
2. Teams may push three players up to stop this, in which case our keeper may have to kick the ball long.

3. We have possession going forward and have good strength in both wide areas of the field. We are attacking in numbers with the security of the defensive midfielder (6) should the move break down.

4. OPTIONS:
   a. (6) drops back behind the center backs, or can replace one center back and mark up a striker and that center back becomes the covering player, whichever way the coach prefers to do it.
   b. Here I show the defensive midfielder (6) dropping back and becoming the covering player.
   c. (8) can drop back (not shown) to protect the team in front of the center backs when we lose possession.

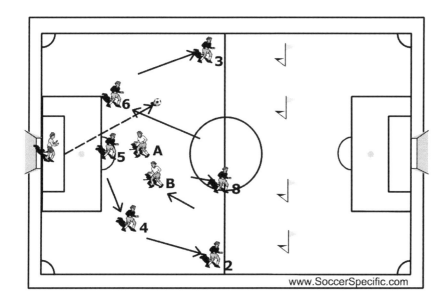

d. (6) can drop into different positions depending on where the ball is and which is the shortest route back. If the ball is on our wide right and in their possession and (6) is slightly to the left, he can drop into the left defender position and (5) can go central. If he is to the right, he drops right.

e. If (6) is closest to the middle then he drops straight back into the sweeper position.

Build this up to an 11v11 session as is shown in other parts of the book, but this is a simple way to start the process of developing play from the back through the number (6).

B) WITH ONE FULLBACK ATTACKING:

Breaking out with a three, with one fullback pushing on and one center back on the same side going touchline wide, it becomes a 3v2 against 2 strikers.

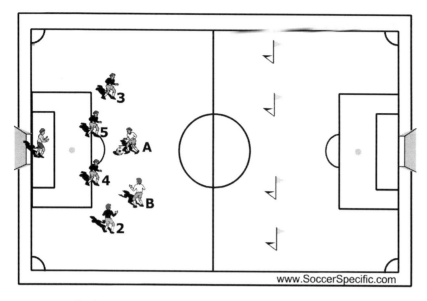

1. A simple beginning, (A) shoots at the keeper and the play starts from there.

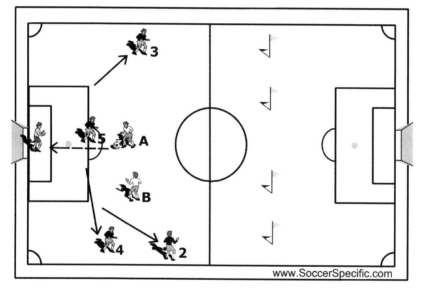

1. Fullback (2) pushes forward, leaving the space for center back (4) to run wide into. Center back (5) stays in the center and Full Back (3) pushes wide on the other side. Both (2) and (3) are TOUCHLINE WIDE.

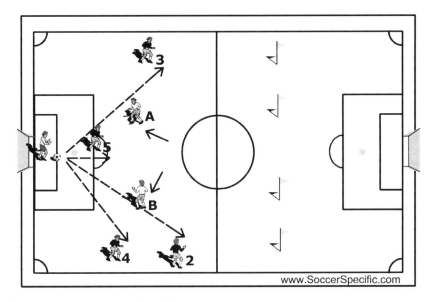

1. Four passing options from the back.

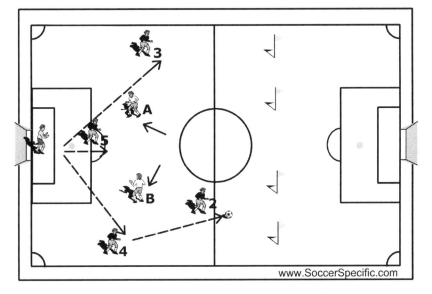

1. Fullback (2) can go inside to receive and play forward.

i) INTRODUCE THE MIDFIELD AND WORK ON THEIR MOVEMENTS

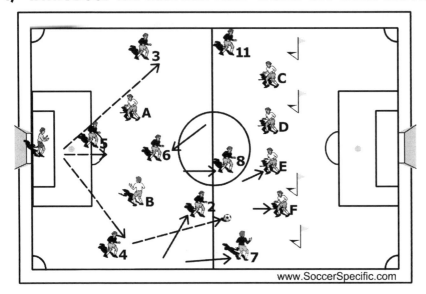

1. (8) runs his marker off to create space for (2) to receive. (7) can also run off the defender to create space. (6) drops in to receive to feet as an option also.

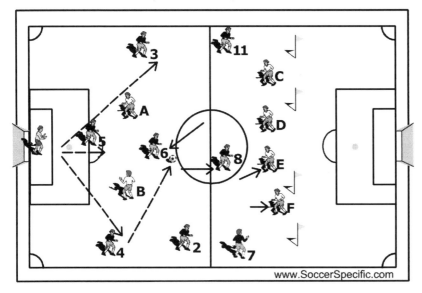

1. (7) runs off (F), (8) runs off (E) and (6) drops in to receive from (4). The keeper has options here to pass straight to (6) or to (6) through (5) and so on. Which option used depends on the positions of the opponents.
2. The players from the back make the field as big as possible to create space between the opposing players to play through. Alternatively, in this instant (4) can pass to (2) and create a 2v1 against (F).

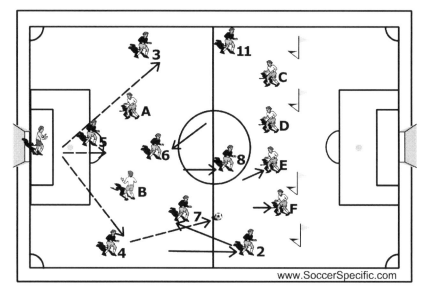

1. Fullback (2) and wide midfielder (7) interchange, inside outside and vice versa. If the defender (F) stays wide, then play to (7) inside.

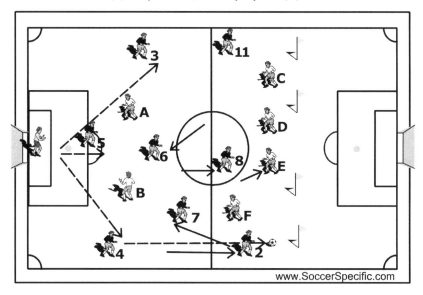

1. If defender (F) tracks (7)'s run inside then pass to (2)

ii) INTRODUCE THE FRONT PLAYERS AND WORK ON THEIR MOVEMENTS

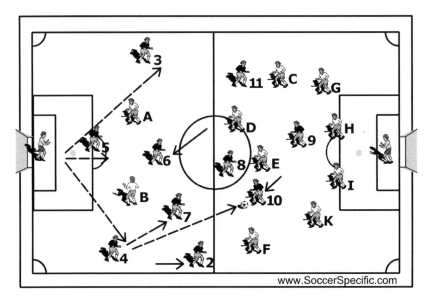

C) ONE FULLBACK ATTACKING AND THE OTHER FULLBACKS OFFERING DEFENSIVE COVER:

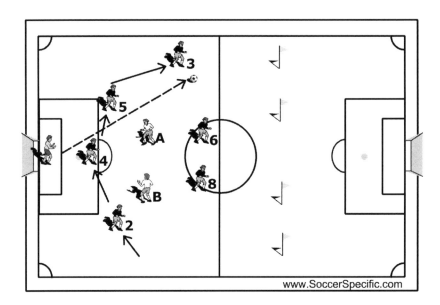

1. Another way to attack from the back is for one side fullback to join in the attack and the other three fullbacks slide over to protect the space he left. This leaves us with good cover, 3 defenders against 2 strikers in the counter attack should we lose possession.

DEVELOPMENT OF OPPOSITE RUNS OF THE CENTRAL STRIKER

A) EXERCISE TO PRACTICE THE OPPOSITE MOVE

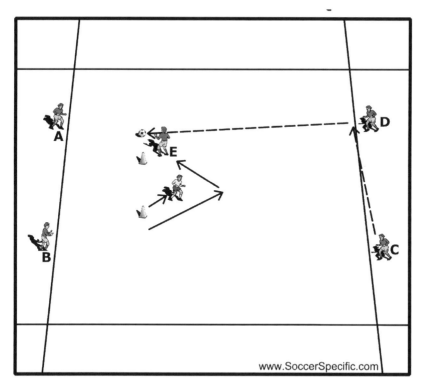

www.SoccerSpecific.com

1. Striker (E) comes short and shows for the ball asking for a pass. Defender (F) follows.
2. Midfielder (C) passes to (D), (D) then passes over the top into (E)'s path as he spins.
3. Defender must play passively. To continue the work, once player (E) receives the ball he must beat (F) back to the touchline. Players (C) and (D) go to the middle and the next two take their place.
4. As the pass is going from (C) to (D) the striker shouts the code word and spins to receive the pass as player (D) is about to pass it. The shout must be early to (D) to make the pass at the exact same time (E) is spinning to receive it.
5. Develop – The player receiving the pass can get it "short or long", to keep the defender guessing. If short, combine with the passer to beat the defender.
6. Key Coaching Points:
   a. Timing of the run (don't go too early or too late)
   b. Angle of the run (back across the defender)
   c. Timing and weight of the pass (into the path of the striker and in front of him) The pass should be paced as such that the striker does not have to break his stride pattern as he receives it.
   d. End Product: getting free for a shot on goal.

B) WORKING WITH THE CENTRAL STRIKER ONLY

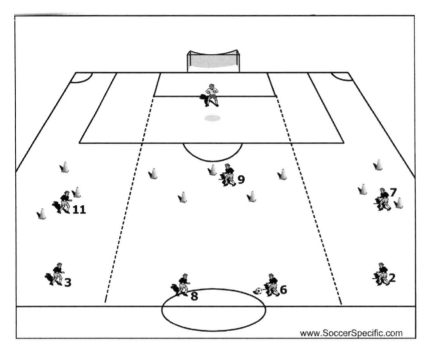

1. The start position of the session. The cones ensure the players check off at angles to the ball. We will focus on the movement of the central striker only.

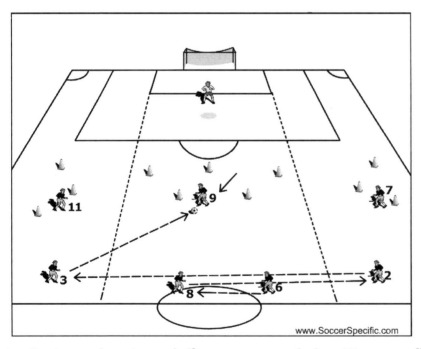

1. Passing and moving at half pace to get a rhythm. (9) comes off at an angle to receive the ball. No defenders yet. The striker must recognize when the man on the ball has TIME to play the ball forward. The striker moves towards the ball dragging the man marking defenders close to him.

2. As the player checks toward the passer as if to receive a pass and is marked tightly by the defender, a sharp spin is made to receive a longer pass behind (into the space created by coming short) rather than the short one the striker seemed to be asking for. A sharp turn/spin into the defender and across the shoulder is the best move rather than the old arc run into space. The arc run is easily tracked by the defender as there is time to see the ball and the player.
3. When the player has time on the ball to pass, expect lots of movement at pace e.g. short to go long.

C) OPPOSITE RUN SHORT TO GO LONG

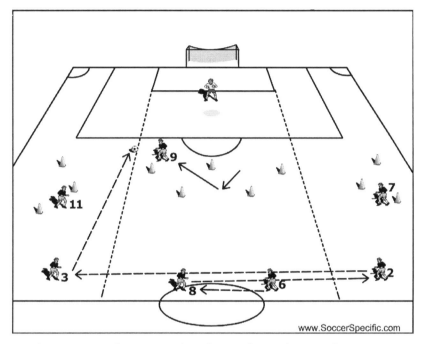

www.SoccerSpecific.com

1. The passing players need to know the striker is playing opposites.
2. The opposite movement is if the striker shows to receive to feet, as above, he is going to spin away and receive in space in front of him in the form of a through ball. If he runs away, then expect a check back to feet.
3. To make the movement clearer the strikers can have a "Code Word" to call as a signal so the player on the ball knows what is happening.
4. They should call it as early as possible. The Italian striker Vialli who played for Juventus and Chelsea was a master at this move. He would draw a defender towards the player on the ball in midfield and within a blink of an eye spin away in the opposite direction with the ball already into his path with the defender left stranded.
5. In a game the team could be prepared to play on the basis that they always make the pass off the first run unless they get a call from the striker using the code word to implement the opposite movement. It isn't always possible in split second situations to recognize how much time a player has on the ball so it may be best just to work the movement off of a predetermined call.

D) OPPOSITE RUN LONG TO COME SHORT

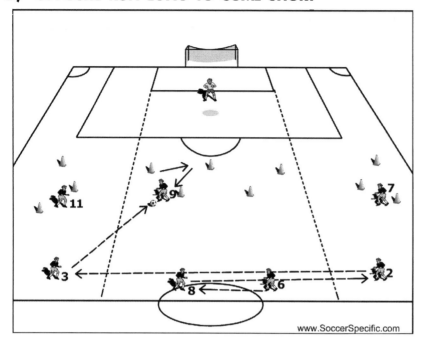

1. The passing players need to know the strikers are playing opposites. This time the striker is moving away to come back. There is time on the ball for the passing player and the opposite movement comes into effect (working off the second run), but if no time the striker knows it will be played first time into the first run.

E) OPPOSITE RUN INSIDE TO GO OUTSIDE

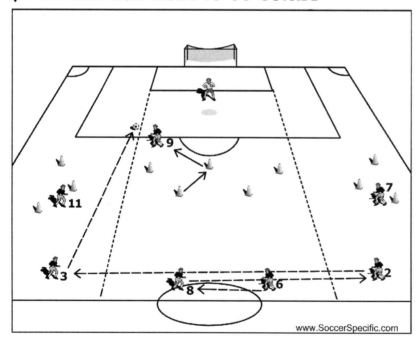

1. Striker (9) runs inside to check back outside.
2. Here, after striker (9) has cut away from the ball and away from the space to open it up for himself on the 2nd run, (3) can play a channel pass to (9).

F) INTRODUCE A DEFENDER

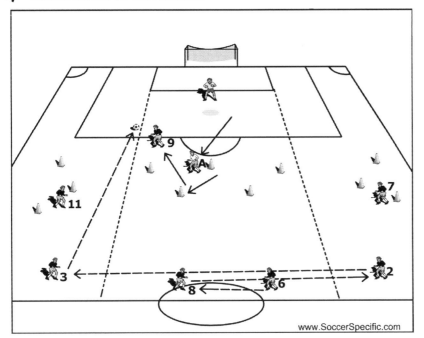

1. Striker (9) draws the defender to the ball and creates space behind for himself. Defender (A) follows and gets tight to him. As the ball is traveling to (3) striker (9) calls out the code word which informs (3) he will check to the ball then check away, wanting the pass behind him and not to feet as the first run would suggest.

G) INTRODUCE A BACK FOUR

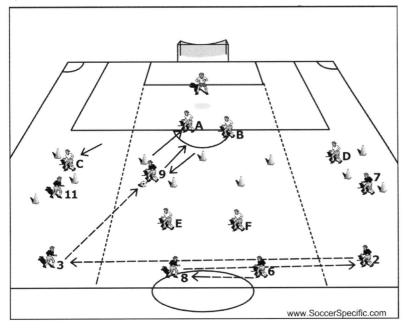

1. Here striker (9) runs off defender (A) who tracks his run. Having called the code word, again (3) knows he will check back to receive to feet, hopefully in space to receive and turn having lost (A) with the first movement (as above).

2. One striker playing against two center backs may look a big disadvantage but the striker can reduce this to a 1v1 by his movement. He can play against either of these players. Above he isolated (A) 1v1 by moving in front of him and away from (B). (B) is now on the opposite side of where the ball is being played and is out of the main area, therefore it is a 1v1 against (A).

www.SoccerSpecific.com

1. Here the pass must be made on the outside of (A) and away from (B) so (B) will have to cover a lot of ground to get in position to cover this run. (C) is drawn to (11) which creates a small space between (A) and (C) to play the ball into. Again the code word has been called to make this movement.

2. Let's say (3) is closed down very quickly and has only time for a one touch pass to striker (9). (9) must realize he hasn't time to do a double and opposite run so he should expect the first pass to feet off his first run.

ADVANCING MOVEMENT "OFF" THE BALL OF THE WIDE ATTACKERS TO GET FREE IN A 4-2-3-1
NOW FOCUSING ON OPPOSITE RUNS TO CREATE SPACE
A) SESSION PLAN TO DEVELOP THESE MOVEMENTS
DRILL / FUNCTION

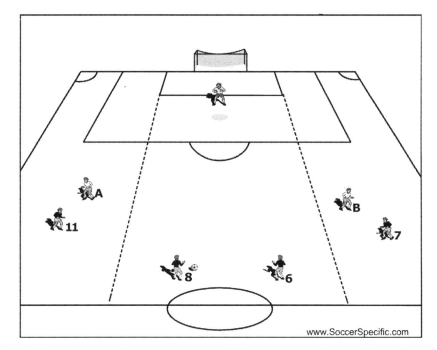

1. You can use the cones as an indicator as in the previous diagrams if you like. Only seven players needed. This keeps the movements simple.
2. Two 1v1 situations teaching both sides how to cut inside and receive a pass inside the defender.
3. Coaching Points:
   a. Start position passing back and forth
   b. Communication: Eye Contact / speech / pointing
   c. Movement off the ball: timing and angle of the two part run (faking the defender)
   d. Quality of the Pass: Timing, angle and accuracy of the pass
   e. Coordinated movements of the passer and receiver
   f. Combination Play
   g. Finish on goal
4. Four Ideas of Movement to get Free:
   a. Run him off and cut inside
   b. Run towards the ball drawing the defender close then cutting across and inside of him
   c. Run him inside to create space outside then check back outside
   d. Run him away and outside away from the ball and then check back inside.
5. Players making all these different runs need to learn to check off of both feet
   a. (11) runs the defender off, then checks inside off his left foot.
   b. (11) runs towards the ball, drawing the defender with him, then checks across him and inside off his right foot.

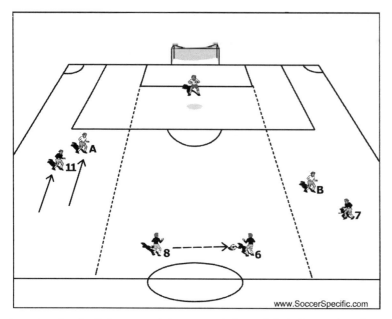

1. As the ball is passed between (6) and (8) the wide player (11) runs off defender (A).
2. We are looking at the timing of the run and the timing of the pass. The run is in two parts; the first one to occupy the defender and the second one to get free of the defender.
3. (11) needs to observe the body language of the player on the ball so he knows when the pass will be delivered and he can then time his second movement off that.
4. You can have the players practicing these movements in your warm up, checking runs, breaking inside off the outside foot. Keep practicing until it becomes embedded in their minds and it becomes a natural movement.

B) CUTTING INSIDE

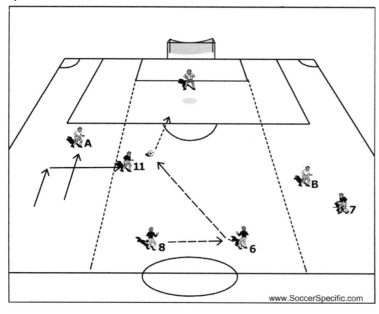

1. Here (11) makes his second run and cuts inside having run the defender off in the first run.
2. Again the key is the timing of each, the run and the pass.
3. If you have a right footer on the left and a left footer on the right then the player cutting inside will come onto his strong foot and be more able to shoot on goal.
4. Here the player breaks inside off his outside foot, the left foot in this case.

C) COMING SHORT TO GO LONG

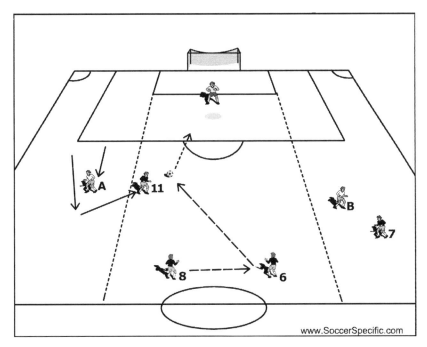

www.SoccerSpecific.com

1. Here we see a different way to get free of the defender, this time coming towards the ball and bringing the defender with him.
2. Once the defender is tight, (11) cuts across his path and into the path of the pass in space in front of him. It is a very sharp cut, not a looping cut that is easier to defend against.
3. Here the player breaks inside off his outside foot again, but in this case it is the right foot. So they need to learn how to do this checking movement off BOTH FEET.

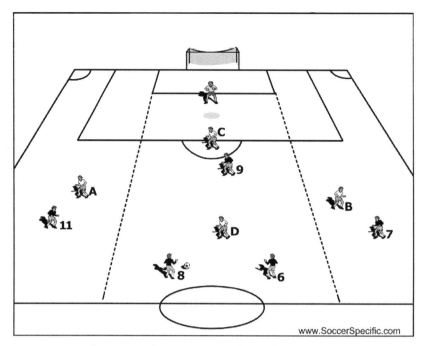

1. Now we have 10 players. We've brought in a central striker, a defender and a defensive midfielder to develop the idea.
2. We are working with the midfield two, the wide players and the striker but haven't introduced the number ten yet.

D) LINKING AND COMBINING WITH THE CENTRAL STRIKER

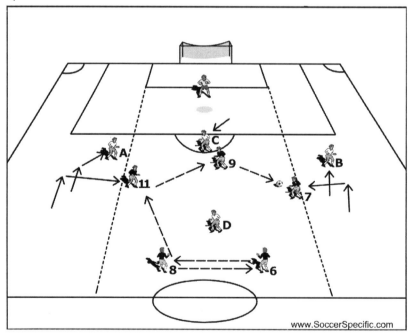

1. (11) runs defender (A) off, then cuts inside and links up with the central striker (9).
2. (7) comes in from the other side and develops the play further, having first run the defender off to create space for himself inside.

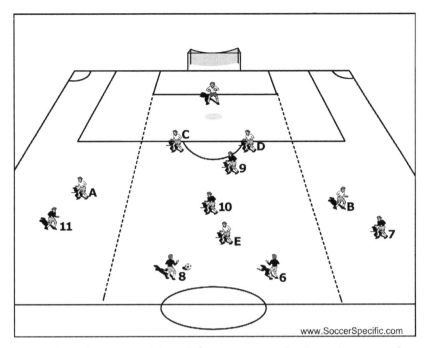

1. Twelve players. Add a defensive center back and an attacking number (10). We are building up the numbers as we go.

E) PHASE OF PLAY

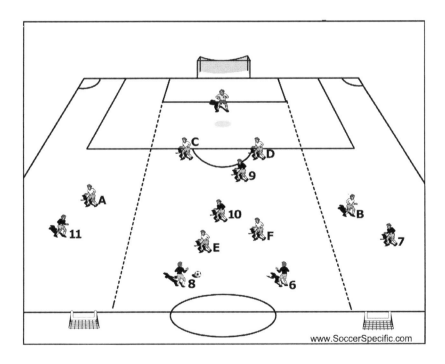

1. Add another defensive central midfield player to increase the difficulty.
2. Introduce target goals for the opponents and it now becomes a Phase of Play.
3. Now we have the 2-3-1 of the 4-2-3-1.

F) INSIDE TO OUT RUN

1. Here we show a different run. Generally, the outside player cuts inside as the second and final run but here he makes the first run inside to cut outside on the second run and open a space up behind. Another opposite run, but going the other way, inside to outside.

1. Showing how the two wide players can cut inside to support the front two; now in a 4-2 against a 4-2 also (same as a lone striker situation but showing it can work in different formations).

2. One is going long and one is coming short but both can be effective. In fact the one coming short can be the best option as it draws the fullback away from the space behind.
3. The one going long means while you still lose him with the check inside he is at least in a deeper defensive position to counter.
4. Obviously the next phase would be to add the fullbacks and link them with the wide players creating 2v1 situations on the outside.
5. It is important to teach the wide players these outside to inside movements because they can be effective in many systems of play not just the 4-2-3-1. The same movements will occur in a 4-2-3-1, 4-2-1-3, 4-3-3, 4-4-2, 4-4-1-1, 3-4-3 and 3-5-2.

G) SMALL SIDED GAME

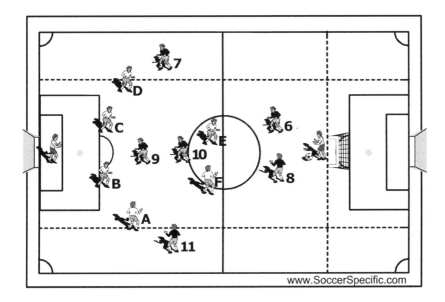

1. Introduce another full size goal and it becomes a small sided game continuing the 2-3-1 theme.
2. Now fourteen players with the addition of another keeper.

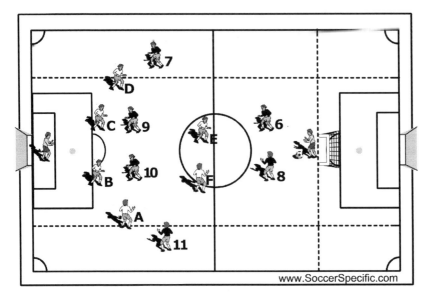

1. We can make a simple switch to a 4-2 from a 2-3-1 which represents the 4-4-2 formation if you decide to do this small sided game with two central strikers.
2. Eventually take it to an 11v11.

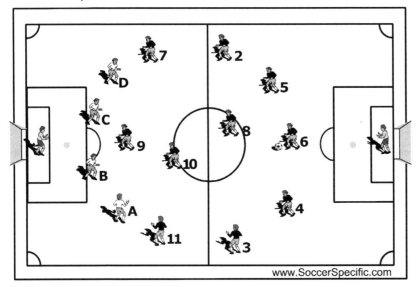

1. The normal attacking set up of the team.
2. (11) is wide looking to accept a pass from (6) and defender (A) is beginning to close him down.

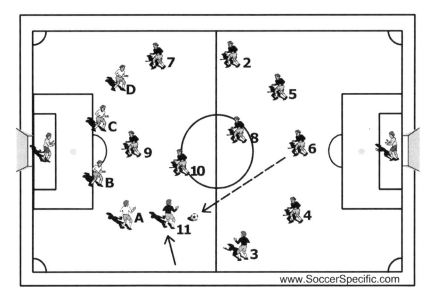

1. (11) goes in TOO EARLY and closes down his OWN SPACE.
2. By doing so he is marked by defender (A) and receives the ball with his BACK TO GOAL to feet and likely standing still.
3. This is ok because he still has possession and has his body between the defender and the ball to protect it, but he is facing backwards away from the opponent's goal and not able to run at the defense. There are better situations he can get himself into to make it more difficult for the defender.

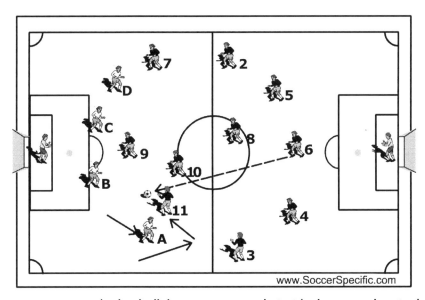

1. Run towards the ball but not too much inside because that is the space we want to keep free. By doing so the defender may follow you to get tight. Once he gets tight, and with the right timing of the pass, you cut across him and inside to receive the pass into the inside space FACING FORWARD and able to run at the defense. This is using an opposite run (come short to go long; go long to come short, go short to cut across and so on).
2. If he does not follow you but stays in the space behind then you can receive the ball and face forward too because you have space in front of you to do so. But

this will be more receiving and turning with the ball. This is fine, but you still have the defender (A) to beat. Hopefully he will get tight to you and follow you and you can use this closeness to check inside and away from him.

3. The pass inside and into the inside space now has to be timed correctly so we need great understanding between the passer and the receiver. This will only come by practicing this in training over and over.

4. Coaching Points:
    a. Timing and accuracy of the pass (into SPACE INSIDE)
    b. Timing of the run
    c. Angle of the run

5. Timing of the pass: If it is too early then it may be intercepted; if it is too late then the player will receive it facing backwards as previously shown.

6. Timing of the run: If it is too early then again, the player will receive it facing backwards as previously shown; if too late then the defender may get to the ball first. Run is in two parts and opposite directions.

7. Angle of the Run: Must be away from the defender and here I show two ways to do it as it is TWO OPPOSITE RUNS, not just one. THe first run to affect the defender and create space, the second to exploit the space created.

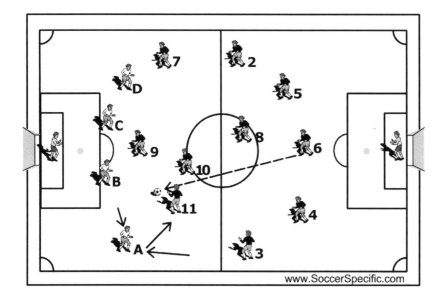

www.SoccerSpecific.com

1. Only if you have time to do it, try to first run the defender AWAY from the space you want to move into. If you make the first run INTO the space you want, you take the defender into it with you, effectively limiting your own options. You may have to receive the pass facing backwards and to feet rather than into space facing forward. We still have possession, but there are better solutions.

2. As shown here, you take the defender away and then check back and inside to receive the pass, which puts you in a great position to be free of (A) and running at (B) with the ball at pace.

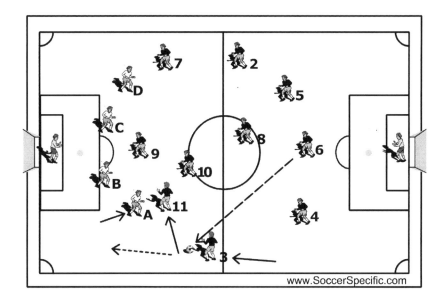

1. If you run inside and the defender is tight and you cannot receive the ball easily then this is still a good run as it creates space outside for fullback (3) to run into.
2. So, the run inside is a good one either for yourself or a teammate, it is the timing and angle of the run that are important.

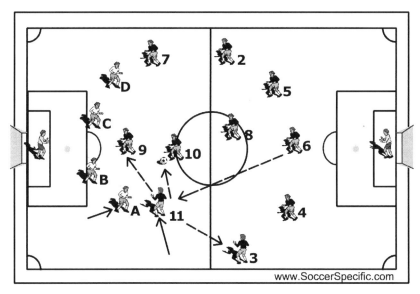

1. Here you have received the ball facing backwards so your own MOMENTUM has stopped but you can still bring other players into play.
2. Here I show three options of a potential pass to maintain possession.

THE TIMING AND ANGLE OF THE MOVEMENT ARE THE KEY HERE. MAKING TWO RUNS INSTEAD OF ONE (IF YOU HAVE TIME TO DO SO) MAY BE THE DIFFERENCE BETWEEN GETTING POSSESSION OR NOT, OR RECEIVING FACING FORWARD OR RECEIVING FACING BACKWARDS. THE FORWARD RUN MAY EVEN BE AS SIMPLE AS A CHECK FORWARD WITH ONE OR TWO STRIDES, GETTING THE DEFENDER OFF BALANCE, THEN A CHECK INSIDE TO RECEIVE THE PASS.

I) MESSI OF BARCELONA

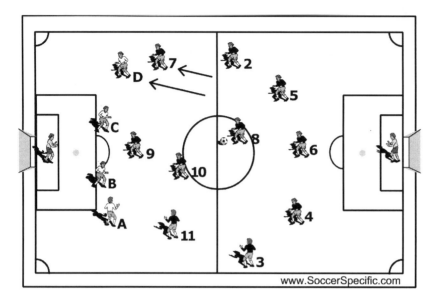

1. Watching Lionel Messi of Barcelona as they play in the build up, even the untrained eye can see that the timing of his movement is exceptional. I am sure this does not just happen and he has practiced this hundreds of times in training. It is a fact that the best players in the world are also the hardest working players.
2. Here Messi (7) sprints forward, attacking defender (D). At the same time he is observing the body language of (8) to see when he is about to release the pass.

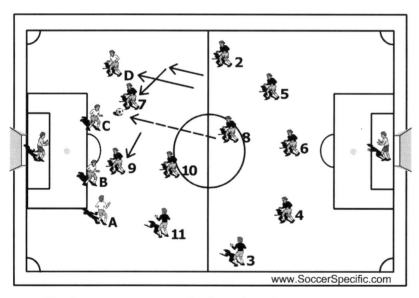

1. Fullback (D) is recovering back and tracking Messi's run trying to stop the ball in behind him. At the correct moment Messi cuts inside to accept the pass INTO HIS PATH and run at full pace to attack the center back (C). (D) is now completely out of the play.
2. If the timing and angle of the pass and the timing and angle of the run are in synch, Messi does not have to break his stride to receive the pass in front of him and he is now at full pace.

3. Striker (9) checks away from the immediate space to allow Messi to run into it and hopefully he can take a defender out of it too, in this case (C). (C) has to decide in a split second to either track (9) or position to defend 1v1 against Messi.
4. If he defends 1v1 then perhaps (9) will be free to play a give and go with Messi.
5. Messi is of course coming inside onto his favored left foot so can also get a strike on goal.

THREE ZONE TRAINING DEVELOPING MOVEMENT OFF THE BALL INTO THE SHADOW STRIKER ZONE 14

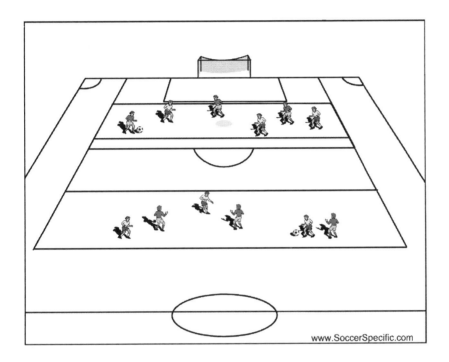

www.SoccerSpecific.com

A) WARM UP FOR THIS SESSION
1. A 3v3 in each end zone
2. A ball each team, passing and moving, but teams are not playing against each other yet.
3. The central zone is the shadow striker zone known as Zone 14 and usually where the number 10 plays.
4. Coaching Points:
   a. The passing player must be aware of when and where the shadow striker drops into the free zone
   b. The receiving player must recognize when the passer is ready to pass
   c. Good communication via visual cues through eye contact or aural cues through speaking makes this work
   d. Movement OFF the ball by the shadow striker to get free and into open space
   e. Timing and angle of the run
   f. Timing; accuracy and pace of the pass
   g. Good receiving and turning skills with an awareness of what is behind before receiving it.
   h. Receive or be a decoy for someone else; depending on where the defender is.

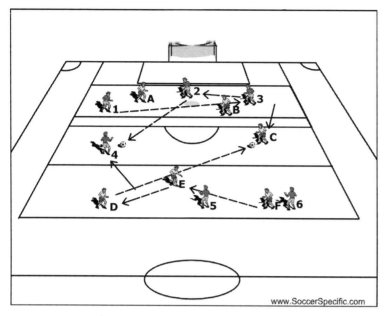

1. Passing and moving, (4) drops in to receive as does (C) going the other way.
2. Movement OFF THE BALL to receive in the middle zone (Zone 14).
3. (4) takes the ball back into his own end zone, as does (C) in the other end zone and play continues. All players are moving, finding space to receive the ball. The two teams pass between each other but cannot tackle each other.
4. Coaching Points:
   a. Timing of the pass
   b. Timing of the run
   c. Angle of the run
   d. Timing of each has to be exact for it to work.

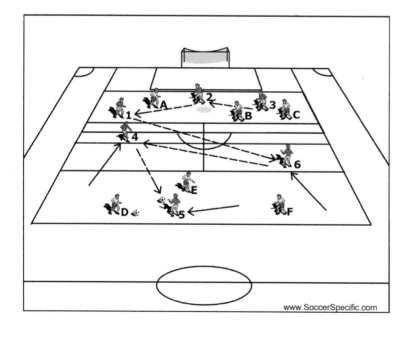

B) DEVELOPMENT:

1. Now 2 players come to meet the ball in opposite halves of Zone 14 and at different angles and depth to each other. Still no opposition so it is free flowing movements linking the two front players now. Do this going both ways with both teams so there is congestion in the middle.
2. Coaching Points:
   a. Timing of the run, timing of the pass
   b. Angles of support of each player in terms of each other's position.
   c. Looking before receiving as the ball is travelling; assessing the next move
   d. Make it a one touch pass in the middle zone (Zone 14) from (6) to (4) to (5) to test the players' awareness
   e. Development: Passing to opposite colors

MOVEMENT OFF THE BALL BETWEEN THE UNITS THROUGH THE SHADOW STRIKER

Two 3 v 1's in the outside areas, the middle area is free and open.

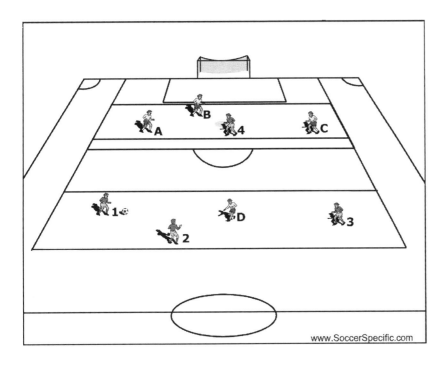

1. Players are passing and maintaining possession 3v1 in one end zone. When a player from the other end zone drops into the free middle zone, the team with the ball look to pass to him to receive and turn and pass into the other zone. They then continue there with a 3v1 keep away.
2. Color coordination and recognition is important here because when the reds pass the ball in they are passing to a yellow and not a red; and vice versa.

A) DROPPING INTO ZONE 14

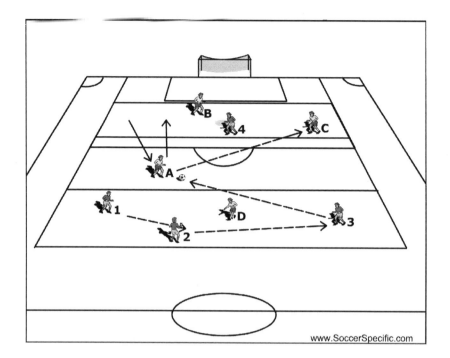

www.SoccerSpecific.com

1. Players are looking at the teammates in their own zone to pass to but also into the other zone for a player to drop into and support and thus switch the direction of play. No pressure to start and the defender must stay in the same zone so the receiving player is always free.
2. Looking for good angles of support at all times; avoid straight line support as it limits vision behind the play. Players try to support in a sideways-on stance to open up their field of vision.
3. Passing can be at an angle, as can the support position of the receiver. A player on the right tries to pass to a player on the left dropping into the middle and vice versa.
4. The cue is more specific now. If a player receives the ball on the right of the grid and has his head up looking to pass, this is the cue for a player on the opposite grid to drop into the middle to receive and turn.

Development 1:
1. Once the receiving player who has checked to the middle receives the ball (on his first touch); that is the cue for the defender to close him down and pressure.
2. This should still give the receiver long enough to receive and turn and pass without losing the ball but we are building up the pressure on that player. It is almost a passive movement because the defender has so far to make up to get close.

Development Two:
1. The defender can close the ball down as the passer moves so now they do not need to wait for the first touch. This changes the options considerably, depending on how good the defender is.

B) DEFENDER CAN TRACK

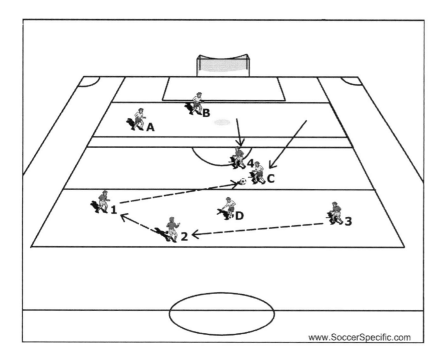

1. Here we show the defender (4) closing the shadow striker (C) coming short at the same time.

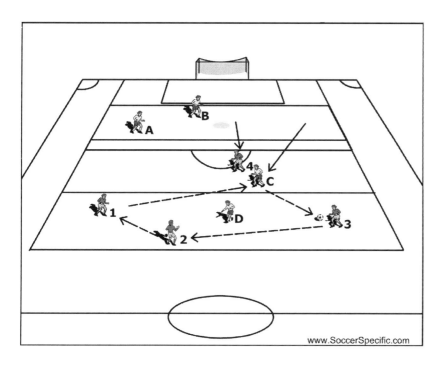

1. Here we show the shadow striker (C) still receiving the ball under pressure but now he can't turn so he lays the ball off into the same zone it came from to another player (3) in that zone.

C) INTERCHANGE OF STRIKERS

1. Here the shadow striker (C) has laid off the ball and checked back into his own zone, taking the defender (4) with him and another player (A) becomes the new shadow striker and gets it to feet in a free area to turn and pass and the 3v1 begins again.

2. You can also liken this situation to a midfield player dropping off the marker and receiving from the back four. Rotate the defenders.

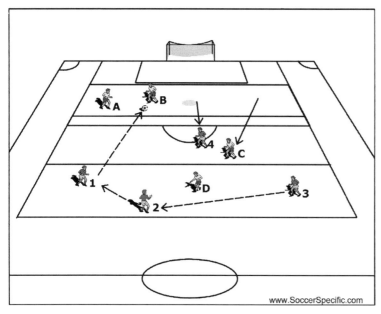

1. Another option for the passer (1) is to avoid the shadow striker (C) who is tightly marked now and whose movement has changed the position of the defender (4). This has opened up a pass to the other players in their other third of the field. Here is the end product above. Two players may go short at the same time; don't worry about this as it may happen in a game anyway.

2. Coaching Points:
   a. The passing player must be aware of when and where the shadow striker drops into the free zone
   b. The receiving player must recognize when the passer is ready to pass.
   c. Good communication via visual cues through eye contact or aural cues through speaking makes this work
   d. Movement OFF the ball by the shadow striker to get free and into open space
   e. Timing and angle of the run
   f. Timing ; accuracy and pace of the pass
   g. Good receiving and turning skills with an awareness of what is behind before receiving it
   h. Receive or be a decoy for someone else; depending on where the defender is.

Important points with regards to awareness:
1. If the receiver (Shadow Striker) goes too early and the passer is not ready to pass (for example if he has the ball but has his head down and so does not see the potential run) then he can check back out and open up the space for the next shadow striker.
2. By then the passer may have his head up and be ready to pass or may even have passed the ball off in his own grid and the next player to get it has seen the 2nd run into the free middle area and he makes the pass.
3. The cue for the 2nd shadow striker to make his run can be the check back of the first shadow striker.

D) COMBINATION MOVEMENT

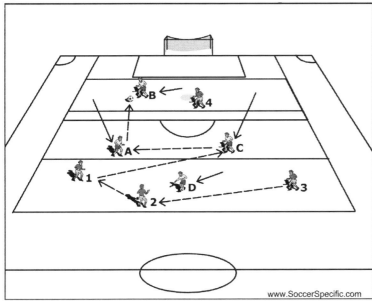

www.SoccerSpecific.com

1. No defenders again. Now the first player (C) and the passing player (1) have to mentally combine to connect with the run and the pass. The cue for the 2nd striker (A) to make his run is off the run of the first striker (C), so again correct timing of the support run is important.
2. Players need to arrive as the ball arrives. If they are too early they can be marked and will tend to stand still (certainly in this practice), too late and a

defender may intercept in a game situation. If they are in too early they should check back again and someone else can take their place.

3. Ensure we maintain the ratio of attackers to defenders in each third of the area; always working to get back immediately to 3v1 in each outside third.

E) A 4 v 1 IN EACH SIDE

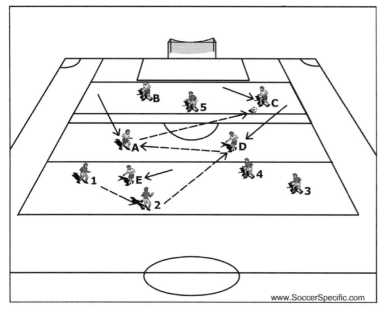

www.SoccerSpecific.com

1. The same idea as before but it is a 4v1 in each outside third now. You can vary the numbers in each outside third based on the ability of the players and / or based on the number of players you have training, 2v1, 3v1, 3v2, 4v2 and so on.

F) 3 v 1; 1 v 1 v 1 AND 3 v 1

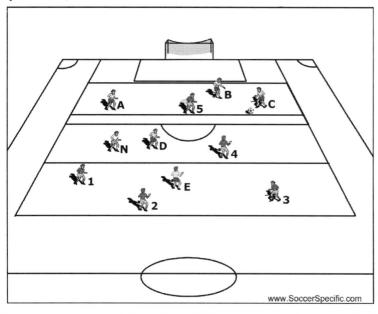

www.SoccerSpecific.com

1. It is always a 2v1 in the middle now, with the neutral player always on the attacking team. Again color coordination and recognition plays a role in the play as the overloaded yellows have to pass to a yellow or neutral player in the middle

and these players actually pass to the overloaded red players in the other side. We now have competitive small sided games in three separate areas on the field.

2. Progression 1: Have the players miss out the middle third players and pass from the back to the front. Players in the middle then support behind in a shadow striker capacity but now going the other way.

3. If the defender wins the ball in an outside third (3v1 against) they have to pass to their own color (or to the neutral player) in the middle; who then passes to the same color in the other outside third.

DEVELOPING THE SHADOW STRIKER (10) IN THE 4-2-3-1 THROUGH A PHASE OF PLAY USING ZONE 14 (NO MANS LAND) AS A FREE AREA

We are focusing on movements and play "In Front" of the opponent's back four

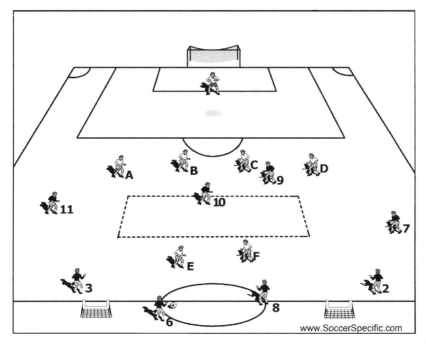

www.SoccerSpecific.com

1. This is the same idea as previously shown with team movement but it is a different way to present it using the Zone 14 (no man's land) area as the FOCUS area and specifically for the number (10).

2. The set up is a 4-2-3-1; the only players not included in the attacking numbered team are the two center backs and the keeper. They will be added when the game goes to an 11v11.

3. The ball starts at the center midfielder here, but essentially it can start from anywhere.

4. Maintain the same start position for simplicity.

5. Dotted area is Zone 14 or "No Man's land" as I like to call it, for the shadow striker to patrol or interchange with teammates.

6. It is a FREE ZONE to begin.

7. As mentioned already the idea is to play a shadow striker (usually known as Number 10 or a false 9) who links up with players around him, but who also can interchange with various players so as to keep opponents guessing.
8. If it is the same player dropping into the free zone all the time then it becomes too predictable.
9. Understanding between players as to where and when is essential here. Try to receive and front up so facing forward on reception (Bergkamp / Baggio / Zola).
10. Here (10) enters the zone 14 area in anticipation of the pass.
11. If this player goes in too early in an actual game situation and takes a defender in then he needs to get out and take the defender out to create space for a teammate to enter that space.
12. This is unselfish play by the shadow striker.
13. Also consider that the position of (10) can change and he can enter the free area from in front of it coming back or from behind it going forward, or from the side of it; so it can depend where he goes in on his START POSITION as the play develops. In this session we focus on him coming back but you can vary it by changing his starting positions to get what you need as the coach. It may depend on how the opposition plays as you prepare your team.

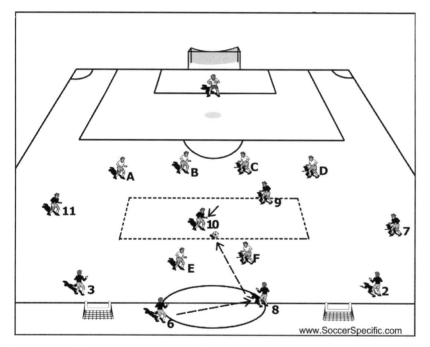

1. Here (10) arrives as the ball arrives and gets free to play. In this instance the first pass and run is free to get the play started successfully.
2. Once (10) gets the ball on his first touch the play is live and the defenders can encroach into Zone 14.
3. Technical Coaching Points:
   a. Support angle / distance of (10)
   b. Receiving skills of (10)
   c. Passes into and from (10)
   d. (10)'s awareness of options BEFORE receiving the pass
4. Player (10) drops into the middle zone:
   a. Correct Timing of the pass / timing of the run

b. With Awareness of options in advance of the ball

c. Body angle / shape; try to be open and facing forward if possible.

d. Good first touch

A) INTERCHANGE OF THE STRIKER AND THE SHADOW STRIKER

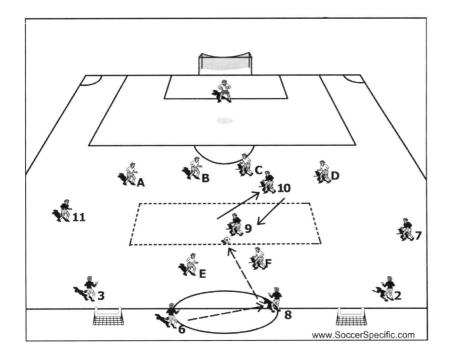

www.SoccerSpecific.com

1. Here we have an interchange between (9) and (10), striker (9) now becoming the shadow striker.

2. This movement may disrupt the defenders enough to get one or both of them free to receive.

3. (9) tries to receive facing at least side-on if not forward. His angle of approach to the ball can help determine this.

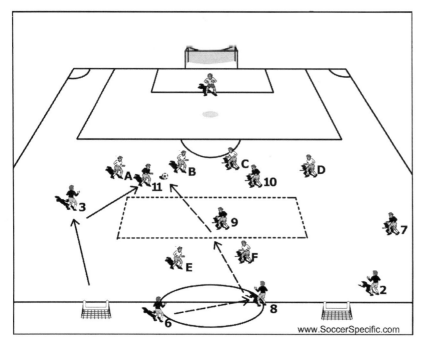

1. (9) receives the pass and as the ball is travelling to him (11) makes an outside to inside run to receive the next pass. His run is into the position and space between (A) and (B).

B) WIDE PLAYER BECOMES THE SHADOW STRIKER

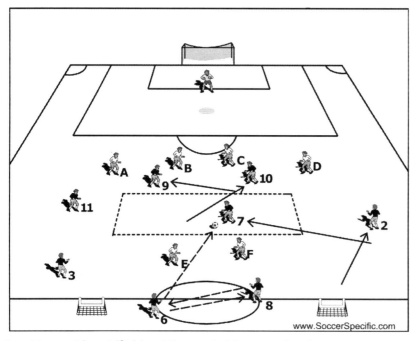

1. Here wide midfielder (7) cuts inside to make the run to receive in Zone 14. Shadow striker (10) has moved out of the zone to free up the space as before but this time for a different player. If he is being man marked he will take his defender out of the space to make room for a teammate, in this case (7).

2. This outside to inside run can prove very effective as it can be hard to pick up. Does defender (D) track him inside or not? If he does then perhaps attacking fullback (2) can get free to receive. If he doesn't then (7) may be open to receive the pass.
3. Again showing various movements (10) may make based on where defenders are and where the best spaces are.
4. All the movement based around the shadow striker for it to be most effective means players must think unselfishly and work for each other and not just for themselves.

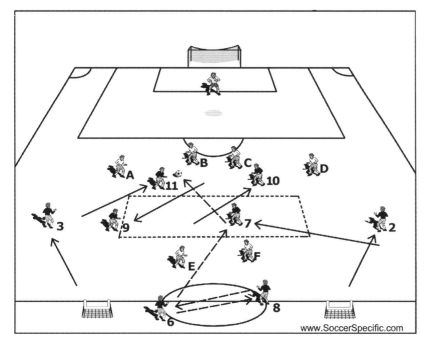

www.SoccerSpecific.com

1. Now (9) makes an interchanging movement with (11). (7) has come inside to receive a good pass facing forward and (11) makes the same type of outside to inside run, but in front of (7), to receive the next pass forward and attack the defense.
2. Various passing options are available to (7), but he chooses this one.
3. This movement by (9) will be even more effective if the defender (B) tracks him and leaves a space open behind.

C) CREATING SPACE BEHIND THE BACK FOUR

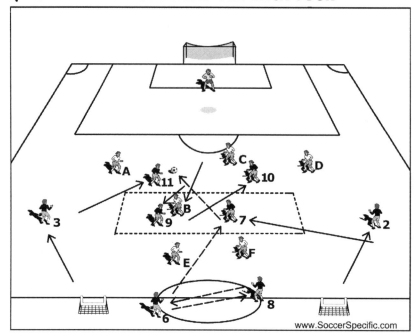

1. Here (B) tracks (9) and leaves the space behind for (11) to run into. Of course (A) can track (11) also but if it happens quickly enough (11) may catch (A) off guard.

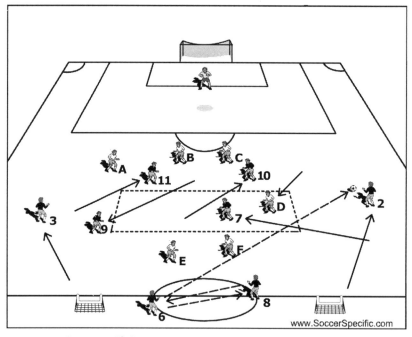

1. Here that unselfish run has created space in the wide area (7) has just come from, especially if defender (D) tracks (7) inside and into Zone 14. This leaves the outside area wide open to attack into.

2. This is the beauty of playing through Zone 14, defenders have to decide do I track the player towards there; or do I pass them on, and who do I pass them on to?

3. Hence fullback (2) gets a great chance to attack and get a cross into the box acting as an attacking and overlapping winger.

4. This interchange of positioning is what we are looking to create as much as we can within the team concept.

D)   ENTERING ZONE 14 FROM BEHIND

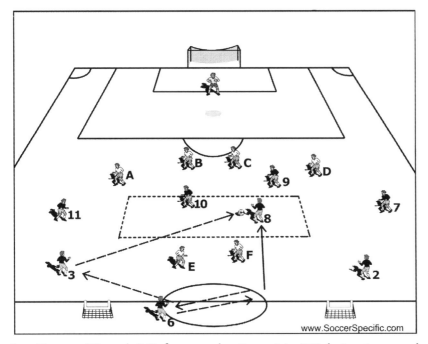

www.SoccerSpecific.com

1. Players (9) and (10) free up the Zone 14, (10) being just on the edge of it. This creates the space for central midfielder (8) to use and he makes a forward run into the space to receive a pass from (3).
2. This is technically a 3rd man run from (8), hopefully on the blind side of marker (F).
3. Making the run from behind and getting the timing of the run and the pass in synch means (8) can receive the ball facing forward and in a good position to run at the defense or work a combination with another player already in front of him such as (9) or (10).
4. This just emphasizes how much movement we can have between various players and various units of players.

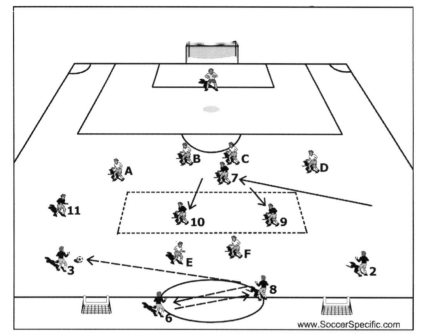

www.SoccerSpecific.com

1. Here we have the CF/WMF/ "Shadow" rotation as one of the many interchanges players can make; this one being more sophisticated than previous ideas with a three or four player development, making movements off each other.

2. (9) and (10) come short to receive. So here we get two players into Zone 14 and wide midfielder (7) makes a run in front of the furthest front player (9) who has effectively become a DUAL shadow striker now with (10) by checking to the ball to possibly receive from (3) if that is the best option.

3. Alternatively (9) may take up a wide position on the right to offer support there. Many options can result from all these movements.

4. The Best option to take may depend on what the defenders do.

5. Technical Coaching Points:
    a. Movement and support positions of (7), (9) and (10)
    b. Awareness of the ball and the other players' positions.
    c. Receiving skills and combination skills with other players
    d. Releasing and passing skills (timing and accuracy)
    e. Support and passing skills of players.

CREATING AN OVERLOAD IN THE CENTER OF THE ATTACKING THIRD

MOVING INTO "FALSE" OR "IN-BETWEEN" AREAS OF THE FIELD OF PLAY TO CREATE A DIAMOND OF SUPPORT

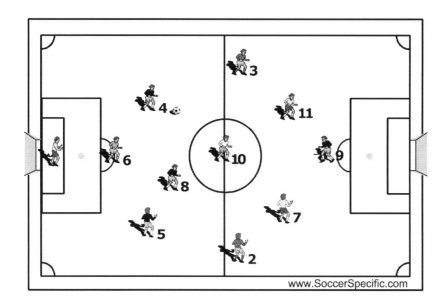

1. Here we show that when the wide attackers cut inside we create a diamond in the center of the field. We overload this area of the field with players. These are positioned in and around Zone 14, the area between the opponent's back defending unit and their midfield unit.

2. With these movements we are asking questions of the opponents in terms of where our players go and who picks them up.

3. The focus is really about movement off the ball and getting players into "false" areas of the field, "in-between" areas I call them; where the opponent's units of players are taken out of their comfort zones (Does the midfield player pick him up? Does the defender step up? Does the fullback track inside? Does he pass him on?) If you do this with a few players at once, it creates great possibilities.

4. We try to overload the zone 14 area and at the same time free up the wings.

5. Most clubs will play with a number 10 operating in zone 14. I am developing a style of play where we can get several players in that zone at the same time.

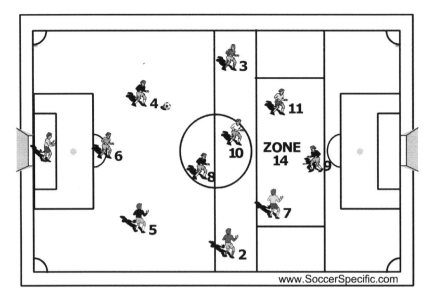

1. In and around the area in front of the back four, but particularly the center backs in a back four, we have a great overload situation. Players are not in what you would term regular positions and they are asking questions of the opponents around them.

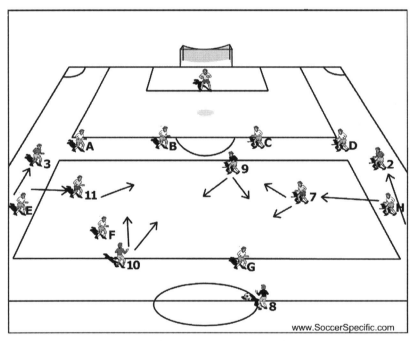

1. Potential movements of each player to confuse the opponents.
2. Here showing the OFF THE BALL MOVEMENT that creates all these options for (8) on the ball.

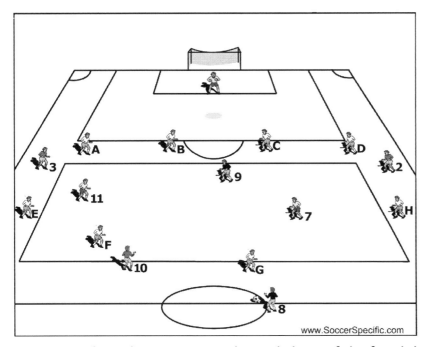

1. Here we have the approximate diamond shape of the four linking players.
2. Through practice and orchestration of these movements in training it becomes second nature to the players and they do it automatically.
3. For the opponents, it should cause confusion as they are not sure who picks up who?

HIGHLIGHTING THE DIAMOND SET UP

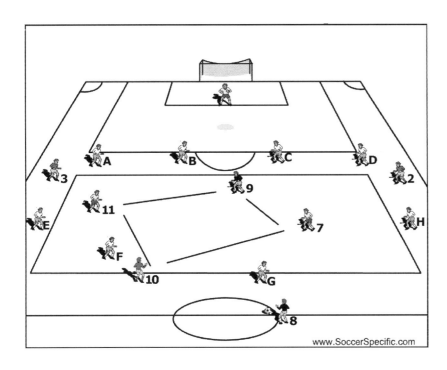

PROGRESSIONAL MOVEMENTS

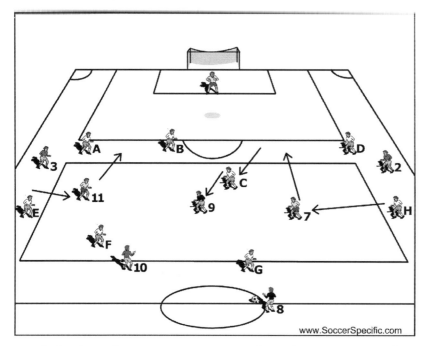

www.SoccerSpecific.com

1. Think about the questions you are asking the opponents individually and collectively with this off the ball movement.
   a. Who picks up overlapping fullback (2)? Defender (D) or Midfielder (H)?
   b. Who picks up overlapping fullback (3)? Defender (A) or Midfielder (E)?
   c. Who picks up Wide midfielder / striker (7)? Defender (D) tracking inside with him, or central defender (C) if he moves into his area of influence?
   d. Who picks up Wide midfielder / striker (11)? Defender (A) tracking inside with him, or central defender (B) if he moves into his area of influence?
   e. Who picks up striker (9) coming short to receive to feet? Does center back (C) track him or does he pass him onto central midfielder (G) or even (F) depending on where (9) goes?
   f. In a split second decision making situation if midfielder (F) decided to track wide midfielder / striker (11) who picks up (10)?
2. Through hours and weeks and months of practice to develop these movements they become automatic and the players do not need to think about them beforehand. They just SEE THE SET UP; like a mental image, and make the combination movements.
3. So, in the game situation with the phase of play happening so quickly, it must be very difficult for opponents to know who picks up whom in that split second.
4. By the time a decision has been made in each instance it will likely be too late and we have the upper hand.

ANGLED SUPPORT; SIDE ON POSITIONING; AND MOVEMENT THROUGH THE FRONT THREE UNITS OF PLAYERS IN A 4-2-3-1

1. Create four zones or corridors across the field and three zones up and down the field.
2. Rules:
   a. A player can't pass straight forward in his own corridor or zone.
   b. A player can pass forward to another corridor / zone (therefore an angled forward pass).
   c. A player can pass back in his own corridor / zone.
   d. A player can pass across a corridor/ zone from side to side.
3. So, players cannot pass forward into the same zone. Therefore the players receiving the pass will always be at an angle to the passer and this will force them to get into a sideways on position, which increases their peripheral vision.
4. By using this set up we educate players to look to support at angles in front of the ball, because the CONDITION of the session forces them to do so.
5. The coach can decide if he wants the same condition going backwards as well, nothing is set in stone.
6. In games you will very often see players coming IN A STRAIGHT LINE to receive a pass to feet from a player behind them. While this can be effective, it would be MORE effective if they come off at an angle.
7. Reasoning:
   a. Straight run / Straight pass / few options / poor peripheral vision
   b. Angled check / Angled pass / More Options and greater peripheral vision
8. Opening up the body and getting side on to receive means the player can see both the defender behind and the ball in front and the options all around him, which means his all round peripheral vision is increased.
9. The attacking player receives the ball side on and can receive and turn and see a bigger picture around and beyond the ball. SIDENOTE: Allow passes that are close to the boundaries created by the condition. If it is within a foot or two let it go in order to maintain momentum.
10. In building the session focus on simple combinations for clarity; for example:
    a. Initially work on the two wide players' movements ((7) and (11)) before the fullbacks are added.
    b. Next introduce the fullbacks and work on the combinations between the fullbacks and wide players, (2) and (7) and (3) and (11)
    c. Next work on the combination movements of the target striker (9) and the shadow striker (10)
    d. Work on the combination between a wide player and a striker
    e. Bring it all together and develop the session using all combinations between units and between players.

A) WARM UP: A TWO TEAM SET UP

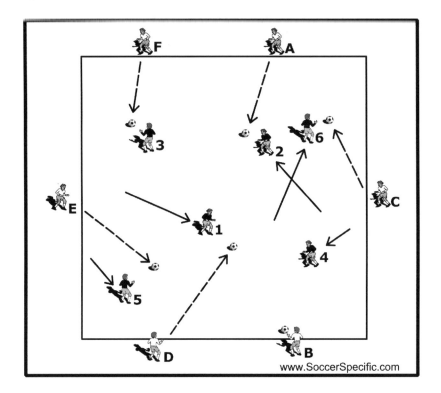

www.SoccerSpecific.com

1. One team inside, one team outside. A ball is with each outside player to begin. Pass to an inside player who receives and turns and finds another outside free player with a pass. Then look to receive from another outside player. The outside player receives and moves the ball side to side until another inside player is free to receive a pass. This ensures all the players are working both inside and outside the grid. Players support at angles to receive, opening up the field of play. Do not do what (4) above has done, where there are no options and no vision.

2. Change to all balls starting with the inside players. These players now look to pass and receive a give and go from an outside player. Rotate the players so both teams have the chance to play in the middle of the grid.

3. Move both teams to the middle; divide the grid into two with each team passing to their own team within their own grid area, keeping teams separate to begin.

4. Mix the play up, let it run through the legs and turn (weight of past), chip the ball into space, use the inside and outside of the foot to receive and turn, play a double pass, look twice before you receive.

5. Competitive: Have the receiving players count the number of times they receive and pass the ball in a set time period. Only count the passes that are accurate. This speeds up the decision making process.

B)   PASSING AND RUNNING ANGLES OF SUPPORT

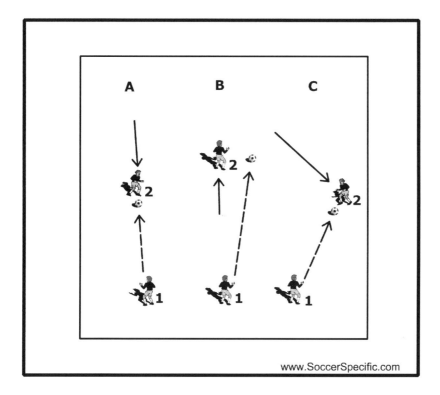

www.SoccerSpecific.com

A: Straight run / Straight pass / No options
B: Straight run / Straight pass / No vision
C: Angled check / Angled pass / Options and vision

1.   Here we show the differences between runs and passes in straight lines or at angles and the effectiveness or ineffectiveness of each.
2.   Opening up the body and getting side on to receive means the player can see both the defender behind and the ball in front and the options all around him, which means his all round peripheral vision is increased.
3.   The attacking player receives the ball side on and can receive and turn and see a bigger picture around and beyond the ball.

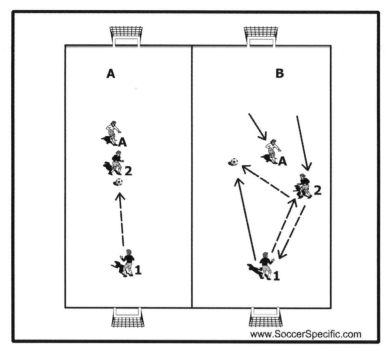

A: No options, no vision, straight lines. It is more difficult to affect the defender and beat him.

B: Check to the side at an angle. The defender follows and is tight but space is created to the side and in front to run onto. (1) can pass to feet or into space.

1. Two 30 by 10 yard areas.
2. Stay in the same corridor for this introductory part of the clinic.
3. The striker can check away to come back to work the defender's position also.

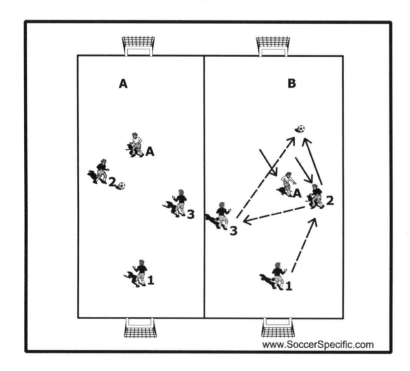

1. Stay in the same corridor for this introductory part of the progression. Defenders start passive to begin.
2. Try to score in the goal. Pass from player (1) to player (3). Player (2) acts as a support player.
3. Players looking to get side on to be able to see the defender behind and the ball in front. (3) must try to get behind the defender if possible to receive a pass and score. This is all about ANGLED SUPPORT and not supporting or passing in straight lines. The striker is always trying to get AT LEAST side on; but preferably facing forward.
4. Ideas:
   a. Check to the ball but at an angle,
   b. Check away then back towards the ball,
   c. Check away and receive the pass in behind and off the shoulder of the defender,
   d. Check to and play a give and go with the support player as in (B).
   e. Defender drops off to stop the pass in behind; so check to feet to receive

C) THE BASIC SET UP USING THE 2-3-1 THEN THE 4-3-1 (OF THE 4-2-3-1)

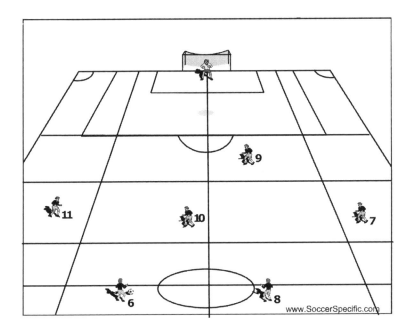

www.SoccerSpecific.com

1. A shadow play with the 2-3-1 of the team (not including the back four and keeper yet). This is basic practicing of passing and moving between units.
2. Initially keep it short and tight for quick movement. So we have four zones just as wide as the penalty area to play in.
3. Have two groups of 6 players going one group at a time to keep the session flowing. By the time the first group is back to the start again the 2nd group has gone and so on.
4. Eventually go to the full width of the field with 4 zones.
5. You can stop the action and show the changes in the interplay. As the passer is about to pass, STOP THE PLAY, show all the positional changes and the potential passing options.

6. Actually fabricate some of the movements to show how they can work.
7. Condition defenders to do certain things. For example, the fullbacks have to either mark the wide player coming inside or the fullback overlapping so the passer has to identify which player is free and make the right decision.

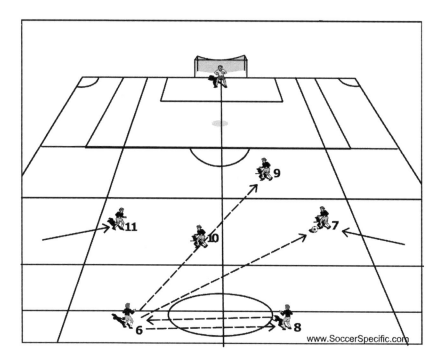

1. Showing a few options for (6). (10) may interchange with (11) and go wide.

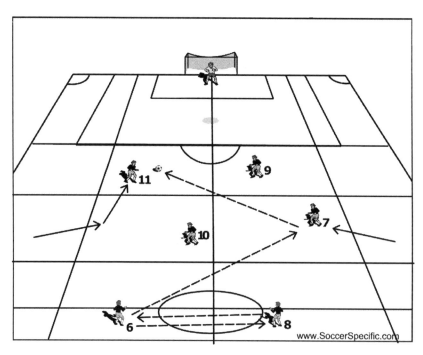

1. Angled passing from (6) to (7) cutting inside from the right to (11) cutting inside from the left.

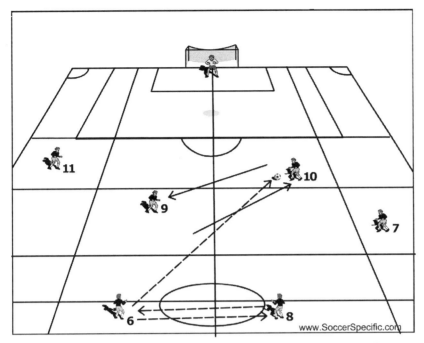

1. Interchange of the target striker (9) and the shadow striker (10). (11) can hit the touchline for the diagonal pass from (10) to get a cross in or come inside for a shorter pass and a potential shot at goal.

D) INTRODUCING BOTH FULLBACKS TO INCREASE THE NUMBER OF OPTIONS AVAILABLE

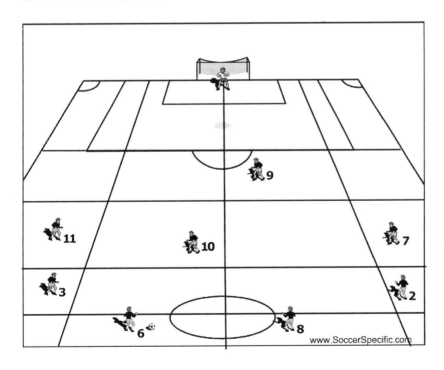

1. Introduce the fullbacks (2) And (3) now. Shadow plays to develop the idea.

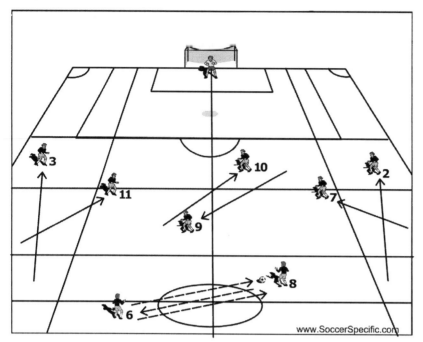

1. Here are some potential movements in front of the passer (8). All very simple but may cause CHAOS in the opponent's defense. We know what we are doing in advance of the ball, the opponents do not, and this is to our advantage. Continue with the movements with the relevant passes and have a finish on goal.

E)   THE BALL IS WITH THE FULLBACK (3) SO HE WONT INTERCHANGE WITH (11)

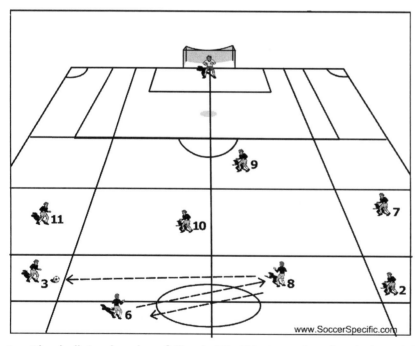

1. The ball is played to fullback (3). This is a CUE for (10) and (11) to interchange and for (7) to come inside and (2) to overlap on the other side of the field.
2. Great off the ball movement for the passer to have many choices.

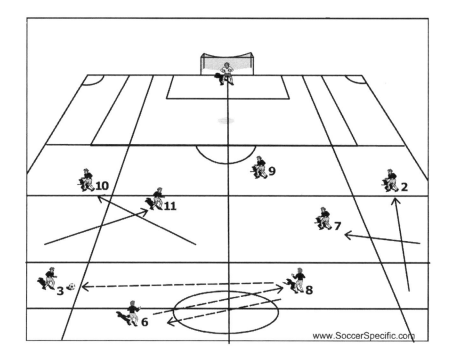

1. Four potential options for (3) in front of the ball. Cannot at this moment in the development of the session play a straight pass to (10) but there are four other options of a forward pass.

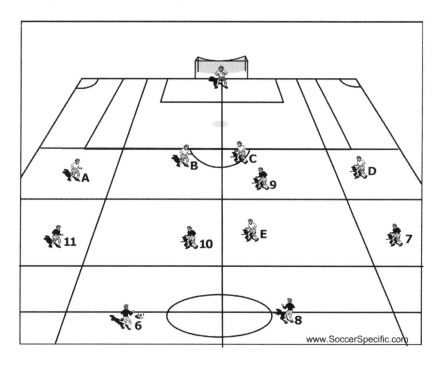

1. Introduce defenders. Bring in a back four and one central midfield player. Now it is a 6v6, or a 6v5 in the outfield.
2. Still developing the play with the shorter and tighter area; the full width of the penalty box; to get quickness of movement and passing.

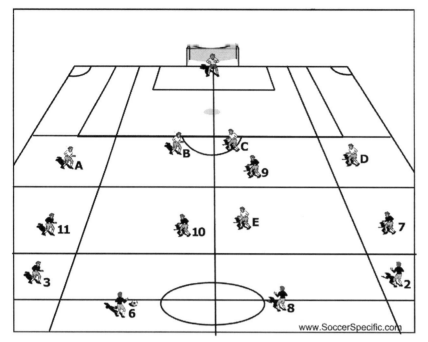

1. Bring in the attacking fullbacks. Now it is an 8v6, or 8v5 in the outfield. Now we can explore all the options this formation offers for the attacking team. Once the phase play works well with this set up, add more defenders to increase the pressure.

2. You can create orchestrated moves between the units of players to show how a phase of play can develop. You as a coach dictate where the ball will go and then eventually when you are satisfied they understand it all, let it go free and have them make their own decisions.

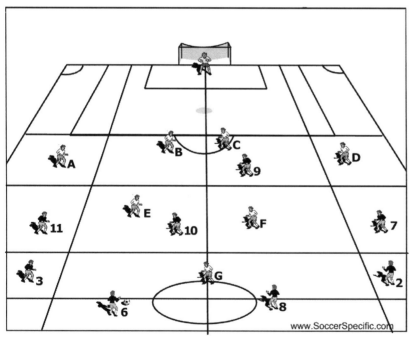

1. Two more defensive players added to make it an 8v8 or 8v7 in the outfield.

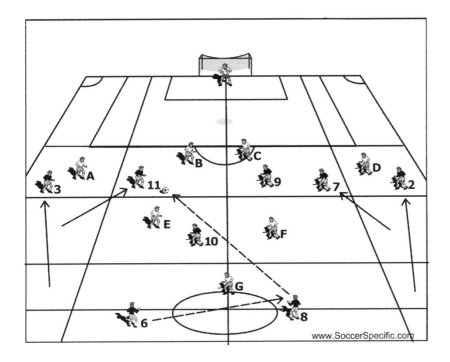

1. Usual interchange between the wide players and the fullbacks. Here (8) passes to (11) coming inside to attack the back four. He can create a 2v1 coming inside against center back (B) with striker (9). If he is a right footer coming inside then even better as he is coming onto his stronger foot and has the option of a shot on goal if in a good enough position to do so.

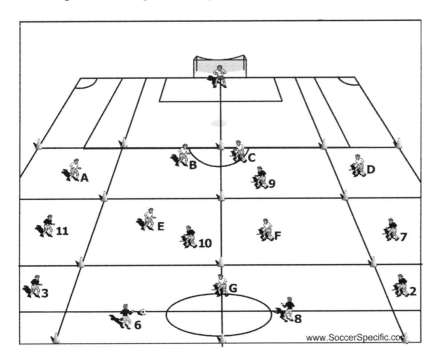

1. Making it clearer with the introduction of cones to represent the designated areas we play in. Ideal if you can get a field permanently marked off with grids.

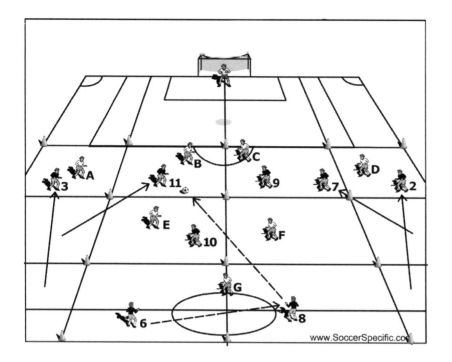

1. A simple pass into (11) cutting inside will open up lots more possibilities as we develop the phase of play.

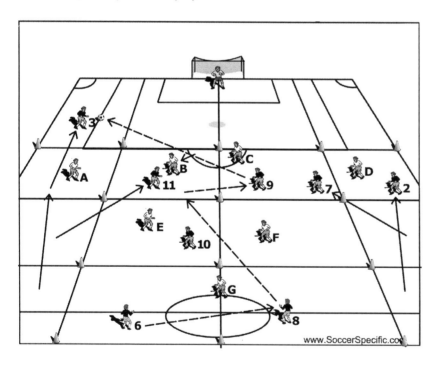

1. A more elaborate development, (11) and (9) linking up to play overlapping fullback (3) in.

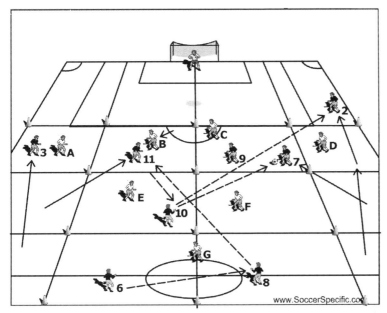

1. Center back (B) closes (11) down and (11) cannot go forward. (10) supports from behind and in doing so offers a simple pass back. At the same time (7) and (2) interchange and offer two potential passes for (10) who can switch the play through both of them. If (9) can get free, he can also get a pass.

F) ALLOWING STRAIGHT PASSES BY PLAYERS SWITCHING ZONES IN FRONT OF THE BALL

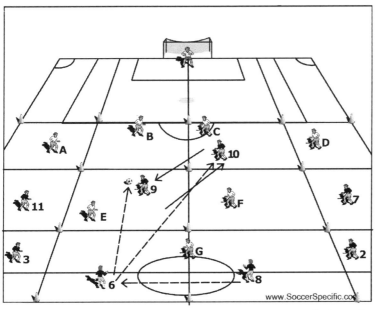

1. New rule: Players can receive a straight pass if they change the zone in front of the passer. Here we have an interchange between (9) and (10). (9) must run in such a way that he times the run so the ball can run alongside him and he does not have to receive and turn or receive with his back to play.

2. The correct timing of the run and timing of the pass is vital here. Also his decision will be influenced by what the defenders do.

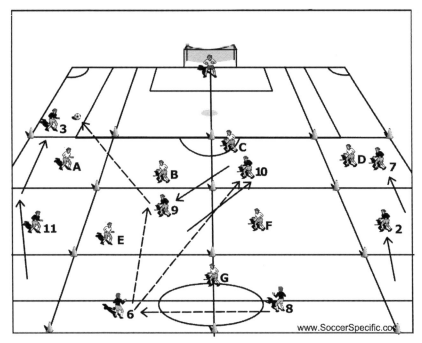

1. For example, here the defender (B) closes (9) down inside and so while he cannot run at the defense he is in a position to play a ball into the path of overlapping fullback (3).

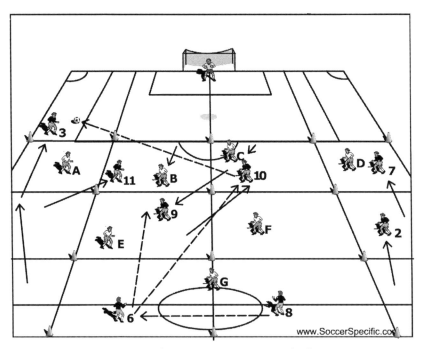

1. Here (9) receives and turns INSIDE (B) and plays a pass into (10) who can develop play further with a wide pass to fullback (3) again. (10) drops into space to be able to get a yard on defending center back (C).

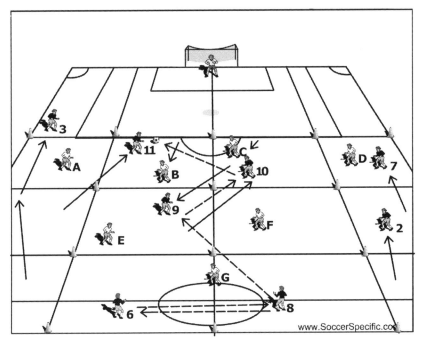

1. (9) drops short to receive. He draws center back (B) with him, creating a space behind (B). (9) plays an around the corner pass to (10) who then plays a pass into the space behind (B) for (11) cutting inside.

COMBINATION MOVEMENTS OF THE FRONT THREE WITH THE WIDE PLAYERS IN ADVANCED POSITIONS

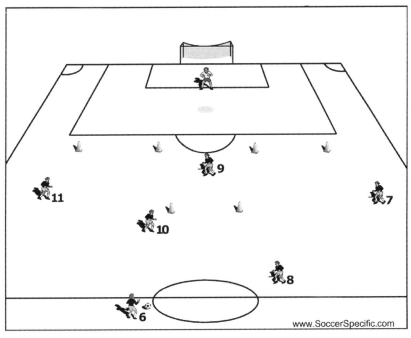

1. Using cones to imitate a back four and a central midfield pair to give the players some defining positions to work from. Still a shadow play but cones or poles make it easier to work the movements.

2. We are working with the 2-3-1 of the 4-2-3-1 system of play for the moment in a phase of play.
3. Showing the movements of (7) and (11), the two wide players in the unit of three, and how they support the striker (9) to become a front three.
4. Coaching Points:
   a. Start positions defined (you can use different color cones for this if you need).
   b. Timing of the runs
   c. Angles of the runs
   d. Timing and quality of the pass
   e. Interchange of positions
   f. We are building the idea up gradually for some clarity.
5. No fullbacks involved yet; we are just focusing on the movements of the wide attacking players (7) and (11).
6. In building the session focus on simple combinations for clarity; for example:
   a. Initially work on the two wide player's movements before the full backs are added
   b. Next introduce the fullbacks and work on the combinations between the fullbacks and wide players, (2) and (7) and (3) and (11)
   c. Next work on the combination movements of the target striker (9) and the shadow striker (10)
   d. Work on the combination between a wide player and a striker
   e. Bring it all together and develop the session using all combinations between units and between players 2. Initially keep it short and tight for quick movement. So we have four zones just as wide as the penalty area only to play in.
7. Have two groups of 6 players going one group at a time to keep the session flowing. By the time the first group is back to the start again the 2nd group has gone and so on.
8. Eventually go to the full width of the field with 4 zones.
9. You can stop the action and show the changes in the interplay. As the passer is about to pass, STOP THE PLAY, show all the positional changes and the potential passing options.
10. Actually fabricate some of the movements to show how they can work.
11. Condition defenders to do certain things. For example, the fullbacks have to either mark the wide player coming inside or the fullback overlapping so the passer has to identify which player is free and make the right decision.

A) FOCUS ON WIDE PLAYERS ONLY

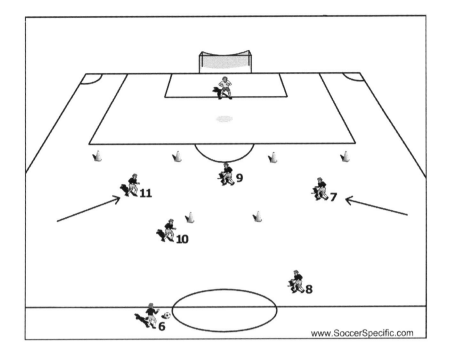

www.SoccerSpecific.com

1. This is the FIRST PHASE OF PLAY
2. Focus only on the movements of the wide players (7) and (11) to establish this.
3. The three midfield player's play at angles off each other. (6) is the defensive midfielder who begins the moves, (10) is the attacking midfield creator, and (8) is the link player between them.
4. Phases of play can be defined here as four developments and their introduction from the first to the second, second to the third, and third to the fourth. It depends on the time taken, the timing of passes and movement and how the opposition react to it, either slowing the momentum down or the attacking team being able to go through the phases quickly. Players have to think on their feet as every phase of play is different.
5. Phases of play:
   a. FIRST PHASE OF PLAY: The initial passing and movement: (it can be the pass from (6) to (8) and the movement of (7) and (11) in synch with each other). So, initial movement to get into position as a three, or a four to include (10).
   b. SECOND PHASE OF PLAY: The next action and movement based on the first movement (which is concerned with a front three now; or a four with (10); after starting in the first phase with a striker and two wingers wide) and a supporting attacking midfielder (10). So, now we are looking at the next interchange of the front three players (7), (9) and (11) and we can then include (10) as part of this offensive diamond.
   c. THIRD PHASE OF PLAY: The continued build up to the end product and fourth phase of development.
   d. FOURTH PHASE OF PLAY: The end product (a shot / header on goal).

1. Now we have a diamond of support up front with many options.
2. All four players position at angles to each other and offer instant support.

1. Bring in two fullbacks (2) and (3) to the phase play.
2. The play is built up as normal with both (7) and (11) tucking inside to do two things:
   a. To create space wide for overlapping fullbacks (2) and (3) and;
   b. To both support (9) inside by getting closer to him and potentially making a three striker set up.
3. Now our focus can switch to the movements of the fullbacks and how they coordinate them with their immediate wide players.

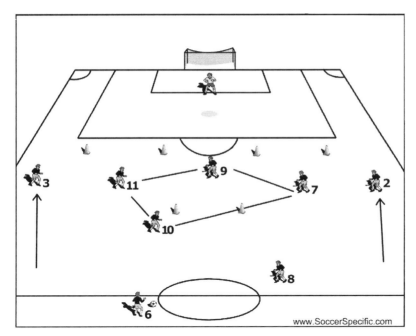

1. We have great potential for structured movements between four attacking players in central areas now. We have four potential individual movements that complement each other and create some CHAOS in the opponent's defense by their interchanging movements in the game situation.
2. Add to the equation the possibilities of the two attacking fullbacks (2) and (3) and we have a great attacking situation for our team and (6) may have many options of a penetrating pass.

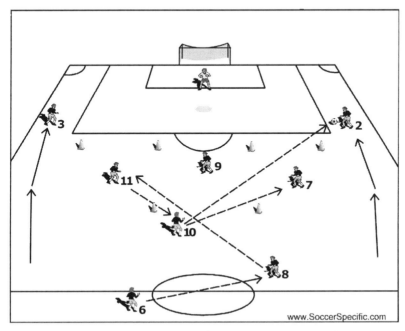

1. Showing a potential phase of play. (10) receives the pass and has a couple of options highlighted here to exploit the runs of (7) and (2).
2. Use the back line of cones as an offside line so the players outside can time their overlap runs.

C) SECOND PHASE OF PLAY

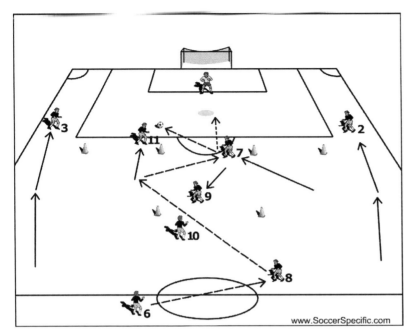

www.SoccerSpecific.com

1. This is the SECOND PHASE OF PLAY. (11) and (7) play a give and go around the center back. (9) has gone short to clear the space for (7).

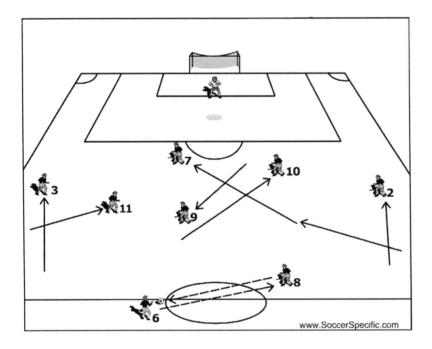

www.SoccerSpecific.com

1. Take the cones out and let it go free.
2. This is the SECOND PHASE OF PLAY.
3. Start Position: (6) and (8) pass between each other. This allows TIME for the players to make their movements and interchange positions. Trial and error ON THE TIMING with this will happen until you get the timing correct as some players have to cover longer distances.

4. Obviously in games it will depend on the moment, the time available before a defining pass is made, the opponent's defensive positioning and our player movements and so on as to which movements occur.

5. For example, (7) may receive the pass earlier in his run (SECOND PHASE OF PLAY), perhaps at the end of the first arrow and beginning of the next depending on how quick the play is. Another pass may occur in between his two runs above, where his final run is rewarded with a pass down the channel.

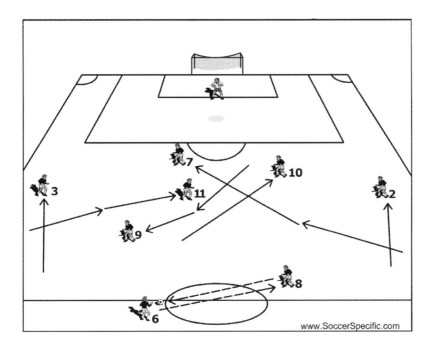

1. SECOND PHASE OF PLAY. Striker (9) continues his run and comes short to create space behind for (7) and (11) to run into. In a game situation if the center back follows him then this movement by (9) will create space for his teammates.

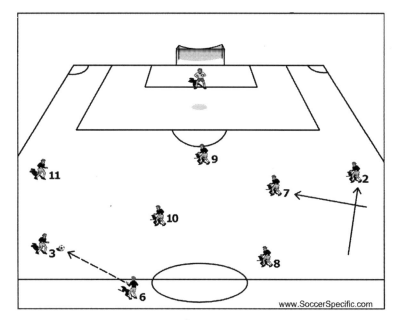

1. Here we find the ball in a wide area and only one fullback (2) attacks down one side and makes the interchange of positions with (7). (11) offers width on the other side.

2. Now we look at the creativity of (7), (9) and (10) in their interchanging of positions to confuse the opponents and take defenders into areas they do not want to go.

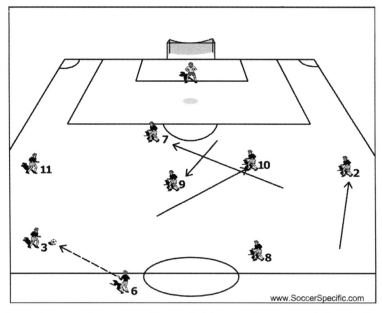

1. Here we have our (2) and (7) interchange and the ball is wide at fullback (3). (11) stays wide as an outlet and (7) links with (9) and (10) to produce a front three to offer three pass options for (3).

2. In this instance (9) can receive short to feet, (7) can receive a pass in front of him down the side channel and (10) can receive a diagonal pass likely behind the 2nd center back in the game situation (having moved off his shoulder to receive).

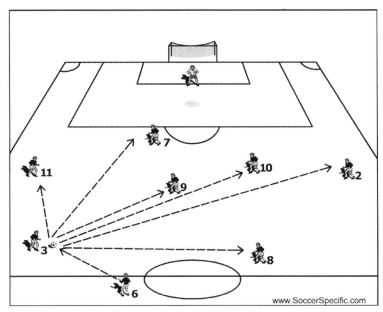

1. Potential passes for player (3) after various movements by several players. The best pass is the one that penetrates the most, likely one behind the opponent's defense to (7) or (10). But if, in the game situation, these passes are not on to play, there are other options available here as shown.

D) BRING IN DEFENDERS

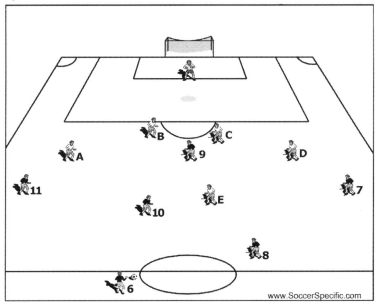

1. Now making it more game realistic once they have performed the movements and passes successfully without pressure and are confident to move to the next more pressurized phase of play.
2. Again, start with just the wide players without fullbacks to clarify their movements without the distraction of having fullbacks overlapping yet.

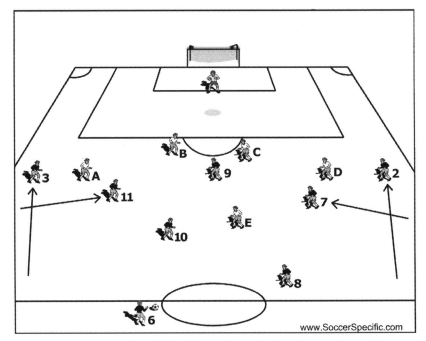

1. Now introduce the fullbacks and work on their relationships with the wide players and how they may affect the opposition.
2. You can create orchestrated moves between the units of players to show how a phase of play can develop. You as the coach dictate where the ball will go and then eventually when you are satisfied they understand it all, let it go free and have them make their own decisions.

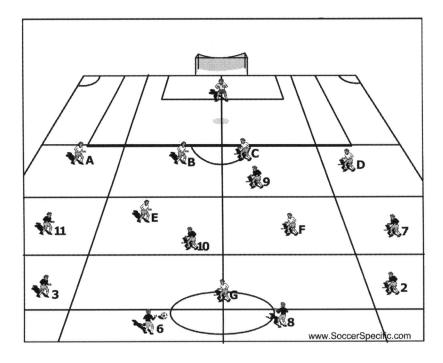

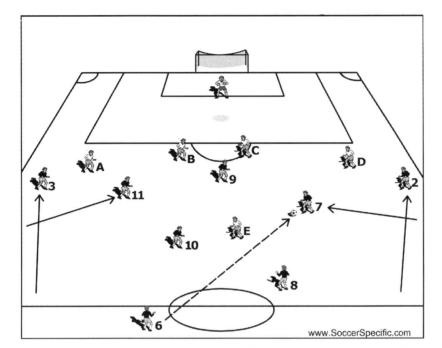

1. In the instant (7) moves inside and (2) overlaps outside, (D) has the dilemma of choosing which one to mark. Here he lets (2) distract his marking and he allows (7) to get free. This now creates a great opportunity for (7) to attack the back four and create a 2v1 with (9) against center back (C) or a 2v1 against fullback (D) with (2), though here (C) is the best option.

2. If (7) is a left footer playing on the right then he is coming inside onto his stronger foot and may get the opportunity to get a direct shot on goal, something he may not try if he is a right footer but coming inside onto his weaker left foot.

3. Playing this system one should consider the possibilities of this with the right fullback (2) who, likely being right footed, can cross with his stronger foot.

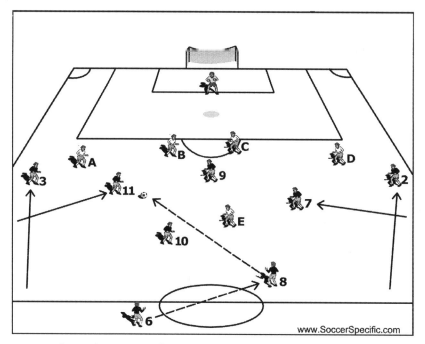

1.   Another idea going the other way, this time (11) being the receiving player to come inside and shoot at goal (especially if he is a right footer coming in from the left) or to make combination plays with his teammates.

E)   THIRD PHASE OF PLAY

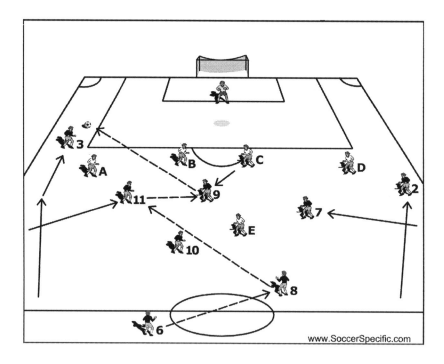

1.   Here (9) drops off into space to receive the pass from (11) and lays a great pass into the path of overlapping fullback (3) to get into a   good crossing position.
If (9) has lots of space here he can receive and turn and run at the defense also.

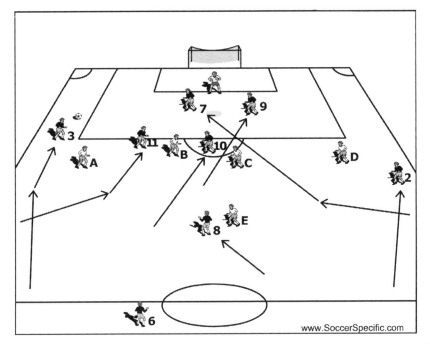

1. Continuing the move on, we show (3) in a crossing position and the following movements of the players to get in position to receive the crossed ball.

2. This is just one idea of many combinations that may occur. (7) near post, (9) far post, (2) beyond the far post if it goes over (9), (11) continuing his run into or around the left side of the box for secondary clearances and (10) moving centrally into or around the box also.

F) FOURTH AND FINAL PHASE OF PLAY

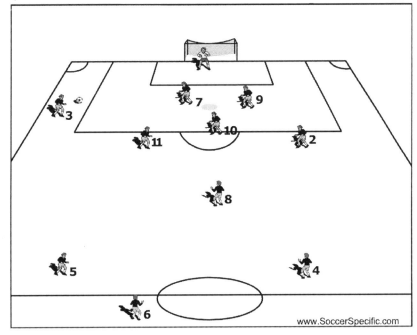

1. End positions covering all eventualities. Also the back four is organized should the opponents COUNTER ATTACK. Likely the opponents will leave 2 strikers up so this adds security behind our attack.

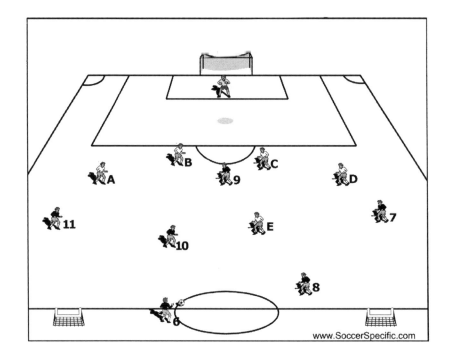

1. Add small goals so the defending team has a target to play to. Make the training competitive by keeping score. First team to score 5 goals wins so both teams have an incentive. Here we have a 6v6 phase of play, and a 6v5 overload in the outfield in our favor.

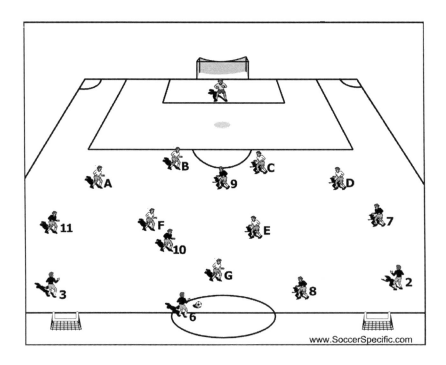

1. Add more players to build the idea. Now it is an 8v8 but it is an 8v7 overload in the outfield.

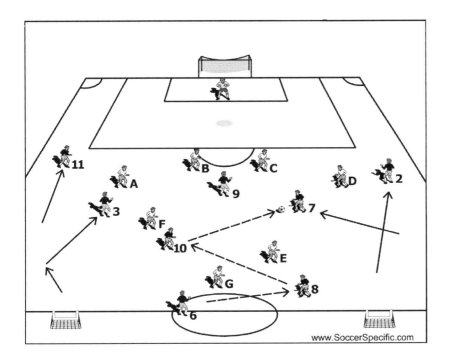

1. Great combination passing between (6), (9) and (10) to get (7) in and in a position to attack the back four. Timing of the run is important by (7) as is timing of the pass from (10). If the pass is too late or the run is too early then (7) will receive with his back to play. Thus it is important the timing of each is in synch so (7) has an opportunity to receive the ball facing forward and in his stride.

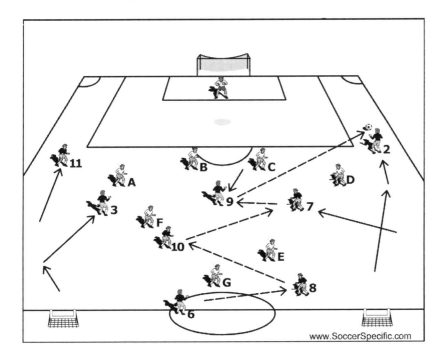

1. Now (7) linking with the striker (9) who plays in overlapping fullback (2).

DEVELOPING PLAY USING SIDE ON BODY POSITIONS IN 11 v 11 AND IN A 4-2-3-1 SYSTEM OF PLAY

A) HERE WE HAVE THE START POSITIONS FOR THE TEAM WITH A 4-2-3-1

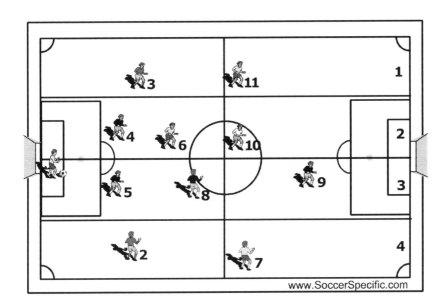

1. Now we have a full size game situation.

B) NOW WE MOVE TO A SHADOW PLAY FOR ELEVEN PLAYERS

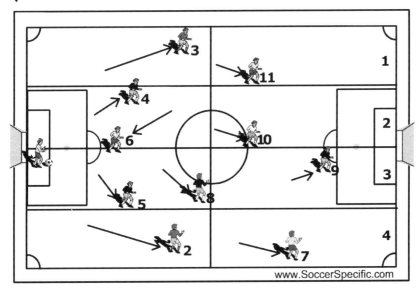

1. The field is divided into four corridors or zones, end to end.
2. Rules:
   a. A player can't pass forward in his own corridor or zone. Diagonally forward passes only.
   b. A player can pass forward to the other corridor (diagonal).
   c. A player can pass back in his own corridor.

3. We begin with the attacking team shape with the start position being the 4-2-3-1 moving to the interchange of players between units, as shown above, especially that of defensive midfielder number (6) dropping back and both fullbacks (2) and (3) moving forward, who in turn push on (7) and (11).

4. Create angled support between (6), (8), (10) and (9) going through the middle of the team and avoid straight line support there.

C) HERE WE HAVE THE MOVEMENTS OF THE 4-2-3-1 INTO THEIR ATTACKING SHAPE

www.SoccerSpecific.com

1. Players looking to get side on to be able to see the defender behind them and the ball in front of them. This is all about ANGLED SUPPORT and not supporting or passing in straight lines.

2. Here if (8) passed to (9), likely (9) would receive the pass with his back to goal. While this is still a good pass and we need to teach each striker to receive like this and keep possession, our theme is receiving sideways on so this pass is not allowed in this particular session. No forward options; no vision with straight lines, so it is more difficult to affect the defender and beat him.

3. So, (8) in Zone 3 is allowed to pass forward to (7) in zone 4, to (10) in zone 2 and to (11) in zone 1 or anyone else moving into their zones ahead of the ball, but not to (9) in zone 3.

4. Having zones to play in will also improve the TIMING OF THE RUNS in front of the ball and the TIMING OF THE PASS. For example, if (8) has the ball, as above, and (11) cuts inside to receive the pass, if the run is too early or the pass too late it may arrive as the player arrives in the SAME ZONE 3 AS (8). If the player (11) receives the ball directly in front of (8) then he may have to be facing backwards to receive it to be able to see where the ball is coming from (unless it is played in front of him to run onto but even then the lack of vision as it is being passed may be to his disadvantage).

5. If the ball arrives as (11) enters Zone 2 then at this stage of the development of play, he can see in front of him and where defenders are (and teammates if they

are in front of him), and have options to choose from. Plus when he receives the pass he will be side on facing forward ready to run at the defense.

6. If he stays in Zone 1 and he has space there also; again, this is a position where he has both options to play and good peripheral vision because his position is at an angle to the ball.

7. The striker is always trying to get AT LEAST side on, but preferably facing forward. So if receiving from (8) in this particular situation a movement to the side into Zone 2 to create a better angle to receive may be the right course of action.

8. Ideas for movement and receiving the pass:
   a. Check to the ball but at an angle,
   b. Check away then back towards the ball,
   c. Check away and receive the pass in behind and off the shoulder of the defender,
   d. Check to and play a give and go with the support player.
   e. Defender drops off to stop the pass in behind; so check to feet to receive

1. Rather than receive the ball from a straight pass with his back to goal, (9) checks away to the side into a different zone to be side on to receive. It may be a matter of only a few yards to make this happen. Now the pass is an angled pass also.

2. Of course the defensive situation he is up against in the real game has to be such that he is able to do this successfully but this just serves as an example of what he could do.

D) DIVIDE THE FIELD UP INTO FOUR QUARTERS LENGTHWAYS AND FOUR QUARTERS WIDTHWAYS
START POSITION: 4-2-3-1

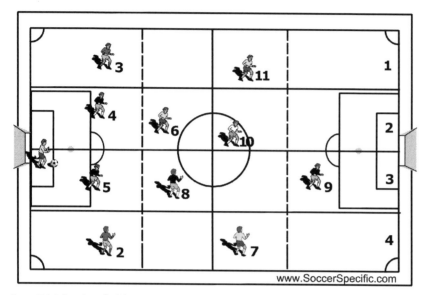

www.SoccerSpecific.com

1. Divide the field into 16 zones with cones. Now you can see the four units of players clearly also in the 4-2-3-1. Same rules apply, a player cannot pass forward into his own zone.

E) ATTACKING POSITION: 3-3-3-1 OR 3-3-1-3

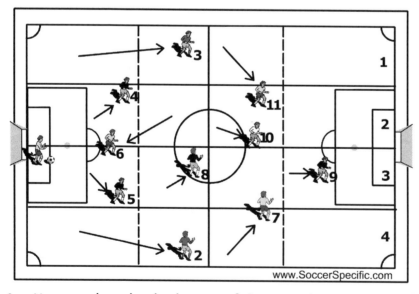

www.SoccerSpecific.com

1. Here we show the development of the team shape in an attacking phase. The changes of position of players are quite dramatic and through this we hope it will confuse the opposition as to who marks who.
2. Having clear boundaries like this may also help the players to position off of each other and create angles for passes.

3. Coaching Points:
   a. Start position team shape and changing team shape as we advance up the field in possession of the ball
   b. Creating angles for passes through conditions and boundaries
   c. Angles of the runs
   d. Timing of the passes
   e. Timing of the runs
   f. Movements off the ball to create space for each other

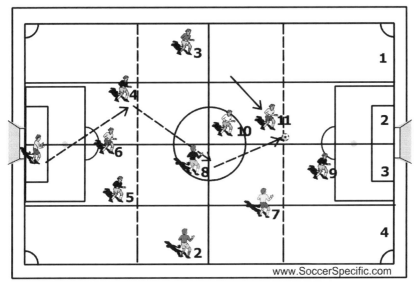

1. Here is a favorite move with a wide player coming inside and receiving an angled pass to attack the goal. (9) moves out the space to leave it free for (11) to run into and is ready to support him in the next phase of play.

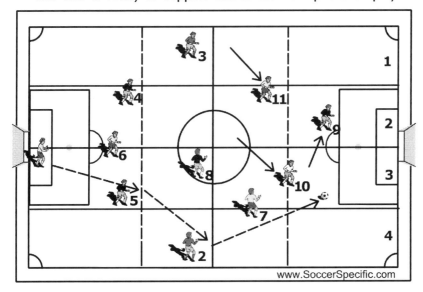

1. Every pass is at an angle from the passer and receiver.
2. The team has transitioned from its start position of 4-2-3-1 into the more dynamic attacking phase. (9) clears the space for (10) to move into in order to receive the pass.

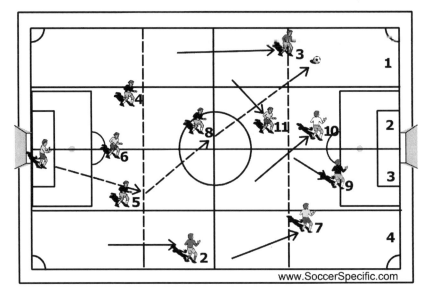

1. Switching the point of attack to overlapping fullback (3), (9) and (10) switch positions to try to create space for each other to receive the cross from (3). (7) positions beyond the far post in case the cross is over hit.

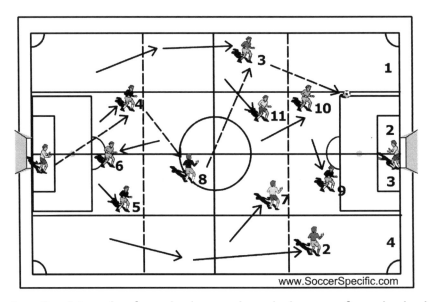

1. Good interplay from the keeper through the team from the back to the midfield to the overlapping fullback who then plays a pass into the space in front of (10) to run onto. (9) has cleared the space there for (10) to run into so we have a nice interchange of positions by these two players.

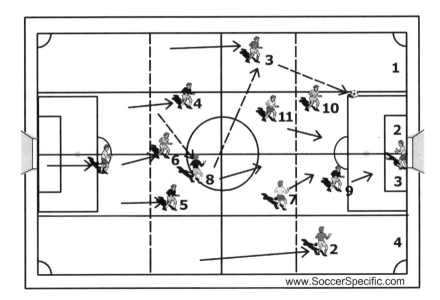

www.SoccerSpecific.com

1. Showing the development of movement up the field from the back now. (9) can attack the near post and (2) the far post if they have time to get there. (7) and (11) cover around the anticipation areas around the box for clearances or pullbacks from (10). (10) may also attack the goal and take a shot from this position.
2. (8) pushes forward to fill the space in front of the back three and the back three and keeper push up to condense the play and force their opponent's strikers (not shown) back towards their own goal. Ultimately the back three should push up as high as the half way line.

DEVELOPING THE PLAN WHERE A PLAYER CAN PASS INTO HIS OWN ZONE TO A PLAYER IF THAT PLAYER HAS COME INTO IT FROM ANOTHER ZONE

Now we are affecting movement off the ball again but using another method of development. Timing of the run and timing of the pass has to be especially good now. So we can have a straight pass now but it has to be IN ADVANCE of the run to get the timing right.

A straight pass in to the feet of the striker is easier because he is already in position but he is also receiving with his back to goal.

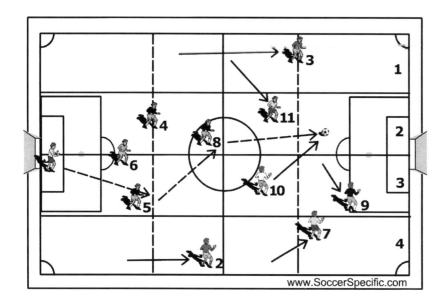

www.SoccerSpecific.com

1. Here we have (8) receiving the pass and (11) cuts inside from Zone 1 to Zone 2, the same zone as (8) to receive the next pass and attack the goal. (9) has moved out of the zone (11) is moving into in order to create space for him. Initially (9) is already in the same zone so cannot accept a pass from (8) but his movement creating space for (11) also means he has moved into another zone and he can receive an angled pass from (8). So his movement creates two possible situations, one to create space for (11), the other to create space for a pass to himself from (8).

2. Likewise as shown here, (10) could make the same run from the other side and from Zone 3 to Zone 2 to receive facing forward and running onto goal with the ball for a shot.

3. So the timing of the run has to be perfect here, where (11) for example does not get ahead of the pass and arrive too early and have to check his run, or (8) does not pass the ball too late.

4. By allowing this new condition the players are made to think about movement off the ball to receive it, and they do not stand still in the same zone as the passer; knowing they cannot receive it there. Therefore the goal of this condition is to teach the players to make greater movements off the ball and usually at angles to receive it even if the pass is straight.

F) ADD CONES OR POLES TO SIMULATE A BACK FOUR

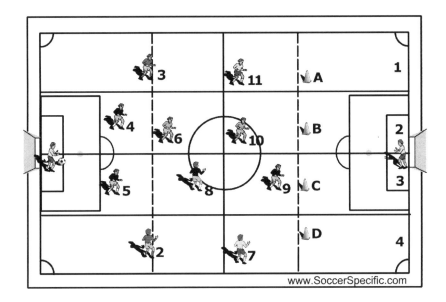

1. It can be easier to create and time your runs when there are guides such as these to work from.

G) ADD CONES OR POLES TO SIMULATE A BACK FOUR AND TWO DEFENSIVE CENTRAL MIDFIELDERS

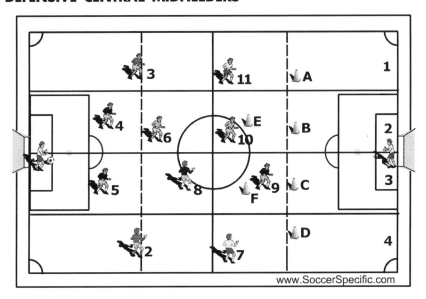

1. Building up the idea we add two central midfield players (represented by the cones). You can do this with the opponent's whole team eventually before starting to build the actual opposing players into the session.

H) ADD A BACK FOUR AND KEEPER TO PLAY AGAINST

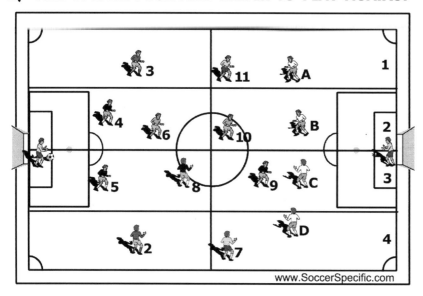

1. Previous diagrams showing different ideas of movement can be referred to here; rather than reproducing the same ideas again.

I) ADD A CENTRAL MIDFIELD PAIR TO PLAY AGAINST

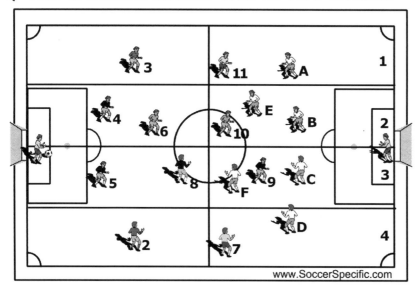

1. Build the session up until it becomes a full 11 v 11 game situation. Have the development at this stage as follows:
   a. Passive defending, players can only intercept, not tackle
   b. Semi Passive, a little more high tempo from the defensive team but still only intercepting
   c. A full on game where the defensive team can tackle and win the ball
   d. To maintain the defensive team's interest we can offer them the opportunity to score but within 6 passes or less as we are ultimately working with the attacking team and want them to have the ball as much as possible.

TO FINISH: TAKE OUT THE ZONES AND LET IT GO FREE

TRANSITION TRAINING

INCORPORATING DEFENDING AND COUNTER ATTACKING AND WORKING ON A CHANGE IN MINDSET OF THE PLAYERS IN A 4-2-3-1 SYSTEM OF PLAY

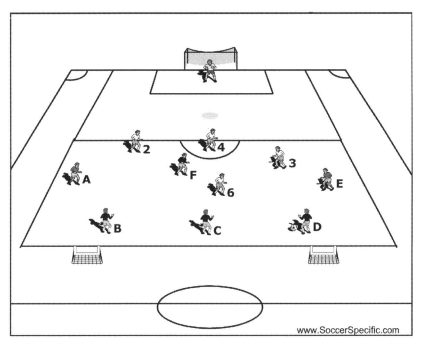

www.SoccerSpecific.com

OBJECTIVE: The defending numbered team has to defend and regain possession then break quickly on the counter attack to score in their opponent's goal (they have a time limit of gaining possession to getting a shot on goal of 6 seconds). Use the penalty box as the offside line.

A) DIFFERENT COUNTER ATTACKING METHODS TO USE

1. **Individual** - ex. Ronaldo takes possession around the halfway line and runs at and past a number of opponents to score or provide for the scorer.
2. **Collective** - ex. Arsenal regains in their own half and with a number of quick but incisive passes produce a strike at goal.
3. **Traditional** - in that the ball is won and delivered early to the back of the defense or up to a forward who then produces a strike or provides for another to strike.
4. **Pressing** - in that a team presses their opponents, regains in or around the attacking third, and within one or two passes strikes at goal.
5. **With Width** – As in this exercise, playing quickly into free wide spaces.
6. **Change of Approach** – Initially we try to counter attack quickly but are unable to make it work, thus we need to focus on maintaining possession and changing the approach to a slower buildup to attempt to score.
7. **Defensive Security** – Ensure as we counter attack that we have defensive security behind the ball should the counter fail and the opponents regain the ball quickly.

In this exercise we will be focusing on counter attacking quickly through free wide spaces. You can introduce and practice the other methods listed above also; and which one is most successful may depend on the makeup of your team.

B) A FUNCTIONAL EXERCISE

1. A 5 v 6 in favor of the attacking team
2. Working on a back three and one midfielder defending to gain possession and counter attack quickly to score into the small goals.
3. Players (A) and (E) play for both teams and so on gaining possession they become (7) and (11) and break wide into the free zones for the counter attacking team. Now it is an overload in favor of the countering team of a 7 v 4. This improves their mental transition.
4. The defending Letters team cannot enter the wide free zones and the attacking team now has 6 seconds to score a goal.
5. Alternatively the defending team on regaining possession has to run the ball over the end line instead of scoring in the goal.

C) COACHING POSITION: BEHIND THE DEFENDING BACK LINE

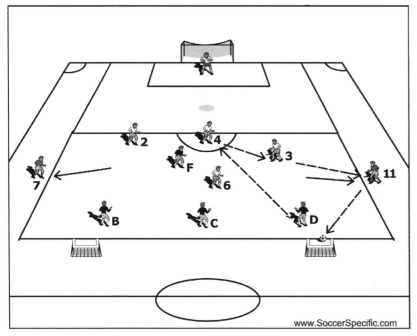

www.SoccerSpecific.com

1. Here a bad pass by (D) has been intercepted by defender (4); (it could be a winning tackle by a numbered player to start the attack; or a shot saved by the keeper to start the counter play).
2. (4) can play it directly to wide player (E) or as he does here through (3). We must break through the wide areas though as that is where the most space is (guaranteed because the wide zone is free).
3. Initially we want success with the counter attack so we make it easy to achieve.

Then, increase the difficulty and insist the wide player cannot score directly but the ball must be scored by an inside player (or the wide player can bring the ball inside to score but then the defender can confront and tackle him).

D) NOW A PHASE OF PLAY

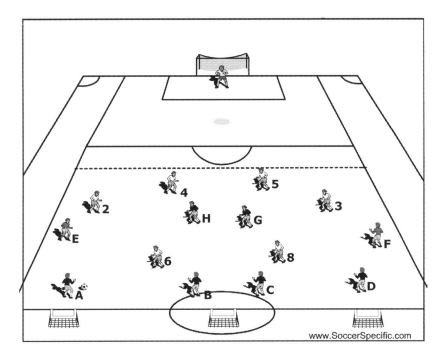

www.SoccerSpecific.com

1. A 7 v 8 in the attacking team's favor to challenge the defending team
2. Half field and three goals.
3. Working on the back four defending with the two defensive midfield players in front of them trying to close opponents down and screen passes into the strikers.
4. An offside line is in place that we encourage the defenders to try to stay in front of as long as they can.
5. Players (E) and (F) play on both teams. When the defenders win the ball they switch teams and play the other way. These two are in different colors to the two teams to identify them as playing for both sides.
6. Possession changes and the defending team are now attacking and the game becomes a 9 v 6 going the other way to help the quick counter attack be a successful one.
7. Score in the small goals and then the letters team attack again.
8. Keep the score to keep the game competitive.
9. Observe the defending fullback (2)'s positioning in particular. He should not press the opposite attacking fullback and leave the wide player (E) free (encouraging patience).
10. COACHING POINTS:
    a. Defensive line trying to stay high using the offside line as a guide
    b. Pressing when the ball gets closer to goal (being outnumbered they cannot push out and press so they have to be patient)
    c. Staying compact as a back four but working on the individual positioning of each player also

d. Midfield two screening passes into the strikers and pressing the ball when they need to
e. Regaining possession and a transition mindset from defending to attacking
f. Playing through the flank players as quickly as possible (initial condition)
g. Playing through whoever is open and in the best position to attack quickly
h. Quality play maintaining quick possession and a shot on goal within 8 seconds

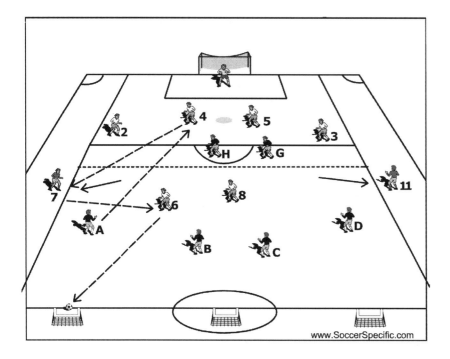

1. Here player (A) makes a bad pass and it is intercepted by center back (4). Immediately players (E) and (F) become attacking players and create width for (4) to pass to them (now numbered 7 and 11 respectively).
2. If possible the team can now counter attack quickly with one or two touch passes. (7) receives the quick pass from (4) and plays another quick pass to midfielder (6) who scores a goal within 8 seconds of the team gaining possession.
3. The three goals can represent the strikers in an actual game situation so it is as if they are trying to get the ball to the strikers as soon as possible.

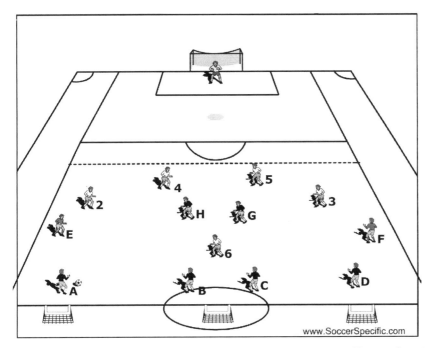

You can vary the numbers of players to increase the difficulty for the defending team both in defending and counter attacking. Here we have a 6 v 8 against that turns into an 8 v 6 going in the other counter attacking direction. You can play around with the numbers to get what you need.

E) ADDING MORE PLAYERS

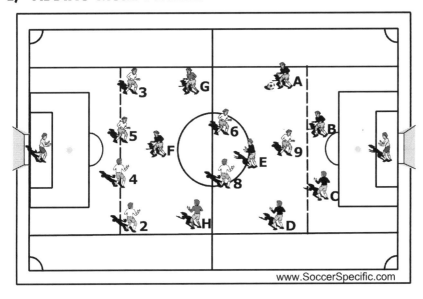

1. As the field size gets bigger and numbers increase, extend the offside line forward so the defense keeps pushing the opponents high up the field. The field is in reality penalty box to penalty box; about 80 x 50. Now we add another goal to the game rather than the small goals previously so it is more like an actual game situation.
2. IT IS NOW A 9 v 8 SMALL SIDED GAME
3. Players (G) and (H) are on the attacking team initially.

4. When possession changes and the defending team are now attacking; the game becomes a 10 v 7 going the other way and in their favor; to help the quick counter attack be a successful one.

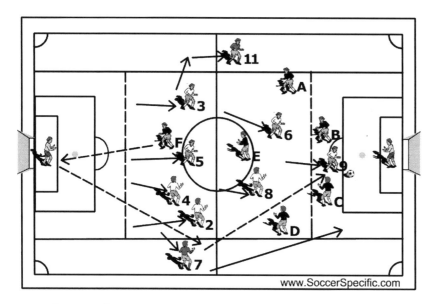

www.SoccerSpecific.com

1. Striker (F) shoots at goal, the keeper saves and he immediately must begin the counter attack.
2. The initial attack is through the flank positions. The red players (once (G) and (H) and now (7) and (11) here attacking the other way) must get touchline wide and into the outside free zones where they cannot be tackled (this is to aid the speed of the counter attack). The keeper throws the ball wide to (7) here and the counter attack begins.
3. So we go from the letters team having an overload of players in a 9 v 8 in their favor to an overload in the counter attacking numbers team of a 10 v 7.
4. This is a great session for the defending team as their reward for defending well and winning possession is to have the opportunity to counter attack and score themselves.
5. More and more professional teams are playing this way now, defending patiently then attacking with pace on gaining possession.
6. This is also a great mental / psychological workout for the players because their thinking has to IMMEDIATELY switch from a defending mentality to an attacking mentality and their bodies have to react accordingly to this with quick actions.
7. Develop: Play 11 v 9 (actually in effect an 11 v 11) on a FULL SIZED FIELD with the two wide players acting for both teams depending on who has possession.
8. Play on the full size field with free zones on each side of the field to play in to ensure the counter is quick and definite and able to happen every time the defending team wins the ball.
9. Develop the idea through different parts of the field:
    a. Through the wide players as above
    b. Through the central midfield players
    c. Through the fullbacks (NOW fullbacks can enter the free zones too in order to make it more game realistic)
    d. Play direct to the strikers if possible

e. Open it up so the opponents to the counter attack can defend in the wide areas too.

f. Now it is a real 11 v 11 game with no restrictions or conditions.

g. Allow a little more time to get a shot on goal as it is now a full field, perhaps 14 seconds initially but bring the time down as they get efficient and develop and improve to perhaps 10 seconds to score from regaining possession and making the first pass.

10. TO RECAP:

a. BEGIN WITH A FUNCTIONAL EXERCISE

b. MOVE ON TO A PHASE PLAY

c. DEVELOP INTO A SMALL SIDED GAME

d. FINISH WITH AN 11 v 11 GAME SITUATION

e. WE NEED 20 PLAYERS MAXIMUM OR WE CAN ALTERNATIVELY HAVE THE WHOLE MIDFIELD FOUR PLAYING FOR BOTH TEAMS SO 18 PLAYERS REQUIRED ONLY

f. YOU CAN VARY THE SET UP BASED ON WHAT YOU ARE TRYING TO ACHIEVE.

g. YOU CAN ALSO AFFECT THIS WITH DIFFERENT SYSTEMS OF PLAY, IT WOULD BE WELL SUITED TO A 4-5-1 (4-3-3) COUNTER ATTACKING TEAM

F) 11 v 11 GAME 4-2-3-1 v 4-4-2 (11 v 9)

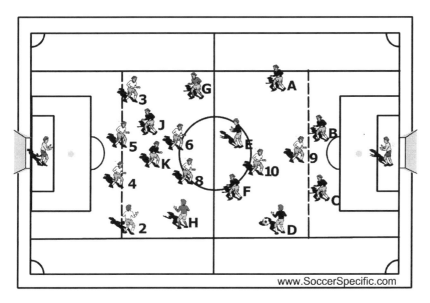

www.SoccerSpecific.com

1. IT IS NOW A FULL SCALE 11 v 11 GAME.

2. Same set up as previously with the same conditions to begin, developing into an open and free 11 v 11 game but always with one team in an 11 v 9 overload.

G) COUNTER ATTACK

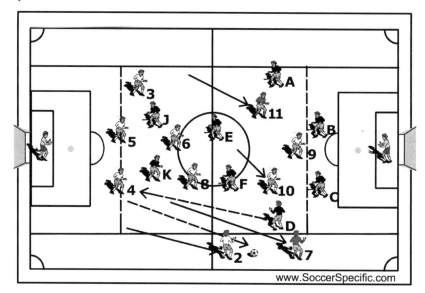

www.SoccerSpecific.com

1. Defending numbers team regains possession and immediately the attacking players (G) and (H) become attackers (7) and (11) going the other way. They spread out into the free attacking lanes to ensure they gain possession and can attack with freedom, able to cross every time.
2. As previously, they have a time limit to get a shot or header on target.
3. The game is continuous but always focused on two themes, defending and counter attack and the conditions ensure this happens.
4. You can develop the idea any way you want, and change the players attacking each way to get different scenarios.
5. Here (D) plays an intended pass to (K) but it is misplaced and goes to defender (4). (4) immediately looks to break and (2) and (7) push on into offensive positions. (4) passes to (2) who now has a 2 v 1 against (D) with (7) and also (10) pushes into the space in front to support this attack. (11) on the other side of the field runs forward to support (9).
6. As the ball travels forward quickly so does the back four pushing the team up the field to condense the play in front of them.

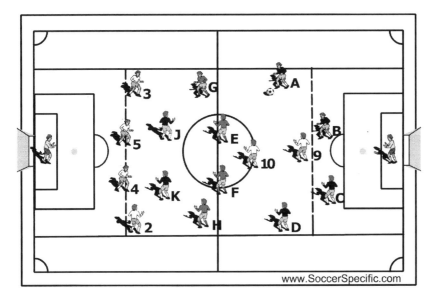

1. Another idea; where the whole midfield four plays both ways. This is more difficult for the defending team to regain possession so a bigger challenge with a 7 v 11 against but also a bigger overload (thus easier) to counter attack (11 v 7).

2. Now you can counter attack through the middle of the field also (to simulate a situation in a game where a central midfield player is free to counter attack).

3. Using this set up you can get the ball to the strikers immediately (who are prevented from turning here but can lay it off to the supporting midfield players who may get a shot in) and so the four midfield players support without immediate pressure.

4. Alternatively have just the central midfield two playing both ways to attack through the middle to increase the difficulty.

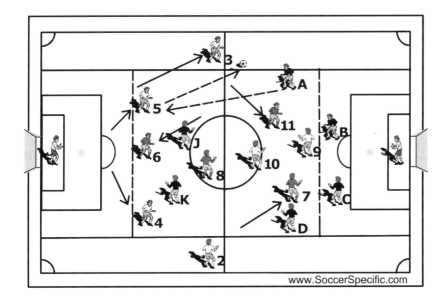

1. Here (6) intercepts the pass and plays in (3) going wide. (11) cuts inside to create the space for this and create a 2 v 1 against (A).

2. As the play develops and (3) attacks, (5) covers across and (6) drops back in to give a balanced defense should the move break down and we will have a 3 v 2 in our favor.

3. An alternate counter attack can be through the middle straight into the striker (9). If buildup is through the back four then it likely will take longer; and the essence of this break is speed, so look to attack from a free flank position or directly to the striker. The striker must be strong and hold the ball up well, and support players have to get there as quickly as possible.

H) STRAIGHT TO THE STRIKER THROUGH ROUTE ONE

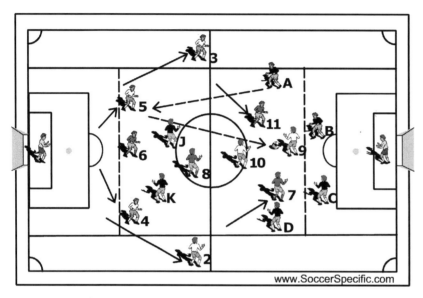

www.SoccerSpecific.com

1. Here we have a very quick break where we go direct to the striker (9) and he gets immediate support from (7), (10) and (11). If there is time, fullbacks (2 and 3) also break forward to support and (6) drops in to cover. This is the BEST counter attack method as it happens so quickly and the defenders do not have a lot of time to adjust from an attacking mentality and positioning to a defensive one. Here the letters team has attacked and both their fullbacks are in advanced positions. So when we win possession and play it quickly we have a great overload in attack.

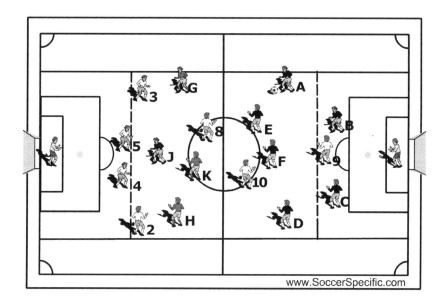

1. Still overloading the attack, now it is an 8 v 11 against the defending team that becomes an 11 v 8 in their favor on the counter attack.
2. The attacking lettered team could alternatively here look more like a 4-2-3-1 depending on how offensive the coach wants them to start.
3. Either way the counter attacking team on gaining possession change immediately from a 4-2-3-1 to a 4-2-1-3.

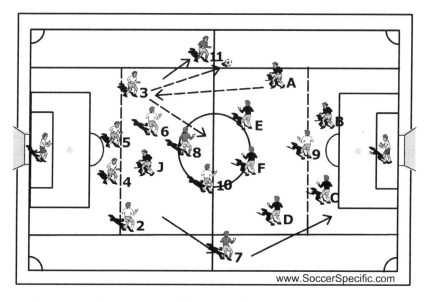

1. A misplaced pass from (A) starts off our counter attack.

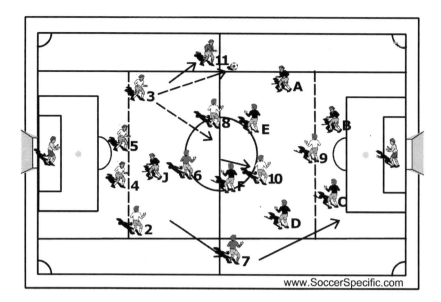

1. (10) also moves forward to support (9) from behind. They can attack with width with (G) and (H) becoming (7) and (11) or through the middle to (K) who becomes number (6) going the other way.
2. This actually equates more to a Starting Position of a 4-2-3-1 with the numbers team; when they win possession; developing into a 4-2-1-3 and ultimately a 3-3-1-3 or very offensive 3-1-3-3 on attack.
3. As soon as possession is regained, players (7) and (11) break out wide to be free to receive and attack.
4. Likely (K) who is now (6) is free so can also be a part of the development of the counter attack.

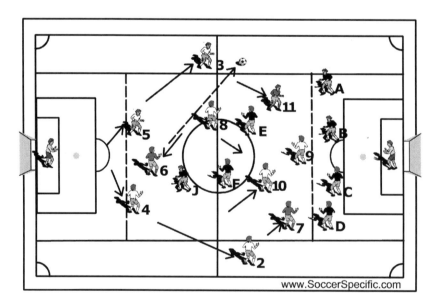

1. If we have time to affect this in full, then here is our normal way to develop play as we break quickly with a pass to fullback (3). He has broken wide to fill the space (11) has vacated by cutting inside to support the striker (9). Likewise on the other side of the field (7) cuts inside and (2) overlaps to provide width on that side

of the field. (6) drops in to cover and fullback (2) and wide midfielder (7) break forward also.

1. Alternatively; here the defending team regains possession of the ball at fullback (3). He has the option of playing to (11) free out wide, or (6) free in the center. Here he passes to (6) who plays a quick pass to the striker (9) and then players move off the ball to support him, behind and beyond.

2. As soon as (7) and (11) know they will not receive the immediate pass from (3); having initially run wide, they break quickly forward again to support (9) for the next phase of play.

1. So, now we have a breakaway counter attack showing wide players (7) and (11) supporting the striker (9) behind and beyond him, plus midfield players (8) and (10) trying to support behind for a lay off and another phase of play will develop going forward quickly.

2. For example (9) lays it off to (10) who plays a through ball to (7) to shoot on goal or cross for (11) at the far post.
3. With just one striker (J) up against us the attacking numbers team can afford to leave (6) pushed on (but positioned in front), and push both fullbacks forward to attack.
4. SO A TWO THEMED SESSION THAT WORKS FOR DEFENDING AND ATTACKING AND CAN FORM THE BASIS OF YOUR TEAM SYSTEM OF PLAY, DEFENDING WITH PATIENCE THEN COUNTER ATTACKING WITH PACE.

COUNTER ATTACKING AND TRANSITION TACTICS

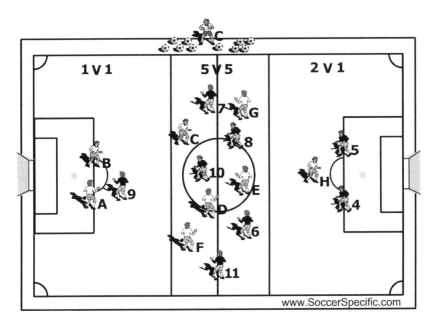

1. A Directional session: Divide the field up into three zones. Start with a 1 v 2 in each attacking zone.
2. Team in possession has to make three passes before passing into the lone striker.
3. The session is designed for working on attacking principles primarily, to create overload situations for the attacking teams going both ways so the focus is on QUICK COUNTER ATTACKING AND THE TRANSITION OF POSSESSION and how to respond to it.
4. TRANSITION: So, we have transition from attacking to defending and defending to attacking happening many times in this session.
5. This is good for the mentality of the players to change their mindset immediately as possession changes and they learn to maintain their focus better. We will develop the main phases of play that result from the attacking shape of a 4-2-3-1.
6. Numbers at the top of the diagram show the balance of players in each third of the field at any one time. We are not including fullbacks yet in the session as we want to focus on breaking from midfield first of all. Breaking from the back and joining the attack in the attacking third will be covered later.
7. DEFENSIVE TRAINING: the RECOVERY RUNS of midfield players are an important part of the learning process also. This system of play can fall down if the two wide players (7) and (11) do not recover back and form a second bank of a defensive four. So, to encourage them to work we ask the midfield players in the middle third when they receive the ball to make 3 passes before they can go into the attacking third. This way the recovering players; usually (7), (10) and (11) have a chance to get back and pressure the opposition.
8. Later, once this is working well, we can change the condition so the counter attack is the main priority and that way the transition from attacking to defending becomes much quicker as possession changes. So once a team win possession there is no condition on the number of passes required and they can play the ball in first time if it is on to do so, to either a midfield player or straight into the striker even from a back four defender for speed of attack.

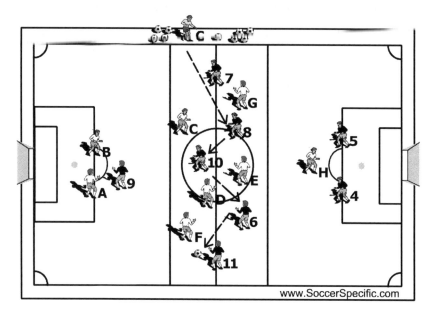

1. Use a full size 11 v 11 field for this clinic. Players make three passes amongst themselves in midfield then pass it into the striker and all three supports quickly to exploit the attacking overload situation.

A)   QUICK BREAK OVERLOAD

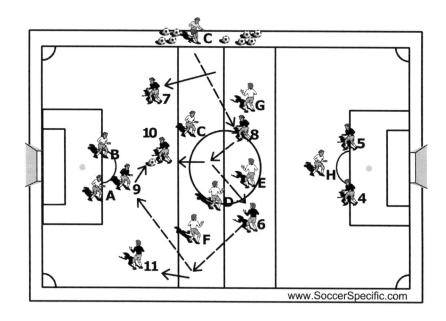

1. Start with a big overload when we attack into the attacking third and introduce a recovering midfielder later when the session is working well to offer a bigger challenge. This leaves a 5 v 2 situation in the middle zone in favor of the other team who are currently defending, if no recovering midfielder is used to begin. This is a good start to the session as it makes it easier to gain success for the attacking team which is ultimately what we are looking to achieve.

2. If the defenders win the ball or the keeper receives it, the ball is played quickly into the middle zone (to a 5 v 2 overload again going the other way) where they make three passes then get the ball into the striker to attack in the other direction.

3. Three midfield players break quickly to support from the 2-3-1 shape of the 4-2-3-1 (making a 4 v 2 over load in favor of the attacking team) and / or one defensive midfielder can recover which would be a 4 v 3 in favor of the attacking team). You can play around and change the numbers to suit what you need, even allowing 2 recovering defending midfield players to get back to create a 4 v 4 situation to really test the speed of attack of the attacking team.

4. Time the break to get a shot in. Ten seconds maximum to score. Working both ways alternately. This is a good conditioning session also.

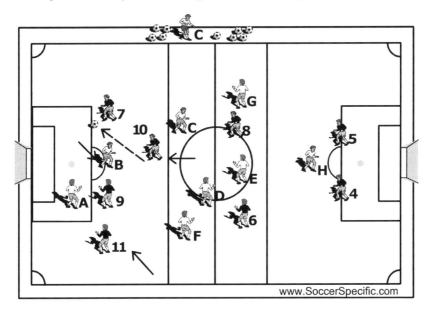

www.SoccerSpecific.com

1. RULES:
   a. Three passes before the ball can go into the attacker
   b. The first ball in has to go to the lone striker's feet.
   c. A 4 v 2 in favor of the attacking team is created
   d. The attacking team has 10 seconds to score as we want to encourage quick counter play
2. PRINCIPLE IDEAS GAINED FROM THE SESSION
   a. Counter attacking and quick play
   b. Different types of counter attack practiced (can be from the back to the front, also directly).
   c. Attacking team shape from an initial 4-2-3-1
   d. Recovery runs of midfield players when we lose possession (VERY IMPORTANT)
   e. It is a very good conditioning game especially for the attacking and then recovering midfield players.
3. Coaching Points
   a. Quick breaks in attack with very quick decision making.
   b. Quick passing and support play.
   c. Early shots / headers on goal.
   d. Regains of the ball and quick counter attacks
   e. Recovery runs of attacking midfield players from the previous attack

B) QUICK FINISH

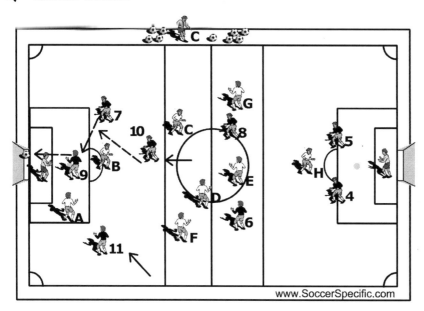

C) RECOVERY RUNS

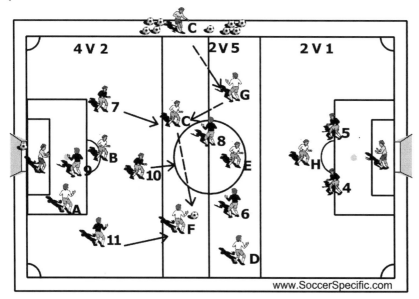

1. Players in the previous attack from the other team must recover as quickly as possible to try to win the ball back before they get it into the striker.

D) FAST COUNTER ATTACK

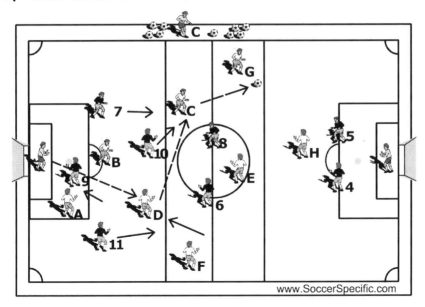

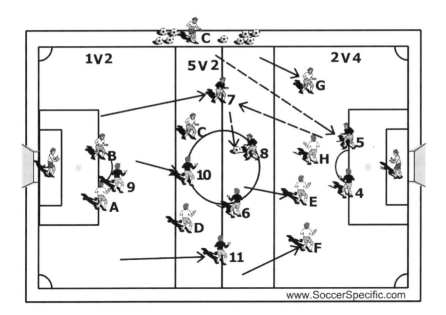

1. The numbered team have been caught on the break but win the ball back, (G) giving it away with a bad pass. Choices can now include quick counter attacking playing through the midfield or a direct ball into the strikers and the midfield can then link up with them.

2. Here we show the ball played into midfield. (D) and (B) run back to the middle zone ready for the next counter attack going the other way. (3) is already on the way to support the strikers from midfield.

3. DEFENDING FOCUSED SESSION: You can work on defending against a counter attacking fast break overload too. To do this require more passes in the middle third before they can go into the attacking third, thus allowing the recovering players more time to get back.

4. Here is the move continued with players breaking forward to attack on the numbers team creating a 4 v 2 overload and the defending team midfield who attacked the other way previously (D and B) recovering back to be ready for the next attack. They must be available to receive the ball should the keeper, (A) or (F) win possession and another transition attack is then under way in the opposite direction.
5. You can also bring in a recovering defender in both sides who comes out of the middle midfield zone to help the defenders.

E) ADD FULLBACKS FOR BOTH TEAMS TO MAKE AN 11 v 11

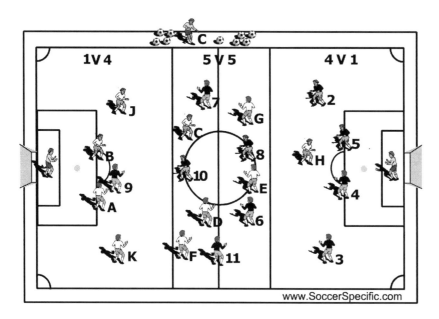

1. A 1 v 4 up front with the defending team at an advantage, and a 5 v 5 in the middle.
2. Once the keeper (or a defender) wins it then a midfield player can drop in and support.
3. Development: Now we develop play from the back. Back four spread out to receive and play from the back.
4. Work on players filling in for each other if the move breaks down.
5. Fullbacks can now transition through the thirds.

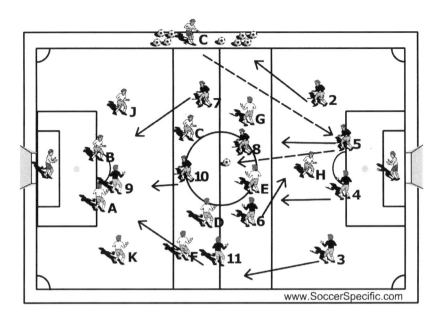

1. (5) gets the ball from the coach as the start position and passes to (8).
2. Fullbacks are now transitioning through the thirds. (8) has the ball and players attack with fullbacks making the forward runs from deep. (6) can cover for them and fill the sweeper position (or fill in one side for a fullback) should the move break down.
3. Striker (9) will be moving the defenders around trying to get free for a pass and the other attacking players try to find space to receive a pass from (8). (8) should have the lots of passing options now.

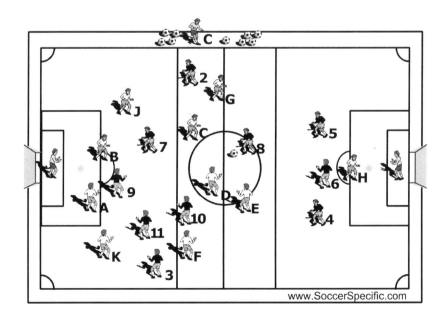

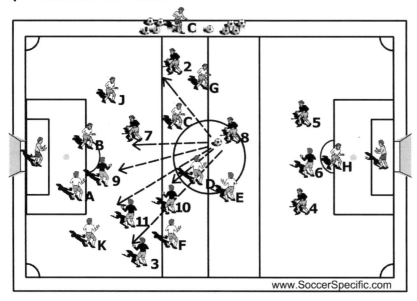

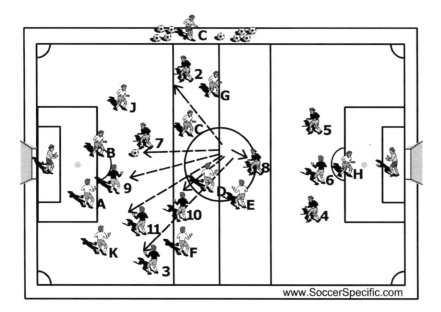

PLANNING
ATTACKING TEAM

1. Midfielders must get the passes in and then break quickly and support the striker as the ball is played into him. Midfielders can run the ball in or pass it in and another player can go in. Vary the support players from here based on where the immediate space is.
2. Strikers must get free from their markers to receive the ball and link up with the attacking quick break midfielders or turn and attack themselves depending on the positions of the defenders.
3. They need to score in a certain short time scale. Decrease the time allowed as they improve at this.

4. You can vary the number of players in striking positions as you develop the session if you want to practice another system of play in counter attacking. Start with one, then two and have these two linking up together to develop an understanding of how to move off the ball to create space for themselves and for each other.

5. As soon as the move breaks down the attacking midfield players who joined in with the striker need to get back to the midfield area they came out of. You can also coach them to rotate where it may be a striker who is nearer who makes a recovery run back to fill in for the midfielder who may have ended up beyond that striker in the attacking third of the field. Nearest player, shortest recovery route back.

6. The idea is to overload the attack so we gain success from the session in an attacking sense.

DEFENDING TEAM

1. Recovering midfield players (7), (10) and (11) get back quickly to counter.

2. Vary the number of defenders already in position and those recovering as you build up the session to change the challenges of the teams.

3. Midfielders and strikers of the team without the ball must be ready to break quickly should they win it back in the defending third. They need to be constantly on the move, getting free from opponents to receive the ball once the keeper or a defender gains possession.

4. When the defending team wins the ball and it is played into midfield it may be a defender who joins in and goes all the way into the attacking third. He can pass it in or run it in. Make sure a midfielder drops back into a defensive position into the defensive third (usually 6) to cover for this. This encourages the players to rotate positions and develop more freedom in their positioning on the field.

GENERAL OBSERVATIONS

1. Maintain the overload situations in midfield once the session gets going to ensure you get it working effectively so there is constant transition from attack to defense and defense to attack, both happening at pace.

2. Eventually open the game up into an actual scrimmage and see if both teams have adopted the quick break mentality you have been trying to teach. Now it is equal numbers in all areas so it will be a good test for the players to see if they can make it work.

DEVELOPMENTS FOR THE TRANSITION GAME

1. 1 v 2 in each attacking and defending zone and a 5 v 5 in the middle zone (the numbers can vary here).

2. Big overload to gain success in the attacking play, three attacking midfielders making a 4 v 2 overload.

3. 1 v 2 in the attacking and defending zones with fewer players in the middle zone but still equal numbers. Midfield can run it in now. Work on the movement of the two strikers to create space and move the defenders around.

4. Development: Allow a midfield player from the middle zone to drop back into the defending zone where his team has regained possession to provide help in the link up play (distances may prevent a good long pass from the back directly to midfield depending on the age group being coached, so this helps). Opponent can't follow them in, so this gives a better chance for the attack to build quickly.

5. Once we are at an 11 v 11 situation: Allow the fullbacks (or center back) from each team (in possession) to break forward into the middle and attacking thirds and now focus on the way they cover for each other, players dropping in to replace each other allowing more freedom in the team in terms of movement around the field. This is important to keep the shape of the team when opponents counter attack.
6. Finally 1 v 4 in the attacking third, meaning when the defending team win it they may have numbers up to break from the back and attack, probably along the flanks.
7. Eventually let it go as a free game; no restrictions.

EARLY CROSSING BEHIND THE DEFENSE IN COUNTER ATTACKING

1. When we attack through wide areas I believe the crosser should cross the ball in as soon as possible and the players should be trained to expect this.
2. This is especially so when a team defends high against you so there is plenty of space behind the defense to cross the ball into. A whipped / bending cross coming back into the path of the players is the best one here.
3. We can create the situation simply like this diagram. As you develop the idea you can bring more players in but use the pertinent players to keep it simple.

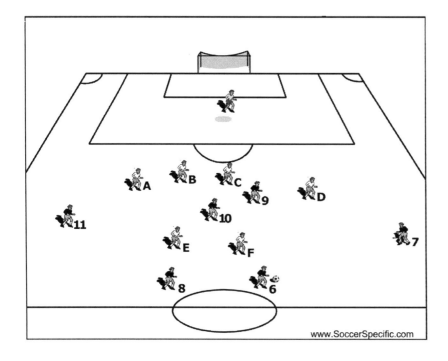

www.SoccerSpecific.com

1. Start position:
    a. The back four defend high (perhaps they have had an attack and pushed up and we have regained possession)
    b. Player (6) looks to play a pass to (7) who is in a clear crossing position.
2. There is a lot of space behind the back four to play the ball into.

A) EARLY CROSS IN BEHIND THE RECOVERING DEFENSE

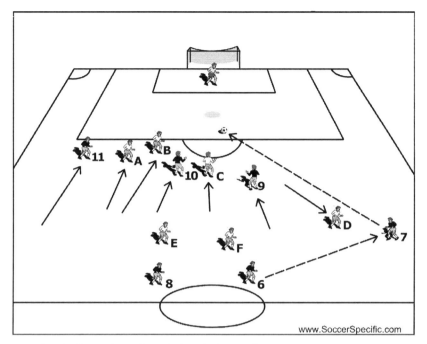

1. The ball is played in behind the defense. It's important to do it early and into space as the defensive back four have to recover back to attempt to win the ball.
2. Now they are facing back to their own goal and at a disadvantage. Our attacking players must press them as quickly as possible. Ultimately they need to try to get to the ball first.
3. Remember also the defenders have to turn and make recovery runs while our players are facing forward already, which gives us an advantage.

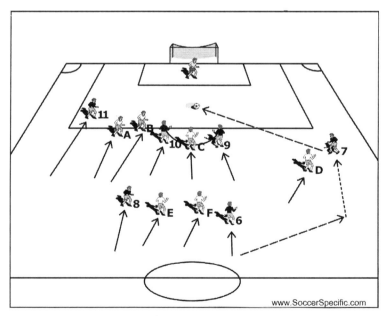

1. Another situation and nearer the goal. An even better situation as the defenders are closer to their own goal and have less space to work in.

2. The cross must be very accurate with less space to play into. This cross will cause a lot of trouble for the defenders recovering back and facing their own goal.
3. The ball needs to be played in an area just out of reach of the keeper; the second six yard box is perfect. It may cause confusion between the recovering defenders and the keeper also, neither knowing which needs to attack the ball; especially if their communication is poor in this moment.

B) A GREAT CROSS CLOSER TO GOAL

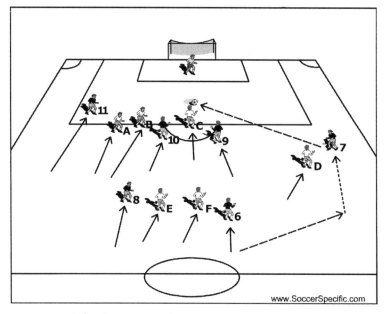

www.SoccerSpecific.com

1. Here defender (C) is able to get to the ball first but is under great pressure from the attacking players. If the ball is whipped in with pace defender (C) will only be able to make a one touch contact as there is no time for more touches in this situation. Being so close to the goal and facing backwards towards the goal is a poor situation for him.
2. A poor touch coupled with the pace on the ball may easily result in an own goal. The worst case scenario would be that we get a corner kick.

DEFENSIVE PRESSING THROUGH THE THIRDS OF THE FIELD IN A 4-2-3-1

KEY COACHING POINTS:
1. PRESSURE
2. SUPPORT
3. COVER / BALANCE
4. RECOVER
5. TRACK
6. DOUBLE TEAM
7. REGAINING POSSESSION & COMPACTNESS

What does this all mean?

PRESSURE
This is when the individual defender closes a player down on the ball to exert pressure on him to give the ball up. It can result in the player on the ball being pressured into making a bad pass, mis-controlling it, or the defender being able to tackle the ball and either kick it away or win possession. These instances all result in possession being lost by the attacking team due to the pressure exerted by the first defender.
Pressure does not always result in change of possession immediately. The defender can jockey the attacker to stop his forward momentum and give time to teammates to get into position to help win the ball back.

SUPPORT
This is the position taken up by the second defender to act as help for the first defender. The first defender by his stance can show/force the attacker towards the support player (second defender). We will talk later about angles and distances of support and communication with the pressuring player. These are the three essentials that are needed for the support player to be effective.

COVER / BALANCE
The next line of players away from these two defenders, particularly the third defender who is next closest to the pressure and support players. This player provides a balance (1st, 2nd, and 3rd defender) behind the pressure and support players. Beyond this third defender you can work with the next closest players and integrate their positioning into your coaching session.

RECOVER
Players in position on the field in front of where the ball is being defended must make it a priority to run back and position behind the ball, if possible between their own goal and the ball that is in the attacking team's possession. They recover back (recovery runs) to help the team by getting more people between the ball and their own goal to make it more difficult for the attacking team to score. They must recover back along the shortest route so they get back as quickly as possible but into a position where they are most effective in terms of the positions of the ball and the opponents.

TRACK
The attacking team's players will make forward runs into dangerous positions on the field and this is where defending players need to follow or track their runs to mark them and prevent them getting free and able to affect the game. Tracking runs can be short or long depending on the distance of the opponent's runs.

DOUBLE TEAM
It is possible to help the pressing player win back possession of the ball by closing down the space (pressuring) around the attacking player on the ball from another angle, preferably from the side opposite from the first pressuring player. Closing the player on the ball down from his blind side can be very effective in regaining possession. In some circumstances triple teaming can occur where three players all close the player on the ball down simultaneously.

REGAINING POSSESSION AND COMPACTNESS

Here the defending team has won back the ball and are now the attacking team and look to play it forward as soon as possible. As the play is developed up the field it is important the team push up the field to add continued support to the player on the ball, but also to affect the positions of the opponents and take them away from their goal should possession be lost again. The whole team moves forward and this will result in the compactness of the players from the back to the front of the team.

A) PRESSING WARM UP

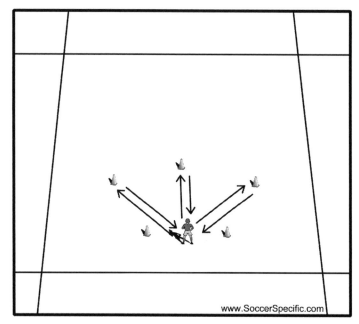

www.SoccerSpecific.com

1. Press each of the three cones and then back to the goal. Make sure the players are not leading with just the left foot. Change the body to do right foot lead, left foot lead and so on doing both sides. Players are checking to the cone and back as before.

1. Press the ball with the intent to show the player somewhere that suits you, the defender. Remember, good pressing includes DELAYING too. Great defenders like Barresi of AC Milan can get out and show to the left and the right. Defenders MUST be able to work both sides. Here, going to the left cone, show inside press with the left, show outside press with the right.
2. BUT, in central goal scoring areas, if you show them one way or the other you actually show them into a shooting position and with as little as 6 inches of space they can get the shot in. Don't show anyone anything and stay flat as you recover back.
3. Move back quickly, tuck knees in and go back in a straight line. You might back off and have left in front of right, or right in front of left, but stay flat. Three cones drill, work the feet in the middle flat and straight back. Side on to side cones straight on to straight cone.
4. So we have acceleration towards the ball, decelerating as they get to the ball, and regaining balance. Get out and hold. Get out and move back 6 inches (Barresi). Out and check back and balanced.

PROGRESSION: Can't get close enough to press the ball.

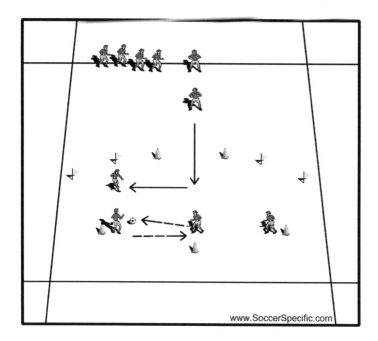

www.SoccerSpecific.com

1.   Now the defender CAN'T press the ball.
2.   The defender can't get tight enough to the ball to influence the player significantly and make him change his mind. BUT, you can make it awkward for him and protect/screen off certain passing routes/lanes. So if you can't get within 2 yards to press the attacker on the ball then try instead to be effective and screen the passes.
3.   Three passers and a series of defenders line up as diagramed. Two goals are positioned 5 yards away from the defender's starting position, one on each side. Have a good supply of balls.
4.   Instructions: The ball starts with the central passer and the first defender moves forward. When the ball gets switched to the outside passer, the aim is now to protect the goal by hustling over to the area in front of the goal first, not close the attacker down. If you tried to close the attacker down first, in the time it would take to get there the open passing lane would be used and the ball would be past you. Occupying the area in front of the goal is a good way to slow the opponent's forward momentum.
5.   So it's "Protect the Goal" and "Press the Ball". As the ball is passed to the center the defender has to get in line with the ball and the side player.
6.   The defender cannot tackle the passers, but can intercept shots to the goal. Play for 10 seconds each defender.
7.   Example: the ball is with the opponent's left back and our defender is our right winger who screens the pass to their wide left midfielder/winger behind. Midfield players can also screen off passes to forward players.
8.   Do center, then defender right; then back then out and next player in, then center then left and back then out then next player in and so on.

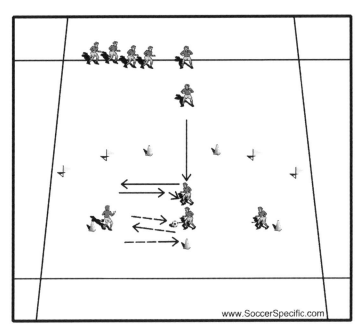

1. Coaching Points:
   a. The ability to change directions and react to the ball is key here.
   b. Plus speed across the field and balance will help the defender to be successful.
2. Great defenders PROTECT and PRESS. So move across then sneak a yard.
3. As the ball is passed, move to protect the goal and press and shut down the angle.
4. Shut off the pass, shut down the ball.
5. The pass goes to the outside player. The defender moves in front of the outside goal to protect it and then presses a yard closer to the ball. The ball then goes inside to the middle player, and the defender moves to protect the inside goal and step closer again. Now the defender can cut the angle of the pass off too so he is protecting the passing route and putting the player on the ball under a little bit more pressure.
6. Variation: Now repeat with 2 defenders, one pressing and one covering.

B) INTRODUCTORY GAME: BUMPING DEFENSIVELY

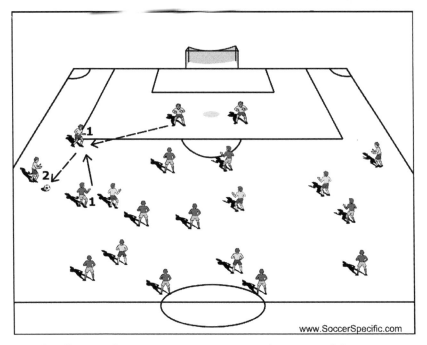

1. This forces players to communicate to be successful.
2. If the ball is passed wide, a back can't step up to defend unless he is told he has coverage, at which point he can be "bumped up" a player. For example, if the ball is passed to yellow 1 and red 1 steps up to mark without coverage, yellow 2 will be wide open.

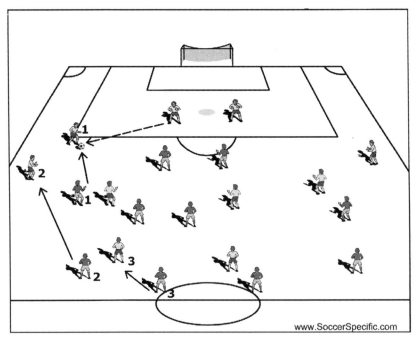

1. On the other hand, if red 3 steps over to yellow 3, red 2 can step to yellow 2 which frees red 1 to go to yellow 1 without a risk of an easy penetrating pass.

2. Throughout this activity yellow passes the ball and red works on figuring out marks and bumping their teammates to provide coverage and support.
3. It starts as a walk through and then progresses up to full speed with freezes done to show better choices when necessary.

C) DEFENSIVE PRESSURIZING SMALL SIDE GAME

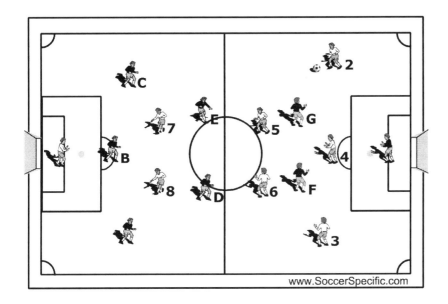

www.SoccerSpecific.com

1. The game is designed to work on pressurizing the player on the ball, prevent a forward pass and ultimately win the ball. Closest player has to pressure the ball. To score, a player has to make a pass from anywhere into the keeper's hands. The ball can be played in the air to the target's hands (to practice quality long distance lofted passes) or on the ground to feet (driven passes). All over the field players must work hard to close people on the ball down quickly.
2. Develop –
   a. As a reward when a team scores a goal, they keep possession so they play to the opposite goal to score. Previously they played to the same goal and the opposition got the ball when they scored.
   b. Go to man–marking. In possession players must get free and defenders must work hard to stop them scoring. Using high pressure as a team, defenders can win the ball back early and close to the opponent's goal to score. Push up from the back to start this.

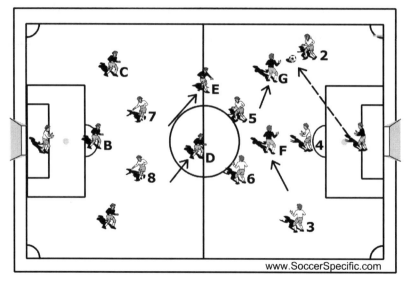

1. Coaching Points:
   a. Quick Pressure on the ball
   b. 2nd defender supplying close Support for first defender (angle / distance / communication)
   c. Deeper Cover from third defender
   d. Recovery runs from players in front of the ball
   e. Regain possession
2. Here the job of player (G) is to pressure the ball as quickly as possible to win it back. (F) supports across, (G) shows the player on the ball inside towards (F) and between them they try to win the ball back quickly. (E) offers a balanced covering deeper position behind them.
3. Players cannot go into the keeper's area.

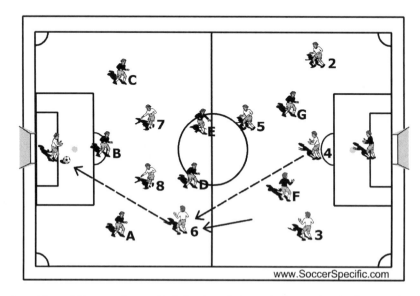

1. Here (6) gets free of defender (D) and chips the ball into the keeper to score a goal. Once this has happened a few times players get the idea they need to work hard to close opponents on the ball down quickly.

2. This game improves the urgency with which players need to close opponents down as they are so easily punished in this game if they don't.

D) FUNCTION: DEFENDING IN THE ATTACKING THIRD

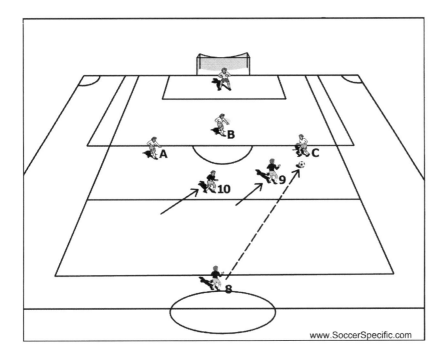

www.SoccerSpecific.com

1. 2v3 against to get strikers used to defending. The back three must work the ball over the twenty yard end line to score. If the strikers win it they get a free run at goal to score as a reward and also to reinforce the importance of winning the ball here.
2. Player (8) can start the play or have the keeper pass the ball to a defender.
3. Strikers must work as a unit to try to regain possession in the Attacking Third and get a quick strike on goal. This is particularly important to train strikers to defend as they are the first line of defense for the team. The players need to realize that the closer to the goal you can win the ball the sooner you will be able to score so practicing defending from the front is an important part of your training. Try a 3v3 if the players are having trouble with a 2v3.
4. Develop: Try a 3v4 but increase the working area to accommodate all the players.
5. The server (8) (or the keeper) can vary where the ball is played to so that each attacking player has the chance to be the first pressuring player.
6. Coaching Points:
   a. Quick pressing by the first defender
   b. Support position of the second defender (angle, distance and communication)

E) REGAINING POSSESSION IN THE ATTACKING THIRD IN A PHASE OF PLAY (8 v 7)

If the letter team win the ball they must play it to the target goals and play restarts.

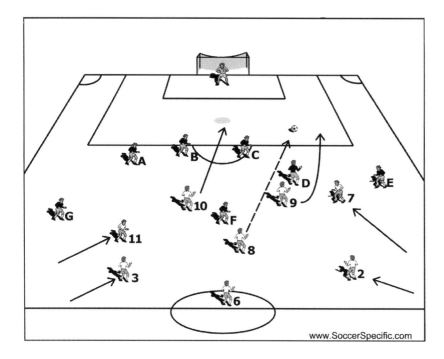

www.SoccerSpecific.com

1. The ball is played in behind the defender. How the players position on the field depends on where the pressing player shows the opponent on the ball. Here the pressing player (9) shows the player inside towards the center of the field. If we can win the ball here we have an immediate chance to shoot at goal.
2. The other players look to fill the spaces around where the ball is likely to be played and be close to an opponent to put them under pressure should the ball be passed to them.
3. Players must act immediately they see where the pressing player shows the opponent on the ball so they have the best chance to collectively win back the ball in a vital area on the field.
4. By winning the ball back early due to quick work over a short distance, they can save themselves a lot of work. Allowing the opponents to clear it easily means they may get it into our defensive third and our whole team has to cover a lot more ground to recover and win back the ball in a less dangerous position for the opponents.

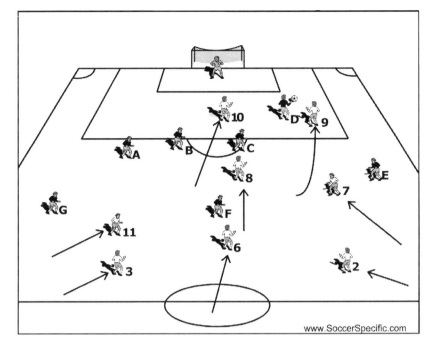

1. This diagram shows where the players should finally position themselves off the position of the pressing player. Here (D) has managed to get turned and face forward. If (D) manages to clear the ball, the pressure may force (D) to hastily clear it and not make good contact and we have several players positioned to collect the second ball and regain possession.

2. Should the clearance be longer and the pressing player can't win the ball or stop the forward pass but can only show (D) inside, the ball is likely to be cleaned up by our center backs or defensive midfielder in an 11v11 game situation. Whatever happens from the three scenarios above (we win it, they kick it short under pressure, they kick it long and clear) we are at least giving ourselves a better chance to win back the ball quickly (by correct positioning) in a dangerous area where we may quickly get a chance to shoot and perhaps score a goal.

F) REGAINING POSSESSION IN THE ATTACKING THIRD IN AN 11 v 11

Defender may get turned or end up facing back, either way show the player inside.

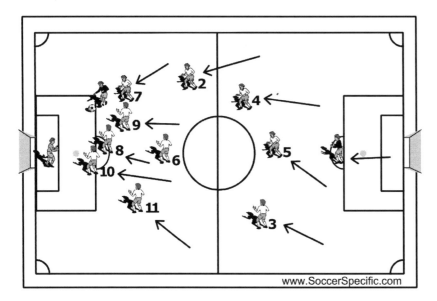

www.SoccerSpecific.com

1. Pressurizing player (7) forces the player on the ball inside towards the support players.
2. Inside means if we gain possession it's a short route to get a cross or shot on goal. Show outside and if the defending team are under pressure the player on the ball can kick it out of play and give them time to reorganize, plus there is no chance of an immediate cross or shot if we win it back in a very wide area. (9) and (7) close down and show inside, (10) closes the keeper to prevent the back pass, (2) (11), (8) and (6) close spaces down close to the ball, (3), (5) and (4) push up but still leave distance from the opposing strikers in case the ball can be played in behind them.
3. Organization – Work with pressing player, support player, then cover players, then defenders and keeper (individual, unit, and team).

VARIOUS START POSITIONS YOU CAN USE

Make it relative to the game plan here.

1. Regaining possession with the ball played in behind the defender, who is facing towards his own goal into or around the box.
2. Regaining possession with the ball passed from the keeper to a defender (or a situation where the defender has possession facing forward).
3. Regaining possession with the ball passed from a defender to a defender (immediate pressure from the strikers).
4. Regaining possession with a ball passed into midfield from a defender; for example: (A) to (F).
5. Regaining possession with the ball crossed into the box (anticipation areas around the box for the 2nd ball from a possible clearance).
6. Regaining possession from a corner (again getting back the 2nd ball if the opponents clear the ball).
7. Regaining possession with the ball played into the box from a long pass from our defense (1st or 2nd ball).

8. Regaining possession with the ball played into the box from a long pass from our defense.

MIDDLE THIRD:

G) PHASE PLAY: DEFENDING AS A MIDFIELD FOUR

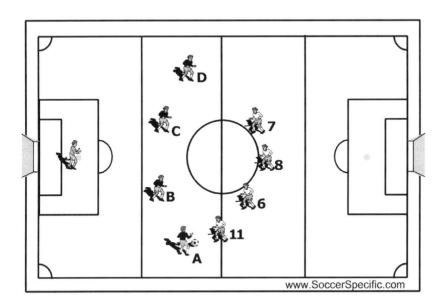

www.SoccerSpecific.com

1. This is a 4v4 in the midfield area. When defending, our two wide players (7) and (11) drop back to form a midfield four and work as a unit with our two central midfield players. The attacking team need to try to run the ball over the midfield line to score, the defending team have to try to win the ball. Once they've gained possession, their goal is initially to get it over the other midfield line and then they can attack the actual goal to try to score.
2. Start position can be just a pass from the coach or the keeper into the attacking midfield players and the defending midfield has to immediately adjust and try to win the ball.
3. The midfield players need to stay in touch with each other, marking bigger spaces as they get further away from the ball. If the ball is transferred across the field the four midfield players adjust accordingly as if tied together.

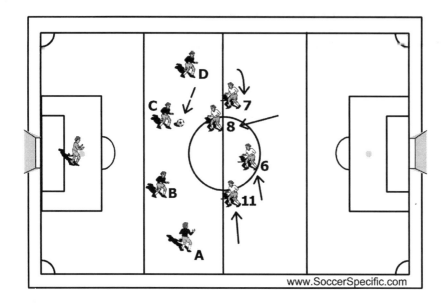

1. Ball is passed inside, (8) closes down (C), (7) tucks in back and across. (6) supports (8) and gets into the passing lane to stop a pass into a striker (not shown) from (C) or at least making it a difficult pass to make.

2. (11) is positioned to close down (B) but also to slide over to close (A) if needed. An alternative would be for a left fullback (3) (not in picture) closing this player down.

3. (7), (6) and (11) mark space in anticipation and in advance of the ball, (8) pressures/marks the player on the ball.

4. This shows the adjustment of the midfield four as the ball travels.

5. Now (7) deals with (D), (8) with (C) though supporting (7) at the same time; (6) with (B) and (11) with (A); but both well "in advance" of the ball should it be switched again.

6. First thought is can they intercept the pass. If not then they adjust as shown. It shows 4 players working together. They must not get too spread out and leave holes between them.

7. They should have enough time to adjust across the field and keep the ball in front of them and still be in a good defensive position.

8. They mark space but are aware of their immediate opponent and each deals with that player should they receive the ball. So they need to be close enough to make sure they can get tight.

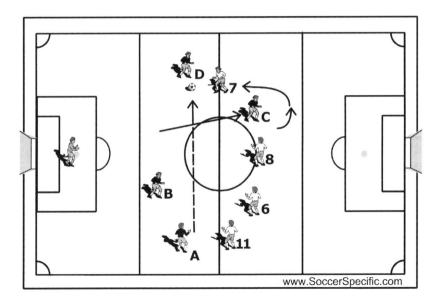

1. Avoid this, where the wide midfielder (11) stays and marks (D) who is totally out of the game now and is not a threat to the team. Likewise players (6) and (8) do not push across. This means big holes appear between the midfielders and the team gets outnumbered, especially around the ball with (7) defending against both (D) and (C).

2. The right fullback or right center back on our team (not shown) could join in to help but it is best if the back four stay compact together and the midfield do the same and each works as an independent unit.

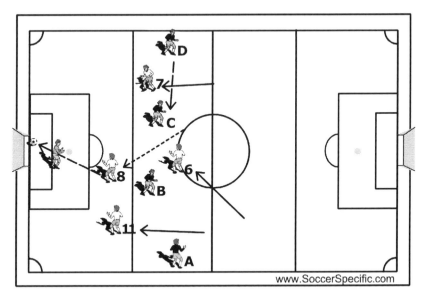

1. Here (8) wins the ball back off (C), runs the ball over the midfield line and continues the run forward to score a goal. The other players push forward and support (8).

2. You could allow recovering players on the other team to go beyond the midfield line to keep the pressure on or allow the defending midfield once they win the ball and get it over the midfield line to attack further without any pressure.

DEFENDING IN THE MIDFIELD THIRD

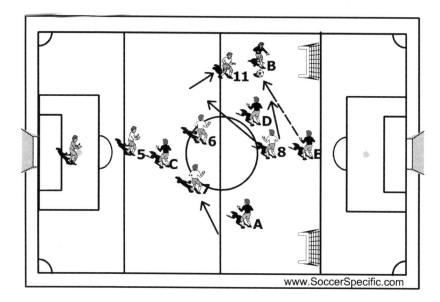

www.SoccerSpecific.com

1. Attacking team must run the ball over the midfield third line to score. If defenders win it they must pass to the target goals and play begins again.
2. Midfield work together as a unit. We show here how players recover back. (8) recovers back and can double up depending where the ball is or recover back to get behind the ball and mark a player (see above)
3. Working across as a unit, the fullback from the back four (not shown) takes care of the widest player on the opposition on the opposite side of the field from the ball when you go into the bigger sized game though midfielder (7) can slide back across as the ball travels.
4. Looking for midfield players to:
   a. Pressure and/or win the ball.
   b. Stop the forward pass.
   c. Force play across the field.
   d. Force play back.
   e. Delay the opposition.

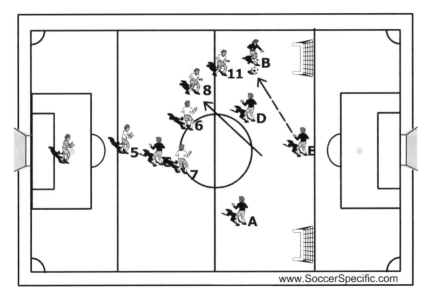

1. (8) has recovered back, (11) delayed (B) passing the ball forward to allow (8) to recover.
2. We have a flat midfield four now, all behind the ball, presenting a difficult barrier for the attacking team to penetrate.
3. Coaching points for supporting player (8):
   a. Recovery runs to get into the support position
   b. Supporting (11) with good angle, distance and communication
   c. Getting in the passing lane to striker (C) to prevent the forward pass
   d. Being in a position to immediately pressure (D) should he get the ball with a pass from (B)

H) DEFENDING IN THE DEFENDING THIRD: THE PHASE PLAY GAME PLAN SET UP

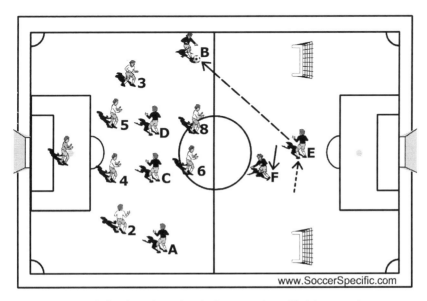

1. Here we defend with a back four and midfield central pairing as in the 4-2-3-1. The start position is where a player moves the ball on his first touch to simulate

open play (as opposed to a set play) and then begins the session by making the required action. This can be a pass to another player or a pass into space or maybe a pass towards an opponent if the session is on regaining possession of the ball.

2. Alternatively the coach may instigate the initial action so that the start of play is how he wants it.

3. Start Position 1 – (E) and (F) do a crossover run and pass the ball to a teammate. This is a simple and effective start position to use to begin the practice (see above).

4. SP2 – You could have (A) or (B) crossing the ball into the 6 yard box for the keeper to take. The defenders are in defensive positions in the box. The keeper can then kick the ball long to (E) or (F) to control and begin the attacking movement with the defenders pushing out at the same time, getting set up to defend and win the ball back.

5. SP3 – Have (B) or (C) shoot at goal and the keeper can kick the ball long as above.

6. Coaching Points:
   a. Pressure
   b. Support
   c. Cover
   d. Recover
   e. Track
   f. Get compact after regaining possession

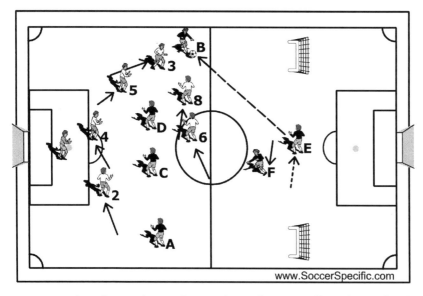

www.SoccerSpecific.com

1. Begin the phase play with equal numbers to allow the defending team a chance of success.

2. Start Position – (E) and (F) do a crossover run and pass the ball to a teammate.

3. Try to keep the ball in front of the back four and outside the penalty area.

4. Play the offside rule so there are true match conditions when you let it go free.

5. Walk through it to begin. Have the ball at each attacking player and show the positions of all the defenders depending on where the ball is. Explain pressure and support positions. Explain when to hold, drop, push out, sprint out (depends on who has the ball and if there is pressure on the ball or not).

6. Once the game starts, when the defenders win it they get the ball to the target goals, push out as a unit and then reorganize and start again.

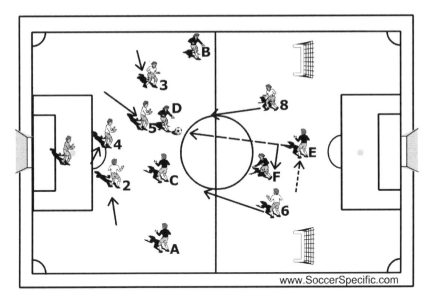

www.SoccerSpecific.com

1. Increase the difficulty as the defenders get success in this phase play. A progression from this is have the two midfielders start in recovery positions on the wrong side of the ball. If at least one holding midfield player stays back this is not likely to happen, but let's do the exercise just in case.
2. The coach can count to three (or more) before the midfielders can recover back to help the back four. This creates a momentary 4v6 against the defending team (outfield players). They must try to delay the attacking team until the recovering midfielders get back into position to help. Recovery runs are via the shortest route back to goal in a straight line.
3. Encourage the attacking team to try to break quickly to attack the goal to increase the difficulty for the defenders.

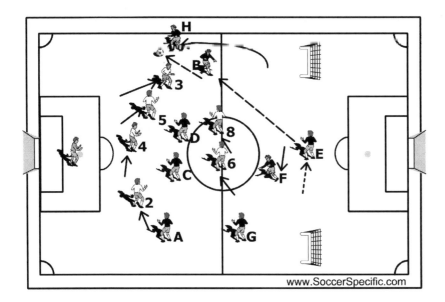

1. Next progression is introducing two wide defenders (fullbacks). This creates 2v1 in wide areas i.e. attackers get behind the defense.
2. (B) and (H) work together to create an overlap situation in a 2v1 overload against (2). This may result in (H) getting into a good crossing position behind the defense. Show the adjustment of back four and midfielders.
3. The challenge of the defending back four is to keep the ball out of the penalty area to keep it clear for the keeper, but here the ball has gotten in behind them in a wide area so they must recover back to cover for the cross.

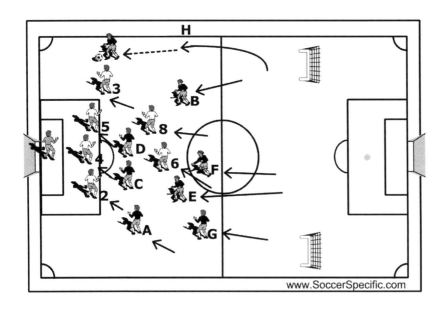

1. Here the fullback (3) has recovered well enough to be able to pressure (H) on the cross.
2. (2), (4) and (5) recover back to position just outside the 6 yard box at the near post, middle of the goal and the far post for the cross if it should come in.

3. Should (3) not be able to stop the cross and recover quickly enough to that position then he should recover back towards the goal as that is where the next danger is.

I) DEFENDING IN AN 11 v 11 SITUATION IN a 4-2-3-1 WITH CONDITIONED SCORING RULES TO ENCOURAGE QUICK PRESSING FROM THE FRONT

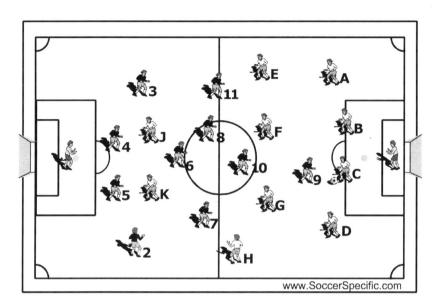

1. Here we have developed the previous practice into an 11v11 game situation, showing our 4-2-3-1 system of play defensively and working with the defending team (numbered team). The coach can serve to the opponent's lettered team in different locations on the field and the team needs to try to win the ball back individually and collectively.
2. The target for the defending team when they win the ball could be to just chip the ball into the opponent's keeper and the defending team has to win the ball again starting from where the coach serves the ball.
3. I have shown zonal defending as a team using a 4-2-3-1 system of play but the same principles apply with other systems using the zonal method of defending and it is easy to practice this method with different formations.
4. Here the opponent's player has the ball. (9) presses (C) to stop the forward pass or even the long ball to our keeper, which means they have scored a goal because we failed to stop the ball being played forward.

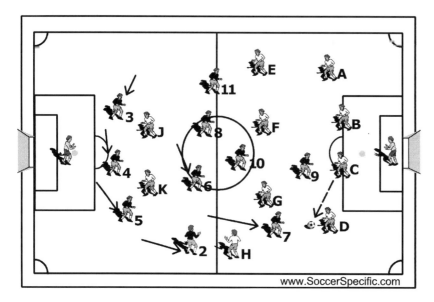

1. (C) passes to (D) and (7) immediately presses the ball to stop the forward pass. Behind him other teammates get close to their opposite number and the back four slide across to condense the immediate spaces.
2. You would use this game where chipping into our keeper means a goal for the opponents only when you decide to work on pressing from the front.

DEFENDING AS A TEAM IN AN 11 v 11 WHEN THE BALL IS BEHIND THE BACK FOUR USING THE 4-2-3-1

1. The start position is player (E) passing to wide player (H).
2. Key Coaching Points:
    a. Pressurizing - Fullback (2) closes quickly as the ball travels. He shows the player inside or outside depending on where the support is and/or how fast and how skilled the defender (2) is. (7) can double up to help.

b. Making play predictable for teammates to adjust their position. Close the spaces close to the ball. (8), (10) and (9) recover back. Leave the far players away from the ball.
c. Support positions – Angle / Distance / Communication.
d. Recovery positions of the strikers should the ball be played to the opponent's back players.
e. Regaining the ball – Strikers and midfield must be ready to break quickly. If the defending team wins the ball they have 6 passes to score and then the ball goes back to the attacking team.

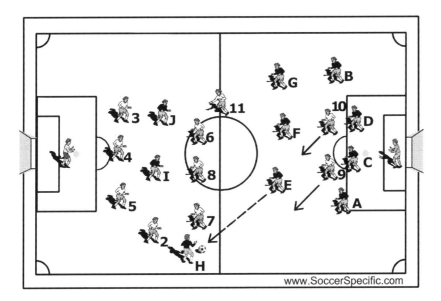

www.SoccerSpecific.com

1. This is how the situation looks when the players have made their movements. Observe how the defending team has compacted as a team in terms of width and length on the field.
2. They have filled the spaces close to the ball, reducing the room to play in. (3) and (11), who have moved across the field, remain focused on the fact that they are responsible for (J) and (G) respectively should the play switch to the other side of the field, hence their body stances are open so they can see both the ball and their immediate opponents. (8) can close down (E) if the ball is played back to him.

A) RECOVERY POSITIONS OF DEFENDERS

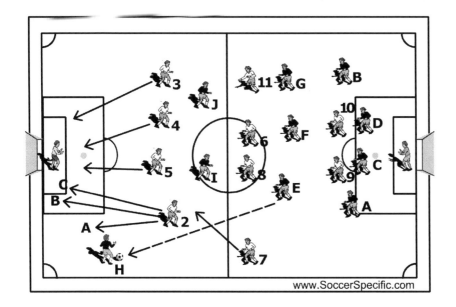

www.SoccerSpecific.com

1. The opponents have gotten behind our team in a wide area. (2) has three questions to answer:
   a. Can I tackle?
   b. Can I stop the cross by getting in the line of it?
   c. Do I recover to the goal?
2. It all depends on how close to the crosser (2) is. If he is too far away he should work back to goal because the danger isn't where the ball is coming from but where it is going to. If (8) can close (E) down as the ball travels.
3. (4), (5) and (3) recover back to mark the danger zones in the box and will mark players who enter those zones. The players are marking the near post, mid goal and the far post areas. (7), (6), (8) and (11) recover to zones in and around the box for pull backs.

IF (5) IS CLOSE ENOUGH HE CAN SPRINT ACROSS TO CLOSE (H) DOWN BUT HE MUST ONLY DO THIS IF HE IS ABSOLUTELY SURE HE CAN MAKE IT AND STOP THE CROSS

4. Key Coaching Points:
   a. If possible stop the cross
   b. Recovery runs of the players, particularly the back four as the ball is now beyond and behind them, trying to get goal side
   c. Positioning at the 6 yard box to address the cross; marking zones at the near post, mid goal and far post areas
   d. Marking players who enter your particular zone
   e. Good communication from the player attacking the cross so everyone is clear who's ball it is and can get out of the way (could be the keeper going to catch or punch it also)
   f. Winning the header, clearing the ball out of the area and pushing out quickly leaving opponents offside

B) CHOICES OF WHERE TO RECOVER TO

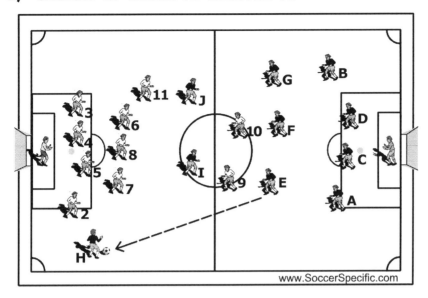

1. This is how it should look once the players have recovered back into position. I have only changed the positions of the defending team but obviously the attacking team will have moved forward and the strikers will be in the penalty box awaiting the cross.
2. Now several major areas where the ball is likely to be crossed into have been filled by the defenders inside the penalty area and the defending team is in a strong position to defend their goal effectively. This is of course the perfect scenario but that is the goal of all the players in this situation, to get as many players back and defending the goal as possible.

C) DEFENSIVE POSITIONS IN THE BOX FROM A CROSS

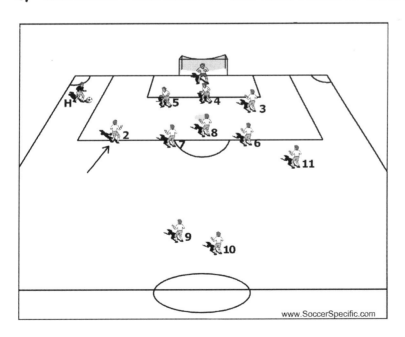

1. I have left the opponents out of this for clarity but rest assured they will have players in and around the box to attack the ball. (5), (4) and (3) mark zones. Here (2) is recovering back to goal having decided he cannot affect the player on the ball as he is too far away. The defenders attack the areas in front of them and don't drop back on top of their teammates. The same applies to (8), (7) and (6). (3) and (11) also have to cover the areas behind them if the ball is hit long. They all pick up players who enter their zones.

2. (5) must resist the temptation to go towards (H) to try to stop the cross from so far away. The danger is in the box, not where the ball is coming from. By the time (5) gets close the cross has gone in, perhaps to the gap where (5) came from and the opposition have a free strike on goal. (4), (3) and (6) or (11) can fill in but we need to avoid too much adjustment.

3. If they win a header the clearance should be high, wide and long. The defense should push up quickly to the edge of the box and beyond if possible (depends on distance of the headed clearance, which the ball goes to and what direction it goes).

D)   TO CLOSE OR NOT TO CLOSE

www.SoccerSpecific.com

1. Here the defender (5) has gone to the ball and before he can get close enough to challenge, the ball has been crossed into the space that he left. A striker may run into this open space now (shown) and score with a free header or shot.

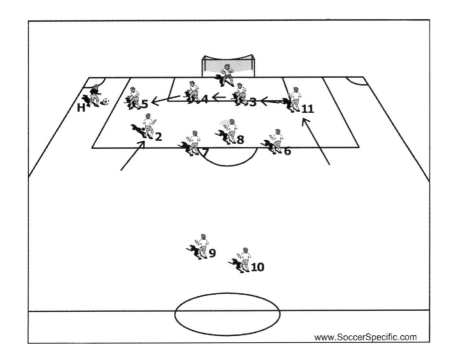

1. If the wide player decides to bring the ball towards goal, (5) is the closest and must close the ball down. (4) and (3) move across to cover the nearest danger zones (rope theory), and (11) drops back in to take (3)'s place. (2) may have got back into a good defensive position, particularly if (5) has held up the attacker to give time to recover.

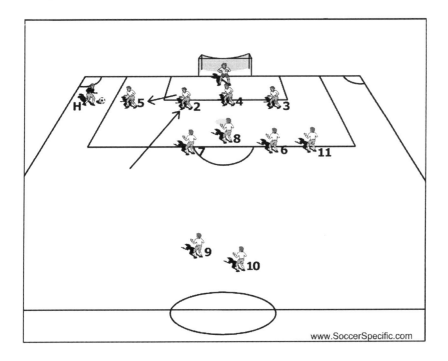

1. If (2) can recover back quickly enough then the other players do not need to adjust their positions.
2. (2) can do the same job as (5) did guarding the area of the near post.

3. The only drawback would be that (2) is now facing the goal so any interception attempted should a cross be made will bo back towards the goal.

4 (2) must bo careful to clear the ball for a corner and not deflect it into the goal for an own goal.

5. If (5) can delay the cross by closing (H) down effectively then this will give (2) time to position correctly facing away from the goal. Now should the cross come in, (2) is in a better position to make a heading or foot clearance AWAY from the goal.

DEFENDING AS A TEAM IN A 4-2-3-1

A) ONE WORD COMMANDS AT THE BACK
We showed the one word commands earlier in the book for team shape and movement in a small sided game and also in a shadow play set up.
Here we take the same idea but apply it to a game situation. While there is some repetition here I felt it necessary to show different ways to do this, without pressure and with pressure.

B) IDENTIFYING WHEN AND WHERE TO DROP; HOLD THE LINE, SLIDE; PRESS THE BALL AND PUSH OR SPRINT UP USING ONE WORD COMMANDS

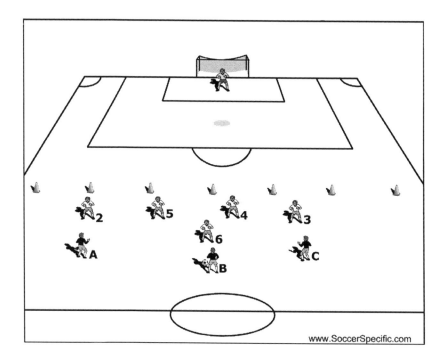

www.SoccerSpecific.com

1. Using the calls UP, OUT, HOLD, DROP, SLIDE RIGHT, and SLIDE LEFT. These are quite self explanatory but UP means edging up a few yards, then reassessing the situation; OUT means sprinting out, potentially many yards.
2. This is set up to practice when to drop, when to hold the line and where to press up as a unit.
3. Start with an overload of defenders to give you a better chance of success.
4. The back four should try not to drop behind the line of cones.

5. Dropping, holding the line or even pressing up (pressing even when you haven't the ball) can depend on the following:

C) DROPPING OFF
(USING THE DROP CALL)
Opponents have the ball, and they make deep penetrating runs in front of the ball; and there is no pressure or very poor pressure on the ball. At this moment the back four should drop off as the opponent on the ball has the freedom to pass forward and can read the timing of when and where to do it based on the back four's position. This is unless the back four are so together and in tune they can push up the moment before the ball is delivered; but this can be a very risky decision.

D) HOLDING THE LINE OR PRESSING UP:
(Using the HOLD; UP or OUT one word commands)
   a. Opponents have the ball. If the attackers make deep penetrating runs and there is very good pressure on the ball in front of the back four by another teammate, thus preventing a forward pass, they should hold the line and let the attackers run offside, or even press up as a unit to make it even more obvious their opponents have run offside.
   b. Opponents have the ball. If there is very poor pressure or no pressure on the ball but also no penetrating forward runs by opponents designed to get in behind the back four, then the back four can hold the line or even press up slightly.
   c. If the opponents have the ball and the player on the ball is facing forward, but has his head down looking at the ball, and is not observing what is ahead, nor any runs made by teammates, even if there is poor or no pressure on the ball; that is a time to hold the line or even step up. The player looking down at the ball is the CUE to the back four to HOLD or step UP.
   d. Opponents have the ball. If there is very good pressure on the ball and the ball cannot be passed forward and the opponents do not make penetrating forward runs beyond the back four, then the back four can actually press up even though we do not have possession of the ball.
   e. This is emphasized even more if the opponents are forced to pass the ball backwards, and cannot immediately play it forward again (due to good pressure). The distance to push up depends on the distance of the ball from the back four and the immediate pressure on the next player receiving the back pass. It can be a substantial step up from the back and may result in opponent's strikers being left offside as a by - product. This in turn pushes our midfield on and further presses the ball if it is in the midfield area.
   f. We have the ball. When we win possession and play the ball forward and maintain possession that is a cue to push up quickly and immediately.
   g. We have the ball. When we win possession and play the ball forward in behind their back four, causing them to turn and chase back, this is ALSO a cue to push up quickly and immediately.

If there is ANY DOUBT in any given situation then the back four should ALWAYS DROP DEEPER to be on the safe side, as that is the easiest decision to make.

E) PHASE PLAY SET UP

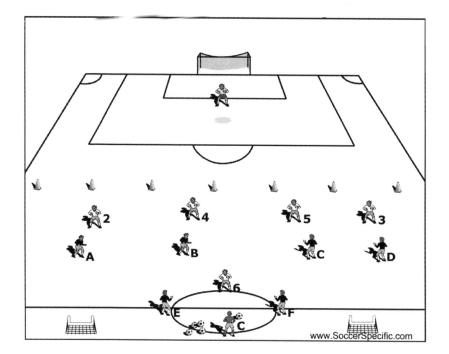

www.SoccerSpecific.com

1. Add players to the practice. We are building this up in numbers with just the one defensive midfielder in to begin. Have the game set up as a normal phase play, attackers against defenders. Attackers have to try to score, defenders try to win the ball back and score in the little goals. The defenders have five passes to score once they win the ball, then it goes back to the attacking side.
2. Use the stepping up method of defending where appropriate. It will not be on every time. The cones act as a guide but defenders can use this method of defending higher up the field in their own half.
3. Coaching Points:
   a. Is there Pressure on the ball or not?
   b. The Timing of when to drop, when to hold the line and when to step up, individually and collectively, and depending on the situation above
   c. Regaining possession or opponents caught offside
   d. A sign they are being successful is when the back four ends high up the field, away from the cones, even though their opponents still have the ball.

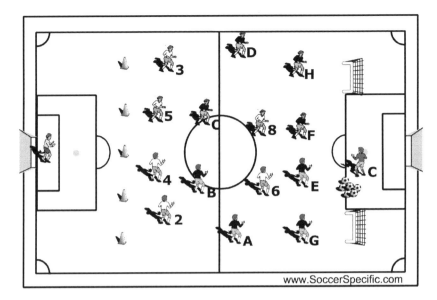

www.SoccerSpecific.com

1. Overload the attacking team now to make it more difficult for the defending team.
2. Here we have an 8 v 6. We defend with our regular 4-2 of the 4-2-3-1
3. Using the one word commands and identifying the moments to implement each one with the team.
4. The coach can start each attack off with a pass.
5. The coach can also be a target for the defenders should they win the ball as well as the side goals. Each represents a front player on their team that they have to pass to, thus when they get it to the goals or the coach they push up quickly using the OUT word.

F) BASIC EXAMPLES OF THE ONE WORD COMMAND CALLS AND WHEN TO USE THEM
UP AND HOLD CALLS

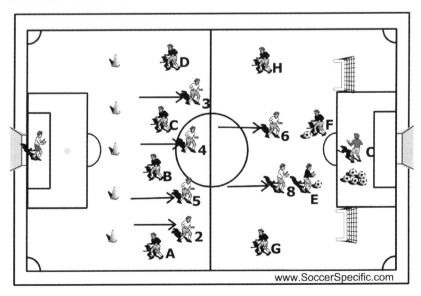

www.SoccerSpecific.com

1. Using two examples here, one with the opponent (F) facing forward with the ball; the other with the opponent (E) facing back with the ball.
2. At (F), where the player is facing forward but is pressed well by (6), if the pressure prevents a forward pass we can edge up still using the UP word. This is braver than HOLD. All the above applies for HOLD also. For instance, if a striker runs forward and the ball can't be passed forward as in the above examples then let them run offside and hold the back line.
3. At (E) the UP call can be used. (E) can't play it forward due to immediate pressure by (8) and he is facing back towards his own goal. This allows the back players to edge up and condense the space and make the opposition strikers work back. Whether (F) is forced to pass back or not, because the ball can't be passed forward due to (6)'s pressure, we can edge up.
4. Here we can see where the players position after pushing up. The opponent's strikers are left well offside and the whole team has moved forward (I have left 4 players in there to emphasize it even more). This puts pressure on the player on the ball in terms of our immediate pressing player but also as a team we are closer to the opponents to help prevent them from receiving the ball or at least be closer to pressure them again wherever the ball is passed.
5. If the opponent on the ball is pressured and is facing back towards hisa own goal then this is a low risk movement. The team can push up also if the opponent is facing forward and the pressing player stops the forward pass but it is more risky and relies on everyone being confident in the pressing player doing his job successfully. This player doesn't have to win possession, just prevent the forward pass and if possible force the player on the ball to pass back or at least to the side and not forward.

OUT CALL

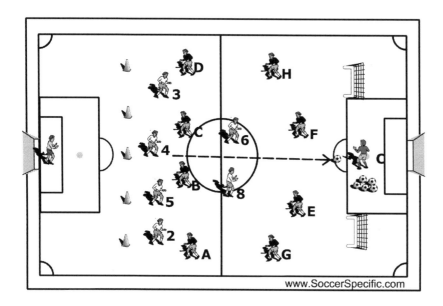

www.SoccerSpecific.com

1. Here the players clear the ball long and have a great chance to get out quickly and effectively. This is the initial set up as the ball is cleared.

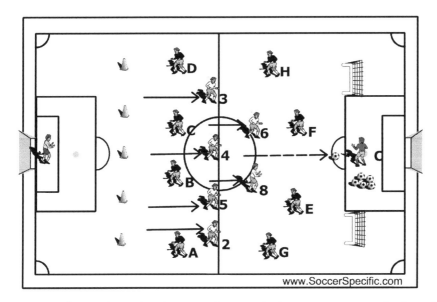

1. We have cleared it long to the coach (acting as our striker) and everyone sprints out.
2. OUT – We have cleared it long and sprint out as quickly as possible, leaving opponents offside (whether we keep possession or opponents get it, we still have time to get out).
3. Players must work forward as a team and push up to the half way line if possible. If the opponents win the ball in their defensive third (our attacking third) we are in a better position to regain possession.
4. This is the best position to regain the ball as the strikers are the first line of defense and if they win it in these areas we have a chance to get an immediate strike on goal.
5. If the team doesn't push out so quickly then the whole team's position suffers. The strikers may try to close down the ball but they lack support as the team is so spread out. This makes it more difficult to win the ball back effectively using a full team press starting with the back four.

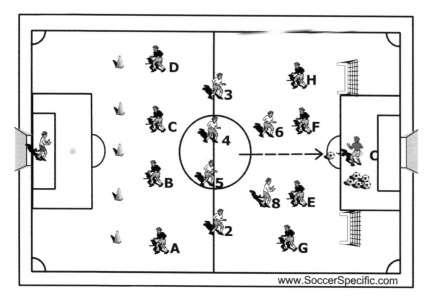

1. This shows four players clearly offside as the back four have pushed up and the team is then condensed up from the back.

DROP CALL

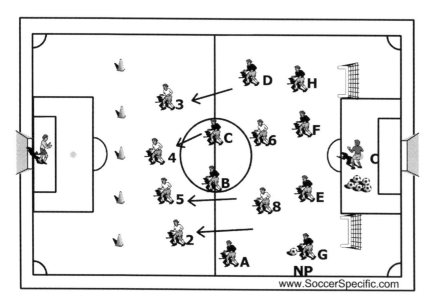

1. The above example shows there is no pressure (NP) and (G) can pass the ball forward early if need be. Strikers (B) and (C) can even time their runs back or across and forward to stay onside as they have time to do so. Generally a defender will have to track the player's runs in this situation so the call DROP will be used.
2. Just a one word signal can organize a back four defense so everyone knows what to do and reacts together as a unit. Midfield players close by can react off the call also.
3. One word calls ensure everyone will know quickly and effectively what they should do as a unit and as a team.

4. Hence the back players can organize their movement as a unit (and therefore influence those in front of them) from 5 one word commands. Midfielders (6) and (8) also drop back (though not shown here).

5. The whole team drops off. Here the defenders have tracked back to stay between the goal and the opposing strikers, particularly the one with possession of the ball. If they hadn't dropped off then the ball would have been played in behind them and the striker would have had a free run at goal in possession of the ball.

6. This can be dangerous if the team defends high up the field and the ball is played behind them as there is a lot of space for the ball to be played into.

7. The team can step up and try to play offside even when the opponents have the ball with no pressure to stop the forward pass, but the timing here is crucial and is not to be recommended. Between bad timing by the players moving up too late and split second decisions by officials this is a very difficult decision to make.

SLIDE CALL

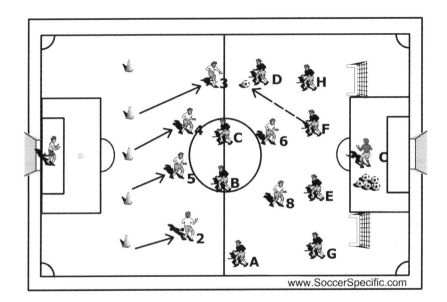

www.SoccerSpecific.com

1. Moving across the field, don't take it literally at 90 degrees. It could be diagonally in a game (45 degrees as above). The furthest players away from the ball are still aware of their immediate opponents but marking in advance of the ball (space). Here (F) passes to (D) and the back four slide over with player (3) applying immediate pressure on the ball. The midfield two (6) and (8) will turn and also slide over (though not shown here).

G) ONE WORD COMMANDS IN AN 11 v 11 USING THE 4-2-3-1 SYSTEM OF PLAY

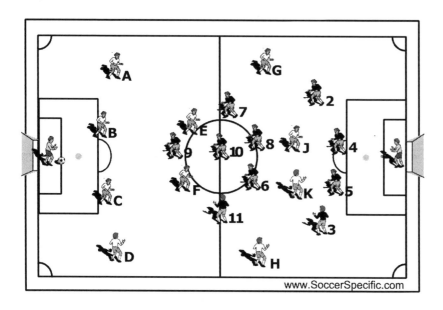

Now taking these ideas into an 11 v 11 game situation

1.   Defending numbered team set up in a defensive shape. Attacking lettered team set up in an attacking shape. The attacking team players STAND STILL and pass the ball between them.
2.   Each player receiving the pass keeps the ball for 5 seconds to show the defending team shape of the numbers team.
3.   Here we show a defensive shape in our 4-2-3-1 against a typical 4-4-2.
4.   For the moment the defending team must only SHADOW THE BALL as it is passed around by the opponent's team, though they all move to press and position.

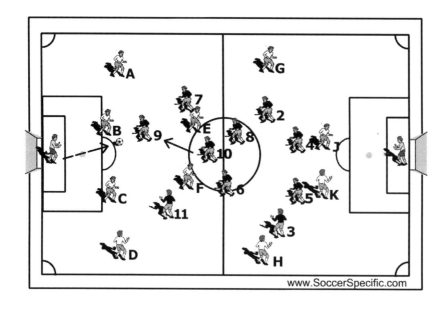

1. I am not showing all the movements with arrows as it will get confusing, but you can see the changed positions of all the players from the previous diagram.
2. Showing (9) pressing the ball, the rest of the team condense play behind. Use the UP call here as there is pressure on the ball from (9) to stop the forward pass and the team can move forward even though we do not have possession. This is when there is pressure and the ball cannot be passed forward so we can push up from the back and not worry about the strikers because even if they get the ball they will be offside.
3. If in the next phase of passing the opponents get in a position where there is no pressure on the ball and they can deliver a forward pass quickly then the DROP call is used and particularly the back four drop off to protect the space behind them.
4. The team takes their shape off the pressing player. It is important he does a good job to delay (or even win the ball if possible). He shows defender (B) inside to the strength of his team.

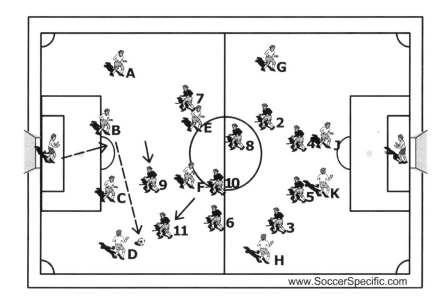

www.SoccerSpecific.com

1. (B) manages to pass to (D). Closest player to the ball now is (11) who presses immediately. The rest of the team follow suit and slide across, condensing the space around the ball. Use the SLIDE LEFT call here for the team adjustment.
2. (11) must try to position so he can stop the pass down the line to (H) and therefore show the player (D) inside; again to our strength. If it is down the line it is a 1v1 potentially.
3. Develop the session: Have the defending NUMBERS team you are coaching able to intercept a pass. Once they do then the game is LIVE and both teams can move. Try to ensure the attacking team starts with the ball and once the play is over the ball goes back to the attacking team again for the defending team to try to win back.
4. Next, have both teams play and coach it as you see it.
5. You can use these words at games for U8 to U18 and even with senior teams if you need to get information to the TEAM without DISTRACTING INDIVIDUALS with direction from the sideline.

6. The older teams U12 and up can have a defender calling the words to dictate what he needs the team to do. I have attached the relevant situations when you can use these words. It is a very fast way of getting information on to the field that will affect the whole team positively. I would like to see teams trying this in training; it is simple but VERY EFFECTIVE.

WHEN AND WHERE TO DROP AS A BACK FOUR AND AS A TEAM

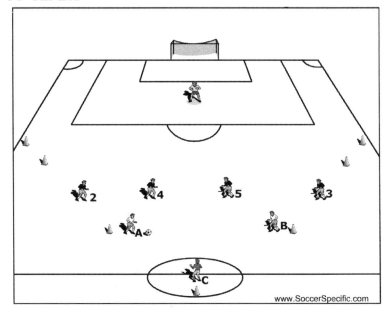

www.SoccerSpecific.com

1. Players (A) and (B) pass the ball back and forth and the back 4 adjust their positions accordingly. You can say that players (A) and (B) represent a player with pressure on the ball so they cannot pass it forward or in behind them. Player (C) on the other hand represents a player with no pressure so he CAN play the ball in behind them.
2. When the ball is played to player (C) this is the cue for the back 4 to drop off quickly as (C) will always play the ball in behind them. The players; (A), (B) and (C); will chase after the ball to apply some pressure.
3. The back 4 as they adjust should get side on and ready to drop. As the ball is being passed side to side the call can be READY or SIDE ON. So they get side on as the ball is passed to (C) and the call is DROP as they know it is going to be played behind them. There are three things happening: getting "set and prepared" and moving as the ball travels, trying to identify and anticipate situations as they develop, "getting side on", and then "dropping quickly".
4. This exercise is designed to help the back four identify when and where to drop back and how to deal with the ball in behind.
5. Timing of the drop is crucial. Too late and they may be passed by a striker who goes on to score a goal. Have one player making the call and identifying each situation as it happens. Vary the distances between the back 4 and the three attackers so the pressure changes. Have a bigger distance to begin so the back four have more time to play and to be successful and gain confidence, and as they get better reduce the distance so they are under more immediate pressure.

A) THE BALL IS PLAYED IN BEHIND THE BACK FOUR

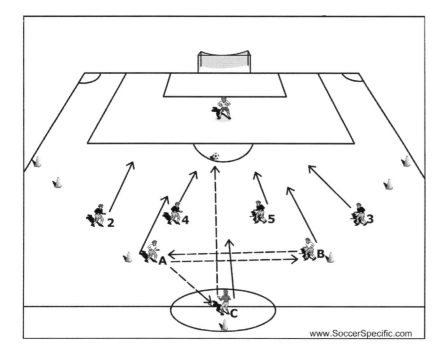

www.SoccerSpecific.com

1. Here we show the players dropping back to where the ball is travelling and the three attacking players applying pressure.
2. Player (3) should weight the pass in behind the back four so they get to it first and are able to deal with it before it reaches the keeper.
3. Pass it to the side of the goal for the keeper (so if the keeper misses the ball it goes for a corner and not into the goal), preferably to the keeper's best foot, but this can depend on time and space and where the attackers are positioned.
4. Two small goals at the sides act as targets for the keeper to pass to when a back 4 player gets to the ball and passes it to him.
5. As players recover back they must not focus solely on the ball or on the attacker, but should be scanning both.

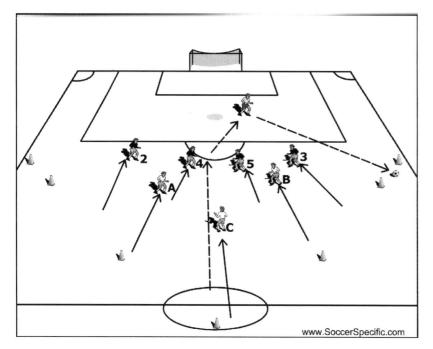

www.SoccerSpecific.com

1. Here the ball is passed back to the keeper who then becomes the first point of attack.
2. If the through pass is too heavy and it goes straight to the keeper then the keeper has to deal with it, either through passing to the side goals or if under real pressure kick it high and long beyond the back four.
3. When the keeper kicks it long the call for the back four is OUT so they get out and up the field quickly.
4. Develop: As the ball is passed back the fullbacks break wide and the keeper passes to one of them to start the attack instead of passing to the side goals. This can be a start position for an 11 v 11 game if you like so you get the theme in every time.

C) AN 11 v 11 SET UP

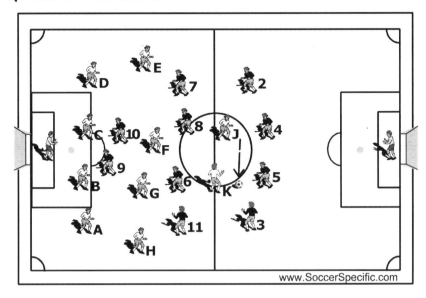

1. Strikers (J) And (K) pass the ball between each other and the back four adjust across and back as the ball moves.

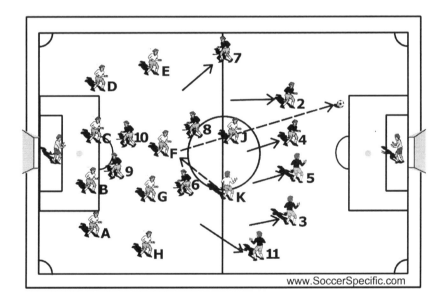

1. The ball is passed back to midfielder (F) who plays a forward pass behind the defense. The back four drop off and recover to get possession and the two wide players drop back into wide areas to receive a pass in the next phase of play if possible. Of course the letters team presses the ball to put the pressure on.

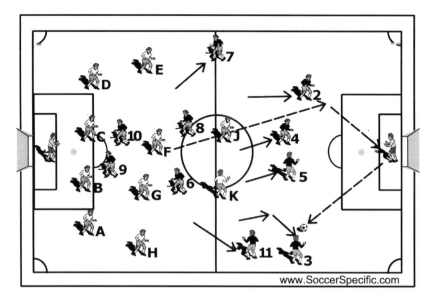

1. As defender (3) sees (2) get to the ball first he knows he is safe to break wide into an attacking position. So now on the right side the keeper from the back pass has two options on the left. Now play as a game until the ball goes out of play and return to the start position.

DEFENSIVE RECOVERY RUNS IN A 4-2-3-1

This is a very important session to practice as RECOVERY RUNS are vitally important to teach to a team. Two ideas regarding this:
1. The players behind the ball DELAYING the continued forward motion of the ball
2. The Recovery runs of the defenders (USUALLY MIDFIELDERS) now in advance of the ball aided by the delaying by teammates

You can start as in the previous session where you have a reduced number of players and eventually build it up to an 11v11.

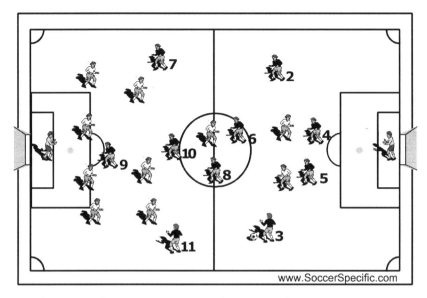

1. Above, we have possession and are attacking. We are in our attacking shape, wide and long.

A) CAUGHT ON THE BREAK

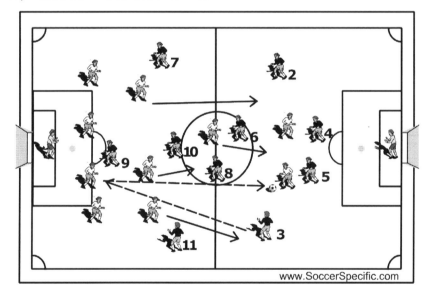

1. A poor pass results in an interception and a pass into the opposing team's striker.
2. While the movements of both teams' players will likely be simultaneous, for clarity here I am just showing one team at a time with their likely movement.
3. Here I show the opposing team attacking after gaining possession.
4. Of course from a defensive perspective we want our closest player (9) to try to press the ball quickly and delay the forward pass or even win the ball back, but if this doesn't happen then our next phase of play should involve the recovery back of as many players as possible.

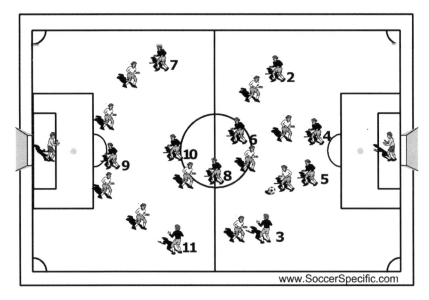

1.   The opponent's approximate resulting attacking team position.

B)   ROUTES OF RECOVERY

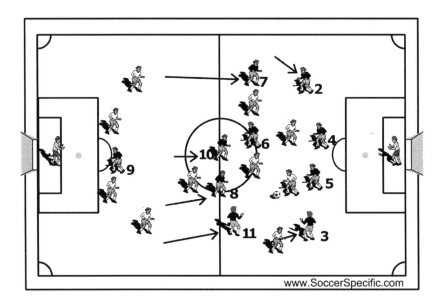

1.   Showing our team's recovery movements. Too often it is like this. They get back but they don't get back into the correct places. They recover too wide.
2.   Also some do not recover back AT ALL and are lazy; which is a big problem also; but let's say here they have at least attempted to recover back.
3.   It is not enough to just 'GET BACK IN RECOVERY". It has to be to the correct positions to be effective.
4.   There are big spaces here between recovering and recovered players.
5.   So while our players do get back here it is not as effective defensively as it should be.

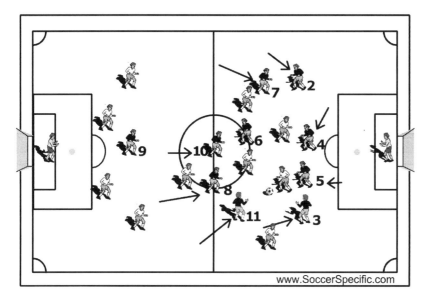

C) EFFECTIVE ROUTES OF RECOVERY

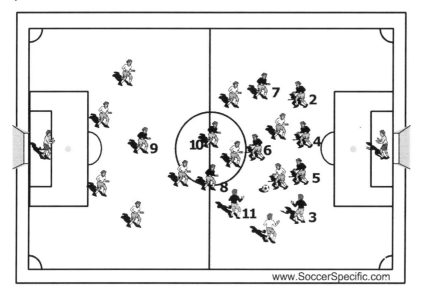

1. Here you can see how we should have the players recover back. They get tighter as they recover.
2. There are very few gaps between the defending players to play through now.
3. Another major part of recovering back is how well the defenders pressing the ball can hold up and delay the opponent's break away.
4. Too often we see these players dive in or try to win the ball in a vulnerable position and often get beaten when all they need to do is be patient and slow the opponents down to allow some time for their teammates to recover back.
5. If (5) were to dive in here then the striker would get a run on our goal and there would be little time for our players to recover back to help.

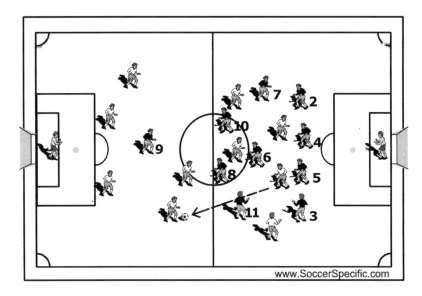

1. Here the striker has been held up by (5). His only option is to play the ball back.
2. By holding him up we have our players back in recovery positions and we are short and tight defensively, forcing opponents on their next phase of play to go wide which again delays and gives us more time to recover.

PLAYING A MAN DOWN (10 v 11)

Defending with 10 men when winning 2-0 and counter attacking

In today's game there are so many situations where teams are given a red card that it would be foolish not to practice with 10 players so you are prepared for this.

A) A PHASE OF PLAY

1. A 1-4-2- against a 4-3-2. Six outfield players (plus a keeper) are playing against nine outfield players. The six defending players are 2-0 up and need to maintain the lead. This is going to build up into a 10 v 11 game situation eventually.
2. We are set up like a 4-4-1 without a number (10) position filled.
3. We have three goals to attack for the six defending players. These represent in an actual game our (7), (9) and (11), so our attacking shape is a 4-2-3 with 10 players.
4. Once the defending six win the ball they can counter attack quickly by passing the ball into either of the goals, as if they were the three attacking players in the game.
5. When they do this successfully they get a goal. Depending on where the ball is won, you can play from the back through midfield and then to the strikers. This is to vary the build up so it does not become too predictable.
6. Having said that, it is best if we can counter quickly when we win the ball to catch the opponents out who are in an attacking phase at that moment and have an overload of players.
7. Start with a tight field only; goal area wide. This creates smaller spaces between players and will help the overloaded defending team of six have some initial success and give them confidence.
8. Coaching Points:
   a. Patience as individuals and as a team, no need to chase the ball as we are winning with numbers down
   b. Keep a compact team shape, short and tight
   c. When having to commit as an individual, delay initially until you know the support is there should you be beaten, then press to win the ball.
   d. Support your immediate teammates' positioning
   e. Cover teammates around and beyond these two;
   f. Recover. When the ball goes past one of our players, try to get goal side
   g. Track. When an opponent makes a forward run, we cannot leave him free
   h. Regain possession
   i. Get compact from the back and squeeze up when we counter
   j. Quick counter attack where and when it is on; otherwise maintain possession as long as possible until the counter opportunity opens up
   k. High or low pressure on the field when we lose the ball, but depending on where we lose it and where the players are positioned (likely low pressure mostly being numbers down and winning because we are not chasing the game; to conserve energy)

B) SIX AGAINST NINE

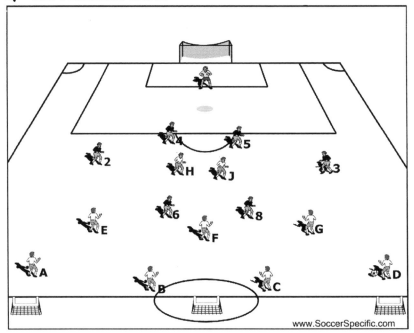

1. After initial success, let's say the defending six who started at 2-0 up won the game 4-0 with two successful counter attacks and did not allow a goal, open the field up and use the full width.
2. It is now a much bigger challenge for the defending team with bigger spaces between them and much more space for the overloaded attacking team to play in.

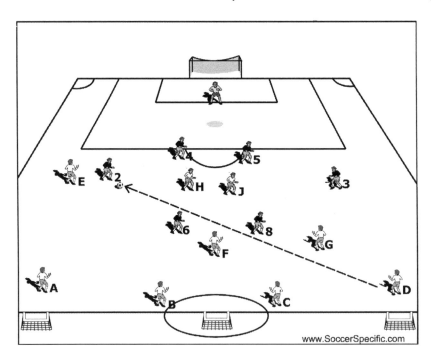

1. An example of a counter attack. (E) has run forward hoping to receive a pass from (D) in behind (2). The pass is under-hit and (E) is out of defensive position and (2) intercepts the pass.

C) IMMEDIATE COUNTER ATTACK

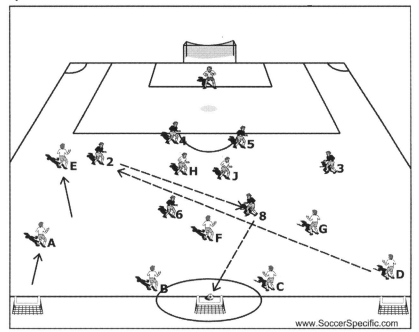

1. (2) is free and has time on the ball. He could play a quick direct pass to one of the goals but instead plays a quick pass to (8) who is free and (8) plays a long pass to the center goal (simulating striker (9) in a game). This counts as a goal for the defending six. The overload team can try to intercept the pass to the goal.

D) INCREASE THE DIFFICULTY

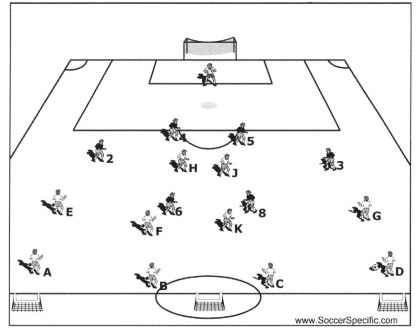

1. Now 6 against 10 players, a much bigger challenge for the defending team. You can bring in the width of the field again if you wish to make it easier for the defending team.

2. If that is successful then widen it to the full width again, you can experiment with field sizes and player numbers to lead up to the 10 v 11 actual game SITUATION.

E) ADD MORE PLAYERS TO OUR TEAM

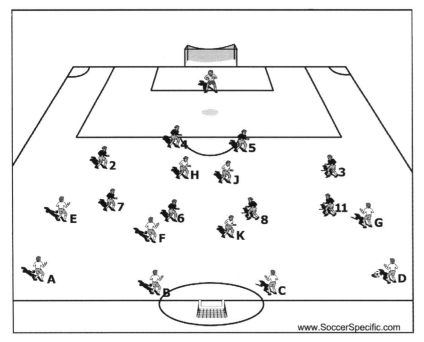

www.SoccerSpecific.com

1. Now bring in the wide players (7) and (11) and take out two of the goals, leaving only the central goal that represents our striker (9). Now it is 8 outfield players against 10 players.
2. Now the defending team counter attack and score by scoring in the single goal still but also if they can play it forward into the path of (7) or (11) who have attacked quickly once we won the ball.

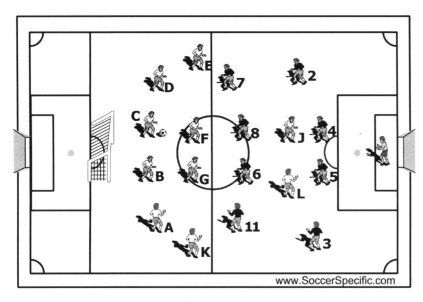

www.SoccerSpecific.com

1. Same set up on the big field.

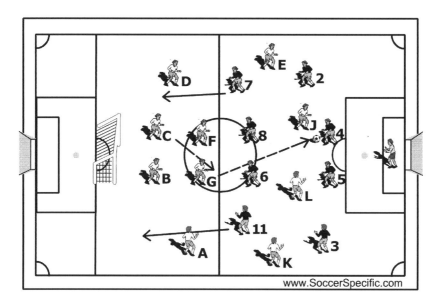

1. Here (C) passes to midfielder (G) who makes a bad pass to a striker. We have won possession now and (4) has time and space to look up. This is the CUE for (7) and (11) to make forward runs to receive the forward pass.

1. Here there are three options for (4). All three passes are into the three furthest forward players in the team. This is the best counter attack if it is on to do so, direct and fast.

2. If the opponents are in a full attacking mode, being 2-0 down they need to chase the game and take chances. In this situation their fullbacks have pushed on and have been caught wrong side.

3. Alternatively if (7) and (11) are not free and the pass directly to the goal representing striker (9) is blocked then we may need to perform a slower build up and keep possession of the ball longer until a counter attacking moment appears.

F) A 10 v 11 FULL GAME SITUATION

www.SoccerSpecific.com

1. We have built the session up with several progressions and now we are at the full game situation.
2. The following are various start positions you can use to create particular situations that will happen in the game.

DEFENDING WITH TEN MEN AND COUNTER ATTACKING

1. PHASE OF PLAY: Play 7 v 9 (4 + 2) against (3 + 3 + 2) with 3 target goals. Defend with depth and patience.
2. 3 targets represent the 3 forwards when we break. When winning possession our player can hit a goal then start again; unless able to dribble forward.
3. Play 7 v 11 (same principle but 4 + 2 v 4-4-2)
4. Play 9 v 11 (4 + 4) against 4-4-2 (win possession 2 wide players spread out immediately).
5. FULL GAME SITUATION: but Play 10 v 11 (should be easier now)
6. Start position 1: CM plays the ball behind their defense in the corner. 2 solutions: we can press and we can't press.
7. Start position 2: Their GK passes to a defender. Same 2 solutions but ST can push one way. Work on distances between units defensively and across units. Keeper / Sweeper.
8. Start position 3: We play to our striker and the ball is intercepted (in the air or on the ground).
9. Start Position 4: Keeper kicks the ball, we win the header, they pick up the 2nd ball.
10. Start Position 5: They play into their STRIKER'S feet. We condense around him.
11. Start Position 6: They play a ball in behind us.
12. Start Position 7: Our Keeper kicks it long to our striker
13. Jockey and delaying: Identify when it is wrong and coach it (such as being beaten 1 v 1 when we can just delay)

14. Show press high if able; or drop off if not; in attacking third
15. When to drop: Cue: Opponent on the ball has head up and is preparing to play the ball forward. Can we press and get his head down first?

A) VARIOUS START POSITIONS:
SP ONE

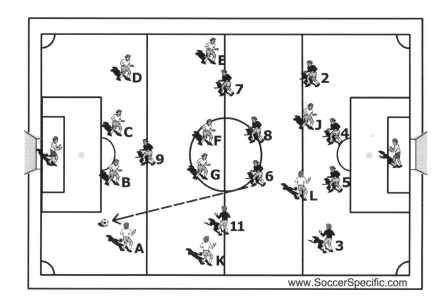

1. Pre - Designed Start positions allow for the coach to create situations in training that he knows will happen in a game at some stage. These are designed to create many different scenarios that your team may face in a game in each third of the field.
2. Structure the start positions so you go from the front to the back of your team and there is a pattern to the development.
3. First one is a ball played behind the opponent's back four. Your team needs to decide:
    a. Can we press from the front? For example, can (9) and (11) get there quick enough to press (A) who likely will be first to the ball?
    b. Can we NOT get there? If so, we drop off as a team and defend from the half way line or the edge of the attacking third line.
4. So we can practice HIGH PRESSURE AND LOW PRESSURE DEFENDING HERE depending on the player positions, but you can also set this up and determine which you use initially by player positioning. So, the first idea is CAN WE PRESS THE BALL IMMEDIATELY? If not, we then must drop off quickly as a team and get as many players behind the ball as possible.
5. Defending deep means it is difficult for them to play the ball in behind us.
6. If we defend high in this situation we must be pretty sure we can win the ball or it is wasted energy on the part of the pressing player or players.
7. If we defend deep then our wide attacking players must have a lot of energy to get up and support the striker and then get back when it breaks down.
8. This is where substitutions can play a part as we defend longer in keeping these wide players fresh.

B) START POSITIONS DETERMINE TYPE OF PRESSURE
LOW PRESSURE

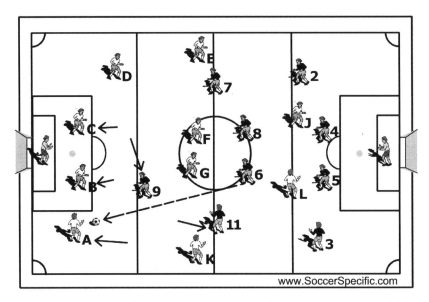

1. Start positions of (9) and (11) are too far away so it would be wasted effort to try to close down so save energy and drop off.

HIGH PRESSURE

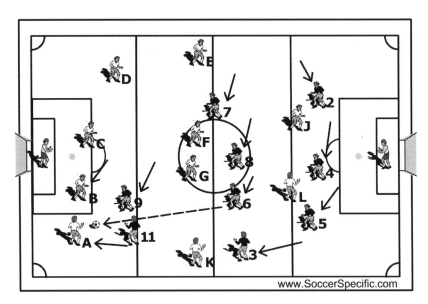

1. (11) and (9)'s start positions are closer to the position of the ball so they can press high. This is the CUE for the rest of the team to adjust behind them. (3) pushes in on (K) and the rest slide across and up to cut down the spaces. It is important that the pressing player shows the player on the ball towards his immediate support.

1. The ball is played from their keeper to the edge of our attacking third (their defending third). (9) presses the ball and tries to win it, or at least force the play one way so the team behind him knows how to position and condense the spaces around where the ball is being forced to go.

SP THREE

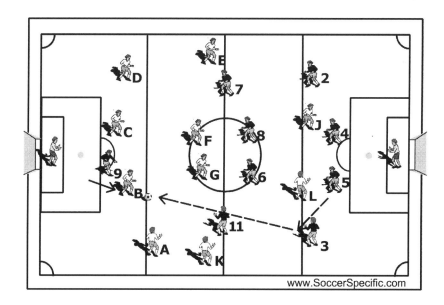

1. The ball is passed into our striker (9) dropping into the middle third and it is intercepted by their center back (B) and they attack from there. Now we have (9) out of the game initially so it is 10 outfield players against 8. All the time the start positions are getting closer to our goal so we have a structured session.

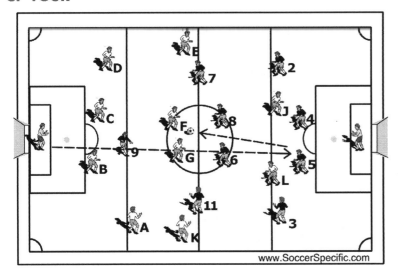

1. Their keeper kicks the ball long. We win the header and it falls at their center midfielder who wins the second ball in the middle third of the field. We must press quickly to try to win the ball back immediately if possible. The next best thing would be to stop the forward pass and delay until we get organized defensively as a team in a stronger way. Example, let's say (8) can't win the ball but he can press to stop the forward pass and slow (F) down. This allows (6), (7) and (11) to tighten up the midfield 4 by tucking in and maybe even delay (F) to allow (9) to double team from behind.

SP FIVE

1. They play the ball into the feet of their striker in our defending third. Now we need to defend around the outside of our box. We must condense around the ball, (5) gets tight and (6) can double team for example. So now the ball starts behind our midfield four and we will need to make recovery runs to try to get goal side and track the runs by the opponent's players.

SP SIX

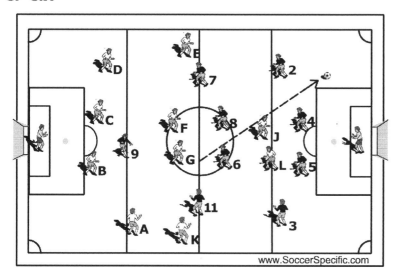

1. They play a ball behind our defense deep into our defending third to get us turned.

SP SEVEN

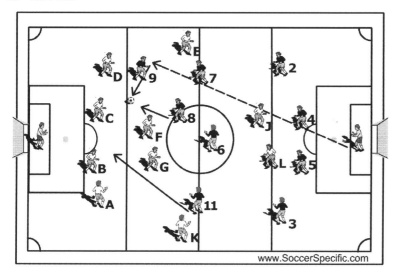

1. Our (9) is good in the air so we position him against a smaller fullback and away from the taller center back. Our keeper kicks it long to him and we look for a flick on for (8) pushing beyond (9) for the knock down and also (11) joining in. This is another counter attack ploy we can use. They do not go too early in case (9) does not win the header and then they are too far forward to defend.

2. Knowing where the keeper is kicking the ball tells the team to slide over and look for the 2nd ball around (9), either in front of him or to the side. And if (D) wins the header, (7), (2) and (4) are in a good position to pick up the 2nd ball.

C) POSITIONING FROM THE KEEPER'S KICKS TO GAIN POSSESSION OF THE 2ND BALL

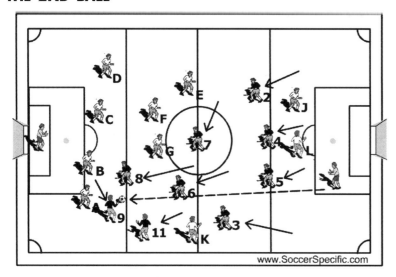

1. To help us win the first and then second ball we must have the players organized. The CUE for where they set up is by the position of the keeper. Here he positions on the left so he is kicking down the left. Striker (9) comes across as the target player. Other players position around him for the 2nd ball.

2. In the immediate area of the ball we may even outnumber the opposition and have a great chance to keep the ball. This long kick from the keeper (2nd ball game) is often preferred in this situation where we are down a player and protecting a lead. Trying to play possession out of the back (1st ball game) can be risky here.

D) DIFFERENT SCENARIOS TO CREATE AND PRACTICE

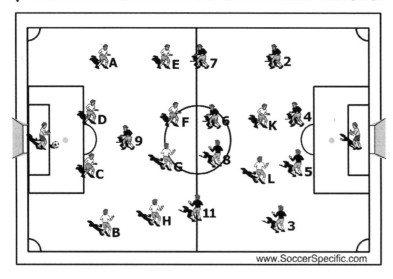

1. Here we are down to 10 men having had a player sent off. It is important we practice playing with 10 men against 11 in training as red cards are often given out quite liberally and all teams can expect at some stage of the season to be playing with only 10 men. Therefore it is important we know what to do when it happens.

2. Different situations in the game will dictate how you deal with this and how you organize your team. Are we winning? Are we losing? Is the score tied? Is a draw a good result or do we need to win?

3. The style of play the opponents use will also affect how we play. Do they play 1, 2 or 3 strikers for example? In this case, my opinion is it does not matter. We still can play with a back four against them. Midfield is the key area of concern.

4. Let's discuss what we can do to get a winning situation from a player down and ensure we are prepared for this by practicing it in training.

5. I have taken the number (10) out here but he may be to player you need up front alone. You have to know your players well and know which players can play this system best in such a circumstance.

6. You may not even necessarily field your best team here. You may bring in two fresh and fit wide players to take on the role of quick support and recovery, which will be important if you are winning and need to keep the lead. This role will be very physically challenging so choose wisely.

7. If you are losing you may put on more offensively skilled players in these two positions.

E) WINNING 1-0 WITH ONLY TEN MEN WHERE WE NEED TO KEEP THE LEAD

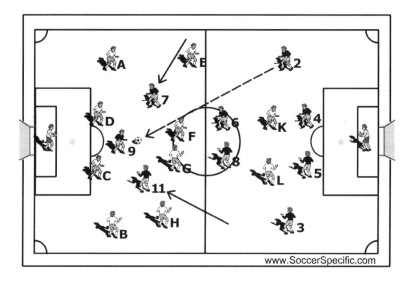

www.SoccerSpecific.com

1. Clearly we are at a disadvantage with only 10 men. Let's say it is the last 25 minutes of the game, we are winning and we have a player sent off. Here are the coaching points associated with this situation AND ONE WAY to enable you to best keep the lead and win the game.

    a. Play a 4-4-1

    b. Have a strong center forward who can hold up the ball to keep possession until support arrives. It will help if he is quick also. If the opponents defend deep then we can play into the striker's feet. If opponents defend high then we can play the ball behind them. If playing it behind them is the best scenario, we may replace a big strong striker with a smaller faster player. You decide from what you see as all games are different and this is where you earn your salary, in the game situation!!

c. Tell your fullbacks to stay in position and play as defenders only. Attacking means they leave a gap at the back that can be exploited, so we need to keep the back four intact at all times.

d. Our two center midfield players stay in defensive position and play a disciplined game.

e. This way we keep a solid defensive base of a keeper, back four and a central midfield two screening in front of the center backs.

f. Have wide midfield players (7) and (11) be the supporting attackers in the team. They need to be very fit and prepared to work hard to support when we attack and recover back immediately when we lose the ball and defend.

g. Use low pressure defending as (9) is alone against a back four, so let them have the ball at the back (unless there is a CLEAR chance to win the ball).

h. Have two banks of FOUR players defending short and tight, making it difficult for the opponents to find space between each player to play through.

i. This means the players have to be at their disciplined best to be patient and wait for any opportunities to attack.

j. Develop a counter attacking game plan where we win the ball and counter quickly. Practice this in training also. While the main priority is to not concede a goal and maintain our lead, we will get opportunities to attack and score ourselves, especially as the opponents push more players forward to try to press and score.

k. So, we have TWO GAME PLANS: one to defend and get players behind the ball, the other to counter attack quickly.

The offensive and defensive shapes will change. Perhaps it will be as simple as a 4-4-1 when defending and a 4-2-3 when attacking or an even more offensive shape if one of the fullbacks gets into an attacking position, leaving three at the back AND MAKING IT A 3-3-3. But we have a defensive team shape of 4-4-1 when we lose possession and recover.

So often the team shape depends on the MOMENT IN THE GAME and who has possession

1. This would be the general set up but situations will happen where it is a fullback who pushes on; when we are generally asking him to stay back. In these circumstances just have another player fill in his position to ensure we have the solid six defensively to protect us.

2. Variables to account for:
   a. What team shape the opponents play
   b. Knowing their areas of strength and adapting to them
   c. Knowing our strengths and using them
   d. We strengthen one area of the field to improve our attack which will inevitably weaken another area, so we need to always consider the consequences.
   e. Playing more forwards means we may weaken the midfield.
   f. Pushing more players into midfield from the back means we weaken the back area.
   g. With one player down we are at a disadvantage and the secret is to find a way to minimize this disadvantage.

F) A LOSING SITUATION 1-0 DOWN WHERE WE NEED TO SCORE

1. How adventurous you play depends on the importance of winning the game.
2. You may play the above style with your two wide players being very athletic and fast and very offensively minded. So, whereas you may play more defensively strong wide players at (7) and (11) who can also attack when need be, but are better at defending when you are winning, in a losing situation you can do the opposite and put better offensive players on.

G) A 4-3-2 STYLE OF PLAY

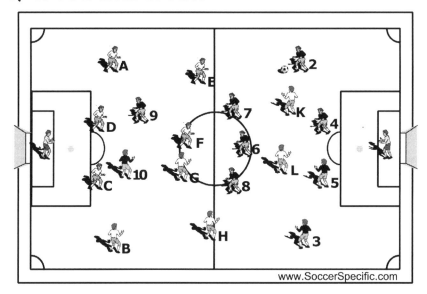

www.SoccerSpecific.com

1. Here we play a 4-3-2 style with two strikers and three in midfield. We can still win the central midfield battle with 10 men depending on how we set the team up.
2. Here we have created a 3v2 in the center in our favor. The problem is their wide players when they get the ball, so our fullbacks have to be more proactive and push on when (E) and/or (H) get the ball as there is no direct midfield player against them.
3. Offensively though, we need to press and score, so our fullbacks are allowed more freedom and our midfield players have to get forward and support the front players. We have to take the gamble and push players forward.
4. Question: At what stage of the game do we do this and go for broke? Depends on the state of the game. Are we confident and playing well? If so, then go for it early. Are we not so confident? Then defend well, make sure you do not concede another goal and wait for the clear breakaway chance to counter. Much will depend on the mentality of the coach and confidence of the players, the mentality of the opposing players and the state of the game at that moment in time.

H) 4-4-1 WHEN 1-0 DOWN

1. Alternatively you may play a 4-4-1 style which at first thought does not look as attacking as a 4-3-2 with only one main striker rather than two, BUT; if your team has a very well developed counter attacking style and it suits your particular players this may prove to be an even more offensive style than playing two up

front because we actually finish up with three strikers.

2. Defend well and be patient, then attack quickly when you win possession with each player knowing his role well.

3. Again, it depends on the makeup of the players at your disposal, your own mentality and how well you have trained the players.

4. So the first diagram showing a counter attacking set up when we are winning 1-0 may also be the best set up when we are in a losing situation trying to get back into the game. You decide.

I) 4-2-3 WHEN 1-0 DOWN

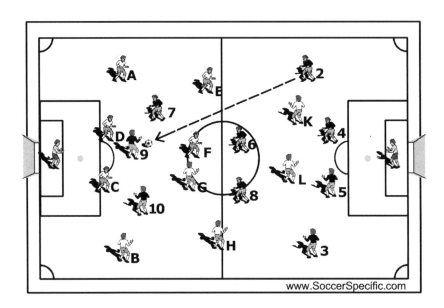

1. Another style to consider is a VERY ATTACKING STYLE OF 4-2-3. Here we will be light in midfield, so our fullbacks need to push up more when the opponents get the ball to a wide player (and be the immediate opponent with no midfield player of our own to close him down). And we will stay and gamble with a 2v2 at the back or slide the other fullback across making a 3v2 (unless they play with a lone striker).

2. Playing into our front three quickly is the key to this system. Again a quick counter attacking style but now with three players to aim for. Being light in midfield may mean we need to bypass the midfield and play a longer game.

3. The difference here to the 4-4-1 is really just the start positions of the wide players, who are closer to the opponent's goal. You could also say this is the end product and finishing position offensively of a 4-4-1 when we counter attack.

J) 3-3-3 or 3-4-2

1. Play three at the back and have more in the attack and midfield combined. We can still have a 3v2 or even a 3v1 at the back in our favor. So should they win the ball and play it forward we are quite secure still in these two situations as long as our players in front of the back three recover quickly and track the

opponent's runs.

2. Playing three means a big mental adjustment for the back players.

3. There are many different ways to play this but ultimately what you will do will depend on the game situation and the strengths and weaknesses of your squad of players and how they match up with the strengths and weaknesses of the opponents.

K) START POSITIONS ARE A 4-4-1

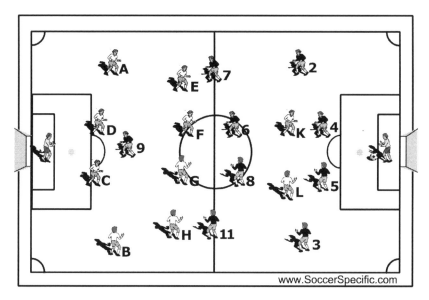

1. Here we have the ball at our keeper and the team starting shape is a 4-4-1.

L) BUILDUP TEAM SHAPE OF A 4-2-3

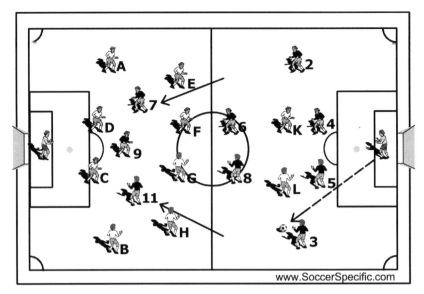

1. Wide players (7) and (11) have pushed on and we have become a three striker attack. The ball is passed to our free fullback (3) to attack down the flank.

M) FURTHER BUILDUP PLAY NOW BECOMING A 3-3-3

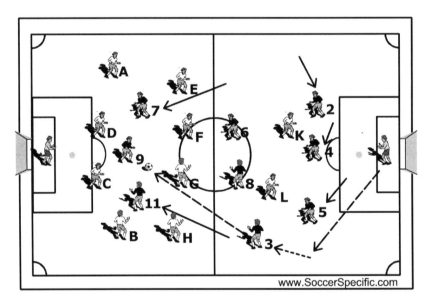

1. Here (3) pushes forward with the ball and enters the midfield area, effectively making it a 3 player midfield. The back three behind him, for security should the opponents win the ball, slide over to make sure they have a 3v2 advantage. Plus we have three strikers so we are now shaped as a 3-3-3.
2. My thoughts on this are that we are best to start with a 4-4-1 and we show the players in training how to transition with the ball with a quick counterattacking style of play.
3. Then it is easy to drop back into a 4-4-1 when we lose the ball and players make recovery runs along the shortest route back to get behind the ball as quickly as possible. With this style of play it is important, if possible, that the closest player to

the ball when the opponents win it delays the forward motion of the opponents to allow the rest of the team to get back into their defensive shape.

N) ATTACKING AND LOSING POSSESSION

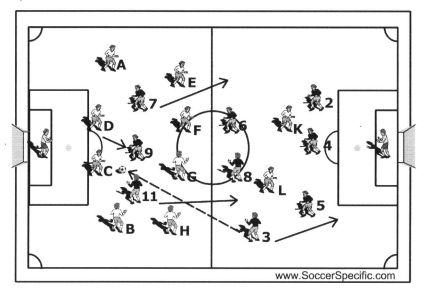

1. Here we are attacking and in our 3-3-3 attacking shape but (3) plays a bad pass which is intercepted by defender (C). Striker (9) slides across to press and delay the forward motion of the opponents through (C).

2. If (11) is the closest player then perhaps (9) will drop back to fill his place and (11) will press the ball and delay.

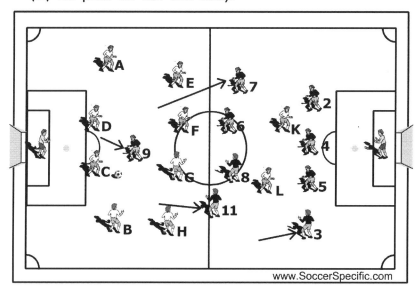

1. Here (9) is able to delay the forward pass and this allows (3), (7) and (11) to get back behind the ball and in a good defensive position, (7) picking up (E) and (11) picking up (H) and (3) becoming a part of the back four again.

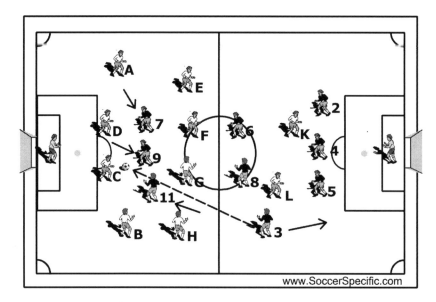

www.SoccerSpecific.com

1. Alternatively if we have enough players VERY CLOSE to the ball, even though the opponent has it we can press from the front quickly and try to win it back at the source. Here (9) and (11) are close so they double team (C) and hopefully win the ball and start an attack close to their goal. (7) can tuck across to outnumber the opponents near the ball. (3) can still recover back and get in position should this ploy not work effectively.

Whatever method you use it is always important to have a game plan for a 10 v 11 GAME SITUATION as it WILL HAPPEN at some stage of the season. How your players react will depend on what you teach them in training; so reproduce the most common moments that may occur on the field.

How your team copes will depend on how well organized you are and how well you have taught them in training. The ultimate test of their understanding in the game situation will be shown by their reactions. For example; if we lose the ball, do we press immediately in numbers to try to win the ball or do we drop off with just one player and delay? Only the players can decide this moment.

THEREFORE, THE PLAYERS NEED TO BE TAUGHT TO MAKE THESE DECISIONS FOR THEMSELVES ON THE FIELD. THIS IS WHY "GUIDED DISCOVERY" IS THE WAY FORWARD, TEACHING PLAYERS TO BE THE DECISION MAKERS.

AS THE COACH ON THE SIDELINES DURING A MATCH YOU CANNOT AFFECT THINGS IN ANY ONE MOMENT LIKE THE PLAYERS CAN. SO IT IS YOUR JOB IN TRAINING TO GIVE THEM THE TOOLS THEY NEED TO MAKE THE RIGHT DECISIONS ON THE FIELD IN THE FLOW OF PLAY. MAKE YOUR TRAINING "player focused" and not "coach focused" in ALL aspects of the game.

These are my thoughts on the theme of 10 v 11. I have offered quite a few alternatives. I know which I like the best, you must decide what suits your players the best and start to teach it in training.

IN CONCLUSION

These are my thoughts and beliefs on how the 4-2-3-1 should be played, both offensively and defensively. No doubt other interpretations exist and all teams who play it will have differences in how they prepare their teams, but this is my way.

The real beauty of this four unit system of play is the freedom it gives the players to interchange between each other and in my mind it is the new TOTAL FOOTBALL.

To make it work you need the best possible technical, tactical, physical and psychological makeup of players and the team. It takes years of developmental training at youth level to perfect this. Barcelona's current crop of first teamers is based on a developmental program used over the past 15 years at youth level with no wavering from the long term plan. Barcelona's set up in central midfield is the same as in this book. They set up like a lopsided triangle which they call a Three. I call it a Two-One but the end product is the same.

One center midfielder drops back to protect the back four and allow the fullbacks to attack, the other central midfielder (Xavi) acts as a pivot between this defensive player (Busquets) and the attacking midfielder (Iniesta). For the front three we have the interchanges of the central striker and the two wide attackers.

Too many clubs and owners think only in the short term and want results instantly. Thankfully, Barcelona has people with long term vision who have shown that if you are patient and stick to your beliefs you will succeed.

No other club in the world has 8 or 9 players in the first team who were developed in their own academy. The results speak for themselves. And don't forget this is one of the top three clubs in the WORLD, if not THE best team there has ever been, not only based on results but also from the standpoint of pure football and how the game should be played.

My book: "Soccer Awareness: Developing the Thinking Player" epitomizes the developmental attitudes and beliefs of the Barcelona system of teaching (one touch quick decision making; with maximum off the ball movement) that led to the creation of these players who represent this successful system of play.

These books complement each other in terms of developing players who fit perfectly into this system of play.

I hope you have enjoyed this book, and please use it as a base to develop your own teams and teach them to play with the freedom this system promotes.

Kindest Regards,
Wayne Harrison